D1602340

Relations of Ruling

Relations of Ruling

*Class and Gender in
Postindustrial Societies*

WALLACE CLEMENT
and JOHN MYLES

McGill-Queen's University Press
Montreal & Kingston • London • Buffalo

© McGill-Queen's University Press 1994
ISBN 0-7735-1164-4 (cloth)
ISBN 0-7735-1178-4 (paper)

Legal deposit second quarter 1994
Bibliothèque nationale du Québec

Printed in Canada on acid-free paper

This book has been published with the help of a
grant from the Social Science Federation of Canada,
using funds provided by the Social Sciences and
Humanities Research Council of Canada.

Canadian Cataloguing in Publication Data

Clement, Wallace
    Relations of ruling : class and gender in
    postindustrial societies
    Includes bibliographical references and index.
    ISBN 0-7735-1164-4 (bound)
    ISBN 0-7735-1178-4 (pbk.)
    1. Social classes. 2. Sex role. 3. Power
    (Social sciences). I. Myles, John II. Title.
    HN17.5.C54 1994   305.5   C93-090666-7

Contents

Preface

The Comparative Project on Class Structure and Class Consciousness was launched under the initiative of Erik Olin Wright in the United States and joined by Göran Ahrne from Sweden in the early 1980s. The undertaking we connected with also included the Finnish project led by Raimo Blom and Markku Kivinen. Our affiliation was simultaneous with the Norwegian group led by Tom Colbjornsen. These five nations constitute the empirical core of this book. Since the initial five, another five nations have completed their surveys and recently produced comparative data (Australia, Denmark, Japan, the United Kingdom, and West Germany), while several others are in varying degrees of preparation (Greece, Hungary, New Zealand, Poland, Taiwan, Turkey, the Soviet Union, and Spain) and are likely to produce data in the near future. This book is the first systematic attempt to present some comparative findings from the original five-nation data set. That data set has been made possible because of the undaunting efforts by Erik Olin Wright to co-ordinate the dissemination of material and the extraordinary organizational skills of the late Bonnie Amim, the former administrative co-ordinator of the Comparative Project, who tragically died on 11 February 1990. Without the talents and generosity of Bonnie and Erik, the *comparative* dimension, which gives this project its essential insights, would not have been possible.

All who approach such a challenging data set will do so in their own way, with their own agendas, so we do not pretend to have exhausted its enormous potential. Moreover, the additional countries will add new dimensions. What we have done is bring to the study our own conception of class, a sensitivity to the salience of gender, and equal attention to the realms of production and reproduction, especially their mutual relationships. We have chosen to "take apart" the concept of class, examine how its components work, and then put it back together. We have been especially cognizant of introducing our concern with ideology, culture, and the attitudes about class and gender, all within a comparative context.

The Canadian survey added to the original questionnaire a greater depth on the division of domestic responsibilities and their effects on labour-force disruptions, greater complexity on authority relationships (including the gendered structure of authority relations), and additional questions on job skills and autonomy. These additional data permit us to pursue some of the comparative questions in greater depth for Canada.

Class analysis has at its core the relationship between capital and labour. Within this relationship, there is a central dynamic that expresses itself at the socio-economic level in the four great classes of advanced capitalism: the capitalist-executive, working, new middle, and old middle classes. The novelty of our analysis lies in our focus on *class structure* as the object of investigation, the structured "relations of ruling" within which men and women go about reproducing the conditions for their own material existence. Our concern has been to identify and account for macro-structural differences in the organization of class relations and less with their micro-behavioural consequences. To use the language of variable analysis, class relations provide the dependent, rather than the independent, variable throughout most of our study. Why has the "old" middle class of independent producers and small property owners been more resilient, and even resurgent, in some countries than in others? Why do some economies devote more labour to the regulation and surveillance of workers than others? These are the sorts of questions we raise in part 1.

Our title, *Relations of Ruling*, is a phrase borrowed from the feminist scholar Dorothy Smith. Its initial appeal was the fact that it provided us with a generic concept that subsumes social relations of both production and reproduction. Our original scheme was to devote part 1 of our study to "relations of ruling" in the labour market and part 2 to "relations of ruling" in the household. Part 1 was to be about class relations and part 2 about gender relations. At the beginning, gender relations meant the division of labour and social relations between men and women in the household. Relations of ruling in the office or factory were "class relations."

We were, of course, sensitive to the fact that class relations could be "gendered," but this meant mainly that there would be gender "differences" in the way men and women are distributed among classes. As our work proceeded, we began to rethink this position, a process that led to the present version of chapter 6, which introduces part 2. There, we revisit the "class analysis" of part 1 to consider the possibility that there is more to production relations than class relations, that relations of ruling in the market not only develop to organize relations between capital and labour but also between men and women.

We also mean to include within the "relations of ruling" the cultural practices that sustain the institutions fundamental to maintaining structures of control in the paid labour force and in the domestic sphere. These we will identify as the class and gender orientations that give meaning to people's accounts of power relations. In chapter 5, we take advantage of our comparative data to address, and to question, long-standing views on the apparent distinctiveness of North American class culture. We challenge prevailing views that the apparent absence of European-like class consciousness among North American workers is the inherited residue of a Lockean-type liberal individualism. Instead, we argue, the cultural repertoire through which North Americans filter their understanding of "classes" reflects the tradition of radical democratic populism that has infused movements of protest against the established order in North America since the end of the nineteenth century. We also take issue with conventional understandings of Canada–U.S. differences in this respect. The Canadian experience has not produced a more European-like understanding of classes and instead is firmly rooted in the populist legacy that has shaped the politics of class on both sides of the 49th parallel.

In chapter 9 we extend our analysis of gender relations to an understanding that includes intranational divisions. Most of the book uses country as a single variable, but in the final empirical analysis we look at key social cleavages, especially in North America. These include the "national question" in Quebec, divisions based upon ethnicity in Canada and race in the United States, and regional divisions in both. We choose to use the "culture of gender" as our site for investigation but maintain our focus on class *and* sex divisions. An issue we concentrate on is how the trade unions have influenced attitudes towards feminist issues.

The major tendencies that have been incorporated into our analysis include the unfolding of postindustrialism, the expanded place of women in the paid labour force, the rise of the new middle class in the hierarchical division of labour, and a recognition of the effects of the social terrains of race, ethnicity, and region. We have also devoted considerable attention to the importance of the relationship between domestic and paid labour. Moreover, we have focused on how people think about class and gender relations, as well as the structural expressions of class and sex. Most obviously we have posed our questions and problems *comparatively*, taking nations as units of analysis and thus avoiding the pitfalls of either American- or European-centric answers with mistakenly universalistic claims. We have also avoided the problem of unwarranted attributions of findings to Canada's uniqueness by making comparisons with not only the United States but also the smaller, more marginal Nordic countries.

A major theme is the unfolding of postindustrialism in the five nations under study here, including the changing nature of goods production and the rise of service employment. Class theorists have often been antagonistic to models of the world in which the benchmarks of history are denoted by transitions from agrarian to industrial or from industrial to postindustrial forms of production. We think this antagonism is misguided: it was Marx after all who put the "revolution in the forces of production" at the centre of modern social thought. Postindustrialism includes transitions in the character of goods production but most especially a dramatic rise in service-sector employment. We are able to demonstrate how the rise of the "service" economy means different things for women in North America and Nordic countries. North American women are concentrated in consumer and business services, usually organized by the private sector, while Nordic women are in health, education, and welfare, usually organized by the public sector. These differences have important implications for the quality of their respective labour-force experiences. Men, in contrast, remain concentrated in goods production in all five countries. The postindustrial experience, then, is highly gendered in its impact and differs dramatically between North America and the Nordic countries.

Related to postindustrialism is the importance of the role of the state sector, particularly as an employer, in our analysis. This is especially acute in comparing the Nordic and North American situations. We concentrate upon two aspects of "sector." These are (1) state-versus-capitalist *property*-ownership sectors, with capitalist sectors subdivided into goods-producing and service sectors, and (2) *activity* sectors, with goods-versus-service sectors, regardless of ownership, and services divided between commercial and consumer activities. Which type of sectoral analysis we utilize depends upon the questions being asked, but all point to the importance of sectors in comparing the unfolding of contemporary labour markets.

What about our approach to class analysis? In a recent "rethinking" piece, Erik Olin Wright identifies "two theoretical impulses" in contemporary class analysis as "minimalist" versus "maximalist" positions, allying himself with the latter.[1] The minimalist strategy is to keep the concept of class structure as simple as possible, while the maximalist impulse is to add complexity by incorporating numerous conceptual divisions to the fundamental division between capital and labour. Our strategy has been to start from a minimalist construction of classes (chapter 1) and to add complexity as the analysis proceeds (see especially chapter 4, where we consider the place of "knowledge workers" and the "new labour aristocracy").

We have chosen to focus our specification of classes around the twin dimensions of commanding the means of production and directing the labour power of others. This produces four main classes, including the most recent one–the new middle class–which has arisen with the full development of corporate capitalism. The new middle class exercises control and surveillance over labour or is part of the administration of the workplace but does not have real economic ownership, characteristic of capitalists and executives, or formal ownership, characteristic of the self-employed.

In 1985 Erik Olin Wright published *Classes*, in which he abandoned the "domination-based" class typology that had originally guided the project's design in favour of an "exploitation-based" typology derived from the work of John Roemer. As our title indicates, we have not followed Wright in this transition. As outlined in chapter 1, the concept of class carries multiple meanings even within Marx's own writings. In Marx the concept of exploitation appears in his analysis of the capital accumulation process, an abstract model of the "laws of motion" of a capitalist economy. As a sociological concept, however, the production relations that constitute a class structure refer to the distribution of effective powers over the forces of production, including the means of production and labour power. Class structures are structures of "empty places," relational maps of the "framework of power in which producing occurs."[2] Social relations of production, as G.A. Cohen writes, are "relations of effective power over persons and productive forces," the instruments and materials used in production and the capacities and skills of those who use them.[3] Class structures in this sense are the political structures humans create to organize their economic activity. Not all "relations of ruling" are class relations; but class relations always imply and are realized in social life as "relations of ruling."

As cultural theorist Raymond Williams writes, "Without arrangements for the collection of statistical data and the development of statistical theory to analyse these data, the society that has emerged out of the industrial revolution is virtually unknowable."[4] We agree. Nevertheless, we recognize that statistics–the numerical representation of information–are not always the most "reader-friendly" way to present information to a broad readership. Most readers are comfortable with information presented in the form of percentages (conditional probabilities) but are less attuned to deciphering more complex techniques such as regression analysis (an alternative method for presenting conditional probabilities). We have tried wherever possible to present our results in percentage form or to use multivariate procedures (standardization) that allow presentation of results in percentage form. The disadvantage of the percentage method is that it does not allow for the more parsimonious presentation of results that other techniques permit. The reader is confronted with familiar numbers but many of them.

A research project of this sort is much like a journey: one never knows what one will find until the destination is reached. Readers who want to know what we think we have found on our journey may wish to begin with our conclusions, summarized in chapter 10 and entitled "After Industrialism." From there they can turn to the beginning and follow us on our journey to determine whether they think their own reading of the evidence supports our conclusions.

Many people and institutions are responsible for supporting and making this study possible. The Social Sciences and Humanities Research Council of Canada (SSHRCC) has provided major ongoing support since 1982. Graduate Studies and Research at Carleton University has filled in the gaps when needed, as has the office of the Dean of Social Science. To these official sponsors we are grateful. SSHRCC funded and Canada Facts conducted our Canadian survey contribution to the Comparative Project. Roger Boe was the project manager during the early years, with Don Black taking over valuable technical work during a crucial period. Ken Innes also provided technical support, as have Ron Santos, Mary Ann Mulvihill, and Wendy Watkins. We wish to acknowledge the major contributions toward the end, as the writing phase began, of Clarence Lochhead and Debra Parnis, who have recently been joined by Grant Schellenberg as the project's graduate research assistants. Clarence is the co-author of chapter 6 and Grant of chapter 3. Clarence also deserves special acknowledgment for his thorough work in checking variable construction and data runs.

Markku Kivinen from the Finnish project has provided us with valuable comments on a draft of the manuscript, and two anonymous reviewers from the Social Science Federation of Canada and

McGill-Queen's University Press have offered thorough comments. Jill Quadagno was especially helpful with her critical reviews of the penultimate draft. We acknowledge the financial support of the Grant in Aid of Publications division of the Social Science Federation. We also wish to thank Philip Cercone, executive director and editor of the press, for his encouragement and assistance.

This work has been a joint effort between the two authors since the earliest days. We have shared the administrative and intellectual responsibilities for the project. This is a book which neither of us would (or could) have written on our own. It has benefited from our different backgrounds, interests, and temperaments. We can witness that writing together takes at least double the time as on one's own, but the product is likely twice as satisfying.

Fondly remembering Bonnie Amim ...

PART ONE

Class Relations
in Postindustrial Societies

1 Class Relations in Industrial Capitalism

> One of the most persistent images that Canadians have of their
> society is that it has no classes.
>
> John Porter, *The Vertical Mosaic* (1965), 3

WHY STUDY CLASSES?

Researchers, at least North American sociologists, seem to spend a good part of their lives trying to persuade a doubting public that it lives in a class society, that classes exist and have real effects. At the time John Porter wrote his ground-breaking study *The Vertical Mosaic*, Canada, like other Western countries, was in the midst of the most sustained economic boom in the history of Western capitalism. Real living standards were rising, mass-produced consumer goods were becoming widely available, and it was difficult to persuade Canadians that classes, if they existed, mattered very much. Certainly, it was difficult to relate the imagery of Marx's exploited proletarians to North American workers, then in the process of acquiring homes, automobiles, appliances, and other accoutrements of a "middle class" life-style. If this was capitalism (a term rarely heard at the time), so be it.

Since the early 1970s, times have been less kind to Western workers. The rate of economic growth has declined, average wages and earnings have not grown and their distribution has become more unequal, and everywhere workers are faced with the insecurities and dislocations associated with globalization and technological change. Despite these changes, it is doubtful that North Americans are any more receptive to class-based analyses of their situation now than in the past. There are several reasons for this attitude.

Classes are not labels people wear on their chests. Class relations, as G.A. Cohen writes, are "relations of effective power over persons and productive forces."[1] They are real relations with real effects that people experience as they go about making a living. But the "bundle" of relations people experience are not homogeneous. And class relations, because they are mediated by relations of race, gender, or nationality, may be experienced very differently by different persons. People can, and often do, have multiple class experiences: throughout their careers and through their parents, spouses, friends, colleagues, and neighbours. Take the example of a woman who works as a clerk all day in an office for a salary, never supervising anyone else, while taking directions from the office manager. In the evenings and on weekends she may be self-employed as a seller of cosmetics or a part-time bookkeeper. Moreover, her experience of class is likely not the same as a man's. She also may have a different class experience because of her spouse's work as, say, an industrial employee or because of the class experiences of those who live in her neighbourhood. Her understanding and evaluation of these relations may be affected by her age, ethnicity, language, or region of residence within the country. Whether she lives in a Nordic country or North America may also have an influence.

A second reason that class relations are obscured in capitalist societies is the institutional separation between state and economy. We slip easily into the language of power – relations of ruling – when discussing affairs of state. But the notion that there are (unelected) economic rulers in the private economy who exercise great power is less widely discussed. Indeed, the concept of power rarely appears in modern economic theory, the source of most of our language for talking about economic matters. And when economists such as John Kenneth Galbraith break ranks to discuss the power exercised by corporations in capitalist societies, they are a source of scandal to their colleagues and reduced to the status of "mere journalists."[2]

Matters are made more complex by the fact that that most Western industrialized societies are not merely capitalist but capitalist *democracies*. The modern state is Janus-faced. Modern capitalism was born out of the struggle to establish the supremacy of the rights of property over and against the supremacy of the state (first feudal and then mercantile) as the central organizing principle both for participation in the exercise of power and for the distribution of wealth and income. The link between property and power was more transparent in nineteenth-century *liberal* states where rights to participate in the affairs of state (to vote and hold office) were conditioned by property ownership (and sex). In contemporary *liberal democratic* states, where political rights are attached to persons as well as to their property, this link is obscured. Workers, as well as capitalists, of both sexes can now influence and take part in the electoral processes of the modern state. Whether and to what extent the relationship between these two sides of the modern state are complementary or contradictory has been a source of long debate in both mainstream and Marxist state theory.[3] Lenin was not alone in observing that the emergence of democratic polities tends to conceal the vast private power exercised by the owners of capital.[4]

Although the modern democratic state puts limits on property rights, the role of property in the exercise of power has not been abolished. Decisions over when and where to invest or whether a plant should be closed or moved to another location are not made by workers or by the local townspeople. Neither are the executives, managers, and supervisors who rule the modern enterprise elected by their subordinates. In short, the capitalist firm is no more democratic today than it was earlier. Instead, the rights that are attached to persons – civil, political, and social – and those attached to property coexist in an uneasy tension, the regulation of which is one of the major tasks of the contemporary state.

How, whether, and why people attach either symbolic or causal significance to class relations is a subject with a long and contentious history (see chapter 5). But whether these relations are perceived as significant is not what determines either the existence of these relations or their analytical importance. In *The Vertical Mosaic*, John Porter directed our attention to the enormous power exercised by a few men (there were no women), who occupied the leading positions in Canada's largest corporations. The fact of this power, and its significance, did not depend on whether or not the larger population was aware of or understood its exercise.

Relations of effective power, or, as we have called them in our title, relations of ruling, are of course not exhausted by *class* relations. Throughout most of recorded history, as Michael Mann writes, relations of effective power between men and women were regulated within the patriarchal household, in which a senior male enjoyed arbitrary power over all females, junior males, and children.[5] And in such societies the "private" sphere of the household was the site of much more economic activity than today. Although the ideal-typical patriarchal household has been eroded as a result of changes occurring since the eighteenth-century, many patriarchal values and practices – neo-patriarchy in Mann's terms – still permeate both public and private life. The historical gendering of class relations during the transition to industrial capitalism has been well documented.[6]

With the decline of the household economy, hierarchically defined gender relations were brought inside the factory gate to become part of a capitalist and, theoretically, universalistic labour market. The subordination of women in the household was reproduced in the relations of power and authority of the capitalist firm. In short, the economic structure of industrial capitalism acquired a social form derived not merely from a logic based on the imperatives of capital accumulation – the logic of the market; it also incorporated social forms derived from the patriarchal household. As a result, class relations became "gendered," a topic we return to in chapters 2 and 6. In part 2 we extend this effort to understand the class-gender nexus by turning our attention to the patriarchal practices of the household and their connection to those of the market.

ALTERNATIVE APPROACHES TO THE STUDY OF CLASSES

Like so many concepts, that of class is highly contested and carries a heavy conceptual burden in the social sciences. In popular parlance, the term is most commonly used to demarcate income classes – to identify, for example, individuals and families with an income sufficient to enjoy a "middle class" life-style. Neo-Marxists in contrast tend to rely on production-based (or "work situation") definitions when speaking of classes: a worker does not become "middle class" simply by virtue of high earnings or by owning a house in the suburbs, filled with appliances. And neo-Weberians (Lockwood, Goldthorpe) typically combine elements of both income ("market situation") and work situation in constructing their class models.

Matters quickly become even more muddled by the fact that there is little agreement, even *within* these broad theoretical camps, over the "real" constitution of classes in modern societies.[7] Some neo-Weberians, such as Ralph Dahrendorf, develop their understanding of classes from Max Weber's emphasis on domination and relations of authority; others, such as Frank Parkin, develop Weber's discussion of "social closure" and emphasize ownership of capital and possession of educational credentials, elements that figure prominently in the work of Erik Olin Wright, a neo-Marxist. During the late seventies and early eighties, debates over the neo-Marxist class typologies of Mino Carchedi, Nicos Poulantzas, and Wright, among others, generated a small growth industry in sociology. Perhaps the ultimate frustration for the student trying to come to grips with "classes" is the fact that after the seemingly arcane debate is finished, the actual

empirical categories generated by neo-Marxian and Weberian analysts are not that different.[8]

What should we make of all this? As Wright points out, the "con-
fusion" can begin to be resolved if attention is paid to the different
levels of abstraction at which "class analysis" is conducted, which in
turn depend on the nature of the questions being asked.[9] Even Karl
Marx, after all, deployed the concept of class in very different ways in
his theoretical analysis of capitalism as a mode of production (as in
Das Kapital) on the one hand and his concrete historical studies of
existing capitalist societies (as in *The Eighteenth Brumaire*) on the
other. Similarly, Ira Katznelson points out that the early debate between Wright and Poulantzas over the use of the distinction between
"productive" and "unproductive" among individual workers was in
fact a pseudo-debate since each author was treating "class" at two
quite different levels of abstraction, the one (Poulantzas) concerned
with the process of capitalist accumulation at the level of the mode of
production (Class$_1$ in Katznelson's terms) and the other with social
relations of actual capitalist workplaces (Class$_2$).[10] The analytical
question in the first instance concerns the trajectory of capital accumulation and its contradictory tendencies, while in the second, the
issue is one of patterned social relations of work lived objectively by
real people in actual social formations. The more useful exercise,
Katznelson goes on to note, is one that proceeds through comparative and historical analyses to sort out what is generic and what is
variable in the relationship between economy and class, understood
at the first, more abstract and general level (e.g., advanced capitalist
economies), and class at the second, more concrete and historically
and spatially specific level.

The reference point for yet a third level of abstraction identified
by Katznelson (Class$_3$) is E.P. Thompson's angry and total rejection
of all classificatory approaches to class structure. Thompson writes:
"I do not see class as a 'structure', nor even as a 'category', but as
something which in fact happens (and can be shown to have happened) in human relationships."[11] The question for him is the classical Marxist question of class agency, of classes as historical actors
and groups that act in class ways. To use a more traditional Marxian
formulation, classes only exist when a "class-in-itself" becomes a
"class-for-itself." A variant of the Thompson view is found in the classificatory perspective of John Goldthorpe.[12] For classes to be "real,"
in Goldthorpe's view, they must minimally have undergone a process
of demographic class formation and acquired an identity as social
groups because of the stability with which individuals and families

occupy class locations, so as to provide a continuity of class experience over the life course and between generations.

It is the variable character of class relations in the second sense that provides the starting point for our analyses: the particular forms and organization of the social relations of production at the level of the workplace. The emergence of classes as historical actors is a topic beyond the scope of survey data, which are the primary source of evidence for this study. Such an undertaking awaits additional sources of data and a broader analysis.[13] We also do not take up Goldthorpe's concern with processes of "demographic class formation." Marxists have often been critical of his preoccupation with social mobility which results from this stance. Poulantzas is perhaps the most condemnatory, commenting on the "stupidity" of the bourgeois problematic of social mobility. For him, "even on the absurd assumption that from one day to the next, or even from one generation to the next, the bourgeoisie would all take the places of workers and vice versa, nothing fundamental about capitalism would be changed, since the places of the bourgeoisie and the proletariat would still be there."[14] Mark Western's neo-Marxian analysis of demographic class formation in Australia provides an elegant and rigorous refutation of this view.[15] But Poulantzas himself gives the case away simply by describing the possibility that bourgeousie and workers might change places everyday as an "absurd assumption." If such a society could still be called capitalist, it would be a strange version of capitalism indeed. Our point is not that processes of "demographic class formation" are unimportant for class analysis,[16] but simply that this is not the question that concerns us here.

This discussion of what our study analysis is *not* about is something of an apology and preparation for the fact that we are about to subject the reader to yet another class typology. This is unavoidable: different questions require different analytical tools. Ours is a study of national differences in social relations of production, not a study of class formation, social, political, demographic, or otherwise. It is the variable character of class relations in the second sense that provides the starting point of our analysis: the particular forms and organization of the social relations of production in five advanced capitalist economies in the latter part of the twentieth-century. Because our analyses are *not* about the *capital-labour* relation (Class$_1$) but about relations between existing capitalists and their employees (Class$_2$), the class categories we develop below are more similar (though not identical) in content to those originally developed by Erik Olin Wright (Wright I) at the origins of the comparative project than those he developed for the subsequent analysis of these data (Wright II).[17] The latter strategy was an attempt to derive empirical class categories from the Marxian concept of exploitation as developed in the work of John Roemer. However, the data collected by the surveys that underlie the analysis are not *about* the capital-labour relation (relations of exploitation), but about the manifestations of this relation in the relations of effective power (relations of ruling) in the workplaces where individual respondents are employed and through which the valorization of labour power is realized.[18] We take as our problematic relations of domination characteristics of both class *and* gender relations, distinguishing our approach from the new exploitation problematic adopted by Wright.

To further clarify our agenda, one final note on what our analyses are *not* about is in order. Much of the contemporary literature on classes has had as its main analytical concern the role of classes as an *independent* variable in models explaining micro-processes of individual behaviour. The subsequent debates have been organized around the problematic of competing class schemes – which explains more variance: Wright I, Wright II, Goldthorpe, and so on. Instead, most of our analysis (but see chapters 5 and 9) focuses on class structure as a *dependent* variable. Our questions are *about* national differences in the organization of production relations – whether they exist and, if so, how to account for these differences. The questions are macro-structural, not micro-behavioural. We attempt to determine, for example, whether and to what extent national differences in the role of the state as an employer, forms of industry composition, the extent and nature of the incorporation of women into paid labour, and so forth have resulted in different "class structures" in five countries.

The demands of such a study, however, do require a starting point, a heuristic model of class structure to serve as a reference for asking questions about national variations. The appropriate starting point for the construction of such a model is history, the actual changes that occurred in the organization of production relations as industrial capitalism matured. This is also the strategy followed by Wright in his original effort to develop a typology of class structure, hence the similarity between our approaches.[19]

ORGANIZING INDUSTRIAL CAPITALISM

Capitalism as a system of production emerged from feudalism, transforming property relations and destroying earlier forms of production. In feudal societies, creating capitalism required the freeing of labour from feudal obligations and of the means of production from aristocratic privilege. In the New World, capitalism required, as

part of its development, the creation of a working class and the sub-
sumption of earlier forms of property that permitted people to "realize their own labour power" (that is, work for themselves). Capitalism required that there be a divorce of labour from ownership of the
means of production for two reasons: to create wage labourers who
must sell their labour power to survive and to concentrate individual
property in collective property.[20] This change did not occur all at
once. During the early stages of capitalism, there were mainly independent commodity producers (working in agriculture, fishing,
manufacturing, etc.). With the industrial revolution, however, the
process of consolidation proceeded rapidly in industry, although
more slowly in resource-based activities (farming, forestry, fishing,
etc.). These activities were the mainstay of the old middle class (the
traditional petite bourgeoisie), including urban sectors in the independent professions (medicine, law, accounting) and retail trade
(shopkeepers). With the rise of corporate capitalism, there was a further erosion of the old middle class but a rise within bureaucratic organizations of the new middle class following from a greater division
of labour in managing the functions of control and co-ordination
over larger labour forces.

Two modern revolutions gave rise to the corporate form that distinguishes twentieth-century industrial capitalism. The first of these,
sometimes called "Sloanism" (because of the pioneering innovations
of Alfred Sloan at General Motors), was the invention of new administrative structures that permitted the creation of large-scale national
and then multi-national diversified corporations. The result was
"managerial capitalism," the creation of a managerial cadre able to
carry out the traditional functions of investment and control over
production, once exclusively the prerogatives of the owner-entrepreneur. The second revolution was the creation of complex hierarchies
for the regulation of labour, symbolically represented by the work of
Frederick Taylor and the growth of scientific management.[21]

The two broad powers of capital that correspond to these two revolutions are the building blocks of the class typology developed here.
The first includes *decision-making* powers over the assignment of the
forces of production to particular uses – when and where to invest,
the mix of capital and labour to be used in production, and so forth.
The second involves the exercise of *authority* over labour, the direction and disciplining of workers.

For the capitalist class the main change was a result of the separation of formal from real economic ownership. Formal ownership includes legal (or juridical) ownership, which may be passive in the
sense of limited to the owner's claim to derive revenue from divi-
dends (*rentiers*). In terms of administration such ownership may be

merely nominal or, if held in sufficient quantity, serve as the basis for real economic ownership that includes control over production, direction of the use to which production is put, and disposal of the products of enterprises, including accumulation and investment. This administrative model, characteristic of advanced capitalist enterprises, can also be applied to the public sector, where executives direct the organizations for which they are responsible based upon the principles of state property rights.[22] Executives, whether empowered by the rights of state or of private property, direct complex organizations of people. Of primary interest to us here is how the rights of property commanded by executives become expressed in hierarchical organizations and are delegated to the new middle class.

The classic work on the rise of modern administration is Alfred D. Chandler Jr's *Strategy and Structure*, in which he documents the rise of executive activities. He notes that often "the executive does not even personally supervise the work force but rather administers the duties of other executives. In planning and coordinating the work of subordinate managers or supervisors, he allocates tasks and makes available the necessary equipment, materials, and other physical resources necessary." As a result, Chandler adopts the term administration to include "executive action and orders as well as the decisions taken in coordinating, appraising, and planning the work of the enterprise and in allocating its resources."[23] Important for our purposes is a further distinction Chandler introduces *within* administration. In part, this distinction involves the scope of responsibility on a long-term versus day-to-day basis, but more significantly it involves the differences between setting long-term goals and conducting the day-to-day operations within the framework of those policies and procedures. This difference Chandler labels strategic versus tactical. "*Strategic* decisions are concerned with the long-term health of the enterprise. *Tactical* decisions deal more with the day-to-day activities necessary for efficient and smooth operations. But decisions, either tactical or strategic, usually require *implementation* by an allocation or reallocation of resources – funds, equipment, or personnel."[24] The modern executive is responsible for strategic decisions, while the new middle class operates at the level of tactical decisions, especially those involving the implementation of strategic decisions. It is this new arrangement of class relations that prompts us to propose a re-conceptualization of classes.

THE HEART OF THE MATTER

The formulation of classes we have adopted here is closest to the early theoretical work of Carchedi. As in Carchedi, the focus is on the labour process and forms of control and surveillance. Classes are produced at the point of production and reproduced throughout social life. At the heart of class formulation are the criteria of real economic ownership of the means of production and the appropriation of surplus labour and/or value through control and surveillance of the labour of others (referred to by Carchedi as the "global function of capital"). These aspects of management or supervision of the labour process are distinct from co-ordination and unity, which are part of creating surplus value/labour, hence, in Carchedi's terms, part of the "global function of the collective worker."

The key class affected by the rise of corporate capitalism is the fully emerged new middle class, which lacks real economic ownership of the means of production (characteristic of what we will call the capitalist-executive class) but exercises control and surveillance over labour, therefore performing part of the "global function of capital" while also (but not necessarily) contributing to the function of the collective worker. The new middle class is neither fully capitalist-executive nor working class. It is important to note that not everyone who directs the labour of others is new middle class since those who only perform the work of co-ordination and unity without conducting control and surveillance are involved in creating surplus value/labour but not appropriating it.

Recall that classes are specified in terms of relationships. The primary relationship in the labour process is control over the creation and appropriation of value and labour. Workers are those who create value and labour; capitalists-executives are those who appropriate surplus value and labour as well as exercising real economic ownership. With the collectivization of social life into larger organizations, a social division of labour emerges and creates a specialized class that exercises control and surveillance over labour or the means of administration on behalf of capitalists and executives yet is itself excluded from real economic ownership; that class we call the new middle class.

Let us follow Carchedi through the argument. The definition of classes begins with "the place occupied by the production agents in the process of production (e.g., under capitalism, whether they are productive or unproductive labours) and on the ownership of the means of production" but goes on to include "the social function performed by the production agents in the production process."[25] A key point in the development of capitalism is the shift from individual to collective performance of tasks by both capital and labour. The function of labour is the production of surplus labour (which Carchedi calls the collective worker). The function of capital is "to carry out the work of control and surveillance" referred to as "the global capitalist." With the rise of corporate capitalism, the new middle class expands so that at the "socio-economic system level of analysis," there are "not only the two primary classes but also the middle classes, i.e. those classes which in terms of production relations are a sort of 'hybrid,' a mixture of the two 'pure' classes."[26]

The distinction between control and surveillance on the one hand and co-ordination and unity on the other is essential. Co-ordination and unity are necessary to any large-scale system of production; control and surveillance, however, follow from the need to "impose discipline on the worker" resulting from the requirement to extract surplus value and/or surplus labour from workers (depending upon the particular relations of production). The latter requirement is particular to maintaining capitalists and executives. They have special powers that are called real economic ownership. Carchedi specifies this as "control of the means of production (i.e. the capacity to determine their use, to hire and dismiss labourers, to decide what, and how much to produce, etc.)."[27] The work of control and surveillance is an extension of real economic ownership and in advanced capitalist societies becomes "the task of a complex, hierarchically organized ensemble of people who collectively perform what used to be the function of the individual capitalist."[28] These collective tasks of capital come to be performed by people who are themselves separate from real economic ownership and have come to be called the new middle class. The middle class that emerges with the development of corporate capitalism does so, in the words of Clegg, Boreham, and Dow, as "both a consequence of the conflict between opposing classes and an expression of the developmental tendencies which are a product of capital-labour antagonisms."[29]

This understanding of the new middle class corresponds somewhat to Poulantzas's notion of the "new petty bourgeoisie." When discussing the nature of supervision in advanced capitalist societies, Poulantzas focused on "the double nature of this labour ... on the one hand as long as supervisory labour is necessary to every labour-process as such, to production in general, then in this sense it is part of productive labour; and, on the other hand, that as long as it concerns the realization of surplus-value, and not the production of it, it constitutes a political control over the working class and, therefore, is not productive labour."[30] Poulantzas contends that it is this difference which distinguishes the "new petty bourgeoisie" (what we are calling the new middle class) from the working class. The "new petty bourgeoisie," in his terms, "exercises specific authority and domination over the working class."[31]

Poulantzas also defines two forms of active control: *economic ownership* is "real economic control of the means of production, i.e. the power to assign the means of production to given uses and so to dispose of the products obtained," while *possession* is "the capacity to put the means of production into operation."[32] The two forms of control are directed at different levels within organizations: economic ownership refers to the activities of accumulation, distribution, and investment while possession refers to the direction of the labour process expressed as commanding either the means of production or the labour power of others.

The key criterion for the capitalist-executive class is real economic ownership, by which we mean the power to direct production to specific purposes and dispose of its products. This involves command over the assets and purpose of organizations at the level of strategic decisions. Executives may also have possession, by which we mean the power to operate the means of production. This is a more specific form of power and includes command of the labour power of employees. Wright recognizes these distinctions in his earliest formulations of class when he distinguishes "economic ownership (control over the flow of investments into production, or more concretely, control over *what* is produced) from possession (control over the production process, or control over *how* things are produced)."[33] As he goes on to say, "Relations of possession concern the direction and control of the capitalist production process. Such direction involves two analytically separable aspects: first, control of the physical means of production; second, control of labour."[34] We contend that people are in new-middle-class positions if they make tactical decisions about administrative processes affecting others *or* if they have control and surveillance over the labour power of other employees with the right to discipline those workers. Those who only co-ordinate the work of others and give unity to the labour process (and are therefore productive of surplus labour and/or value) are not part of the new middle class, connecting instead with collective labour.

It is important to recognize that we are discussing classes in relation to one another, within which we then locate individuals. For these classes, the primary relationship is between the capitalist-executive class and the working class, but there are also secondary relations or alliances involving both the old and new middle classes and either the capitalist-executive or working classes. The old and new middle classes have some level of commonality around the notion of "independence" or "individualism" but one is within a relationship between capital and labour (the new middle class) and the other outside that relationship (the old middle class, which owns its own means of realizing its labour). One type of middle class derives from commanding the labour power of others, the other from command over realizing its own labour power. The capitalist-executive class has in common with the old middle class the protection of property rights, while the new middle class and working class have in common wage relationships with employers (the capitalist-executive class).

Based upon its material conditions, the old middle class has in common its individual relationship to property, providing it with the ability to realize its own labour power (that is, it works for itself or with household labour). This characteristic means the old middle class is necessarily small in scale and likely to oppose large organizations of capital or labour. It leads to populist opposition to both corporate capital and industrial unions. The old middle class will tend to organize in co-operatives or professional associations, which bind together to give it political voice (interest associations) or protect markets (co-operatives) or sources of capital (credit unions).

The old middle class is defined by the criterion of working for itself. The classic petite bourgeoisie owned its own property and was thus "independent" from the capitalist class. A more intensive analysis of the fate of the old middle class under advanced capitalism reveals that many members retain formal ownership of their means of production and possession of their immediate labour process but have often lost control over real economic ownership (thus becoming dependent commodity producers, experiencing proletarianization without becoming proletarian).[35] Throughout advanced capitalist societies there has been a process of the commodification of labour, which has meant the decline of the old middle class, with most openings occurring in the working class (becoming proletarian) but many in the new middle class as well.

OPERATIONALIZING CLASS

No task has been more puzzling for researchers of social stratification than the operationalization of class. There are legitimate debates of a theoretical, methodological, and substantive order. We have chosen to begin with a broad conceptualization, introducing refinements and specifications within four broadly constructed classes. As suggested, the problem is, in part, one of levels of abstraction. At the highest level of abstraction there are only two great "classes" within capitalism, capital and labour, with capital seeking to appropriate the value that only labour can produce. At a more intermediary level of analysis (and the one we have chosen to enter), there are four major classes that appear within industrial capitalism. Each is defined in relation to the command of capital (the means of production) and the labour power of others (the source of value). They can be illustrated as follows:

Command Means of Production	Command Labour Power of Others	
	Yes	No
Yes	Capitalist-executive	Old middle class
No	New middle class	Working class

While the principal opposition within capitalist societies is between the capitalist and working classes, two other major classes mediate between them. Members of the old middle class (or traditional petite bourgeoisie) control their own means of production required for realizing their own labour (work for themselves) and do not have significant command of labour outside their own households. The new middle class (or modern petite bourgeoisie) exercises control over the labour power of others on behalf of capital but does not have real economic ownership over the means of production or control over its own means of realizing its labour (as the old middle class does) because it is itself employed. The above chart does not adequately capture the two (often overlapping) ways the new middle class is identified by administering either people or policy. Commanding the labour power of others is made clear, but the other way of having non-binding policy-setting powers as delegated by executives is not well portrayed. In fact, the new middle class includes those who administer through tactical decisions the strategic command over the means of production exercised by executives *as well as* those with control and surveillance over other employees.

The capitalist class includes senior managers who have real economic ownership and command the labour power of others. The working class has only its labour power to sell, being the subject of capital as mediated by the new middle class. Members of the working class are divorced from the means of realizing their labour, so they must sell their labour power to capital, and they do not themselves command the labour power of others (as does the new middle class). Capitalists and senior managers command, besides the labour power of others, the means of capital accumulation, the products of labour, and, through the new middle class, the use of labour and direction of the labour process.

Just how these criteria are operationalized empirically is also subject to considerable contestation, and, it should be said, there is a necessary degree of arbitrariness about the decisions taken in the concrete operationalization, depending upon the type of information available or the questions asked. We have chosen, for purposes of outlining the four broad classes, to proceed as follows:

1 Capitalists-executives are defined as those who employ on a regular basis three or more people or who command the means of production (make decisions) concerning the number of persons employed, the products made, their amount, methods of production, budget, or distribution, with binding decision-making authority either themselves or as a voting member of a group. Executives must also be located within the top, upper, or at least middle-management levels of their organizations. This condition was adopted for measurement reasons (to be discussed in chapter 4) as a way to distinguish strategic from tactical decision-makers. The capitalist-executive class, then, includes two groups of people. Capitalists are self-employed with three or more employees. Executives are senior managers who make direct decisions about the products or services delivered, the number of employees, and budgets.

2 The new middle class includes those who exercise "control and surveillance" over other employees or play a role in the lower-level management of people and budgets. Control and surveillance is operationalized in terms of the ability to affect the promotion of subordinates, prevent their gaining raises, cause them to be fired or suspended, or issue formal warnings. Lower-level management includes employees below the executive class who make decisions about products or services, numbers of employed, budgets, policies on work performance, or procedures as part of a group or subject to approval. In short, the new middle class includes non-executive employees who can impose sanctions on other employees or have some policy-setting authority.

3 The old middle class is the self-employed with two or fewer employees.

4 The working class has an absence of command over the means of production, labour power of others, or its own means of realizing its labour.

Producing these operationalizations required a complex set of questions reproduced in appendix 1. Numerous detailed decisions have been made that influenced the data produced. Several of these are significant when drawing comparisons with other typologies with which readers may be familiar, especially with that originally developed by Wright.[36]

For conceptual reasons (discussed above) and measurement reasons (discussed in chapter 4), our "executive" category is a much narrower and smaller category than Wright's managerial category. Our "new middle class" includes lower-level managers (administrators) and supervisors with sanctioning authority. Another difficult decision is where to draw the line between "capitalists" and the old middle class. Most would agree the old middle class is self-employed and contributes its own labour power. Indeed, the key notion is its ability to realize its own labour rather than being compelled to sell its labour power to others. But just how many others can the self-employed themselves employ before they are regarded as small capitalists? We have selected the cut-off between two (still old middle class) and three (the bottom line for capitalists). At a common-sense level, this means that those who work for themselves and hire one or two others to assist them (often family members controlled by patriarchal relations) still rely primarily upon their own labour power whereas those who regularly employ three or more others are beginning to rely primarily upon the labour power of the others. In practical terms, this is also the break-point used in the Canadian labour movement, specifically by the United Fishermen and Allied Workers' Union in its rules for membership eligibility.[37] It is necessarily somewhat arbitrary but more grounded than any other criterion we have encountered. Finally, we have not followed the practice of including unpaid family workers among the old middle class for both theoretical and measurement reasons that we discuss in the endnote.[38]

We have theoretically identified a set of production relations between capital and labour. Empirically, we rely upon respondents as reporters of these work relationships and their place within them, a practice strongly criticized by Carchedi, who argues that with survey data "all one can do is to enquire into how classes affect individuals. However, the basic unit of analysis remains the individual, not classes."[39] He contends that "once one starts with a 'micro-individual logic,' the only way of reaching the social level is by aggregation of individual units. But aggregation of individual units cannot explain the social, i.e., what constitutes the units as units of a whole."[40] We disagree. Classes are specified outside individuals, as are the key social relationships that constitute classes at the socio-economic level of analysis (and informed by the highest level of abstraction concerning surplus value/labour and productive/unproductive labour). We claim that individual reports of social relationships help both to locate individuals within class relations and to specify the nature of those

Table 1.1
Class by Nation (percentages)

Class*	United States	Canada	Norway	Sweden	Finland
Capitalist-executive	10.2	6.2	6.8	6.6	7.4
New middle	28.3	24.9	24.8	19.2	16.3
Old middle	7.8	11.3	9.2	6.0	12.9
Working	53.7	57.6	59.3	68.2	63.3
	100	100	100	100	100
(N)[a]	(1,494)	(2,115)	(1,713)	(1,186)	(998)

[a] See appendix 1 for a description of samples.
* National differences in size of class compared to the United States are significant at .05 level of confidence or better in all cells with the exception of the old middle classes in Norway and Sweden.

relationships. The individuals/agents occupy places/positions within a structure of classes, so their reports can reveal differences in class structure for different nations and their experiences of class. We can use their reports to explore how class relations affect individuals and their attitudes and actions. We do not claim that such reports exhaust the whole of class as a social phenomenon or practice.

To summarize, the capitalist-executive class controls production and the employment of others, while the new middle class are employees who assist the employer's control through sanctioning authority or administration. The working class works for others and is the subject of the control processes. The old middle class is self-employed, so its members work "outside" the dominant relations of production and basically have at their disposal the means of realizing their own labour. The resulting distribution of classes for the five countries, based on national surveys conducted at the beginning of the 1980s (see the appendix 1 for sample details), is shown in Table 1.1. At this aggregate level, the United States has the largest capitalist-executive class, the largest new middle class, and the smallest working class. The U.S. distribution contrasts most sharply with the pattern found in Sweden and Finland, where the working class is decidedly larger and the new middle and capitalist-executive classes considerably smaller. In what will become a familiar pattern, Canada and Norway are virtually identical, standing between Sweden and the United States.

The class distributions in Table 1.1 provide us with a first approximation of the distribution of effective powers over persons and the forces of production in the five countries, but only that. They provide a starting point – an empirical referent – for asking questions about origins, processes of transformation, and their composition. To set the stage for the analyses in the chapters that follow, we turn briefly to a discussion of origins, the historical residues of the rather different trajectories followed by each of our five nations during their initial period of industrialization.

ORIGINS: HISTORICAL RESIDUES OF INDUSTRIAL CAPITALISM

The contemporary organization of production relations in advanced capitalist societies is the "effect" of history. For most of the twentieth-century, the "old middle class" has been a class in decline, but this decline has proceeded at different rates in different national economies. Sloanism and Taylorism took form in the United States early in the century and were succesfully exported to the majority of advanced capitalist countries, but usually with important modifications.[41] All five countries are advanced capitalist societies, but they occupy different places within the international division of labour. As blocs, the Nordic countries have their roots in estate-based feudal societies and emigration, whereas the North American ones are built on colonialization and immigration. The United States made a revolutionary break from the British Empire, while Canada's movement from that empire has been more evolutionary, shifting into the domain of its continental neighbour after the Second World War.[42]

Canada occupies a peculiar place within the international division of labour. Like Sweden, Norway, and Finland, Canada is an advanced capitalist society with a strong reliance upon resource exports. All four countries were "late" industrializers, but Canada failed to take the path to independent development and has become intimately associated with the U.S. economy. It continues to have a foreign-dominated industrial sector and has relied upon immigration for its labour force. The Nordic situation is one of internal empires of Sweden over Norway (until 1905) and Russia over Finland (until 1917), with relatively homogeneous national populations. They are late industrializing countries, but made their breakthroughs in the twentieth century with fairly autonomous development: first Sweden, then Norway, and finally Finland.

The social, economic, and political links between the two North American nations on the one hand and the Nordic countries on the other lead us to look for broad similarities in their class structures. But the class experience of the two regional blocs has not been homogeneous. Canada's relation to the United States, it has often been argued, has produced a "distorted" class structure north of the border (see chapter 4). And the United States was constructed from two distinct economic formations: an industrializing economy in the

North and Midwest and a slave-based plantation economy in the South. Although Sweden, Norway, and Finland share important markets on more equitable terms than Canada and the United States, Finland tends to supply more labour, Norway resources, and Sweden industrial products.

Our understanding of the Nordic class structure builds upon the historical background provided by our collegues in the Comparative Class Structure Project. Historically, Finland has had a higher proportion of self-employed rural peasants and a smaller industrial working class than the other two Nordic countries. The working classes in each Nordic nation have quite distinct roots. Agricultural and forestry labourers made up over half Finland's working class in 1920, compared to a fifth in Sweden and Norway. By the 1950s manufacturing labourers were in a majority in the Norwegian and Swedish working classes.[43] In Finland, agricultural and forestry workers continued to dominate. Swedish industrialization occurred in a period when manufacturing was still labour-intensive and in the absence of strong craft-based production, with the result that industrial workers have tended to dominate the Swedish working class. For the crucial 1930 to 1950 period, the Swedish industrial working class was a much more significant force than in Norway and Finland, facilitating the establishment of Social Democratic Party hegemony in Sweden. In Norway, in contrast, "the middle class (white-collar employees) have held a stronger position than in Sweden. Wage earners in Norway have to a lesser extent been dominated by the working-class than in Sweden."[44] Finnish workers were fewer in number than the old middle class until as late as 1960 because of the extraordinarily large independent, self-employed population in agrarian and forestry activity, thus providing the material basis for powerful agrarian political parties.

Some of the residues of this history *seem* apparent in our results: Finland's large old middle class, broad similarities between Canada and the United States, a larger new middle class in Norway than in the other Nordic countries. But what of more recent changes, particularly those that have distinguished the postwar years and the very dramatic transformation that has occurred in both the division of labour (the shift to services) and the composition of the labour force (the growing participation of women in the labour force)? While the long arm of history may underlie and help to explain national differences in class structure, recent theoretical debates concerning the trajectory of class relations in capitalist societies have focused on these more proximate reasons for expected changes and differences, debates we take up in chapter 2.

2 Filling the Empty Places: Class, Gender, and Postindustrialism

> In the social production of their life, men [*sic*] enter into definite relations that are indispensable and independent of their will, relations of production which correspond to a definite stage of development of their material productive forces. The sum total of these relations of production constitutes the economic structure.
>
> Karl Marx, *Critique of Political Economy*

Class structures are arrangements of "empty places," relational maps of the "framework of power in which producing occurs."[1] By themselves, however, class structures are abstractions, empty analytical boxes without history or content. While the language of classes provides a way to speak about the *social* form of economic activity, it tells us nothing about its *material* content – the forces of production and the material division of labour – or about the *persons* who fill the "empty places."

Class descriptions tell us about *social* relations of production, "relations of effective power over persons and productive forces."[2] They describe relations of effective power among the parts, but as George Cohen points out, there cannot be an economy without persons and productive forces. A class description of the nineteenth-century American South that counted only the number of slave-owners, overseers, and slaves, without reference to the fact that this was a plantation economy engaged in the production of cotton and other commodities or the fact that slaves were of black African origin while slave-owners were from white European stock would be incomplete, to say the least. The history of all societies is marked by the way particular types of persons are inserted into the economic structure and by the stage of development of their productive forces.

The stereotypical worker who emerges from the pages of the history of *industrial* capitalism was distinguished both by his sex and by the nature of the work performed. The male, blue-collar worker was typically employed in the production of goods (mining, manufactur-

Table 2.1
Selected Characteristics of Working-Class Men

Percentage of Working-Class Men Who Are in:	*United States*	*Canada*	*Norway*	*Sweden*	*Finland*
Blue-collar occupations	63	58	59	63	75
Goods & distributive industries	61	62	66	71	79
State employment	22	27	35	35	27
Unskilled jobs	80	75	79	78	78

ing, construction) or their distribution (trucking, railways, shipping). He was usually employed by a capitalist firm, not the state. His work required little formal education, and the tasks he performed were routine and repetitive. He was also the raw material from which the labour movement (whether craft or industrial) was formed and upon whom the fate of class politics depended.

From the vantage point of working-class men, this traditional imagery is not far from the mark (Table 2.1). The majority of male workers are in blue-collar occupations (crafts, factory operatives, and labourers); they are employed in industries associated with the production and distribution of goods (manufacturing, transportation); relatively few work for the state (public administration, state-provided services, and publicly owned enterprises); and most are in relatively unskilled jobs (our measure of "skilled" workers is described in chapter 4).

In effect, the historical stereotype of the blue-collar, semi-skilled industrial worker remains the modal experience of working-class men even today. What has changed is that such men are now a distinct minority in the class structure of the advanced societies. In the 1980s, blue-collar, working-class men made up less than 30 per cent of all wage salary workers in the five countries. Indeed, their share of the employed labour force (i.e., excluding the self-employed) is virtually an international constant, ranging only from 26 per cent in Norway to a high of 29 per cent in Finla.id.

The relative decline of the industrial working class in general and of the male working class in particular is a result of changes in both the material division of labour and the social composition of the people employed by capital. The first of these changes has to do with the shift of employment from the production of things to the production of services; the second is a result of the massive entry of women into the paid work-force. Both changes, it is now argued, require us to rethink our understanding of classes and class structure. An understanding of classes derived from the period of industrial capitalism is at best incomplete. A new material division of labour (postindustri-

Table 2.2
Services by Total Employment, 1963–86
(percentage)

	1963	1975	1986
United States	58	65	69
Canada	56	65	70
Norway	–	56	66
Sweden	46	57	66
Finland	36	49	56

Source: Based upon OECD, *Labour Force Statistics: 1966–86*
(Paris: OECD, 1988), Table 7.

alism) and the feminization of the labour force have made our traditional ways of looking at things anachronistic. But while there is broad consensus that these changes are important, there is less agreement over their consequences and implications.

POSTINDUSTRIALISM AND THE MATERIAL DIVISION OF LABOUR

The remarkable capacity of capitalism to revolutionize the forces of production – to increase productivity and reduce the amount of labour required to create a product – was remarked upon by Karl Marx, as well as by Adam Smith, and can now no longer be in doubt. Traditionally, 50 to 70 per cent of the labour force was required to produce the food required for survival; today, that figure has fallen to 3 to 4 per cent in the developed capitalist economies. Since the fifties, the trend in manufacturing has been similar. In Canada, where the shift to a service economy is most advanced (Table 2.2), less than a fifth of the labour force is now directly engaged in manufacturing. In the brief period between 1981 and 1986, the percentage of full-time equivalent jobs in processing, fabricating, and machining occupations declined from 18 per cent of all jobs to 15 per cent.[3]

As Joachim Singelmann has shown, the transition to service employment in North America dates to the 1920s, considerably earlier than in other nations.[4] Canada and the United States did not follow the classical trajectory described by the Fisher-Clark thesis of employment shifts from primary to secondary, and subsequently to tertiary industries. The shift of employment from agriculture into goods and services occurred simultaneously. "In both countries," Singelmann concludes, "the decline of agriculture led to a concomitant growth of transformative and service industries, with services overtaking the transformative sector by the turn of the century."[5] The employment share of the transformative sector (agriculture, resources, manufacturing, and construction) peaked in Canada during the 1950s and in the United States in the 1960s. These North American peaks occurred sooner and at lower levels than in Europe. This early start is reflected in the higher levels of service employment evident in Canada and the United States by the 1960s. By 1986, however, both Sweden and Norway were close to North American levels, while Finland had reached a level comparable to North America in the 1960s.

Since the 1960s, it has been commonplace to subsume these developments under the conceptual rubric of "postindustrialism." In its original incarnation, the concept of postindustrialism was deployed by mainstream practitioners of what Anthony Giddens calls "industrialization theory" to make sense of unexplained emergent trends and patterns.[6] If such trends could not be adequately understood with a theory derived from "the logic of industrialism," then presumably a theory based on "the logic of postindustrialism" was required.[7]

Our use of the term is less ambitious. As Fred Block observes, the concept of *postindustrialism* (like post-Keynesianism or post-Fordism) is a negative one.[8] It does not designate the kind of economy or society we are moving towards, but only the kind of economy and society we are leaving behind. It means simply that societies have moved beyond "industrialism" – a historical, not a logical category. But our use of the term also differs from Block's, for whom postindustrialism represents "the development of new productive forces that come into conflict with capitalist social relations."[9] The judgment that postindustrialism represents a transformation which cannot be absorbed within capitalist social relations is at least historically premature. It is not *capitalist* social relations *per se* that are threatened by postindustrialism but a particular historical form of those relations.

Postindustrialism is not the only metaphor that has been adopted to capture this transition. Many analysts prefer to describe the current period as "post-Fordist." As developed by the French regulation theorists (Aglietta, Boyer, Lipietz), the concept of Fordism directs our attention to the form of capitalism that emerged out of the Depression and the Second World War, based on mass-production technologies on the one hand and the extension of mass consumption on the other.[10] For our purposes, however, the empirical terrain subsumed by the Fordist metaphor is too narrow. As Rianne Mahon observes, the analyses of postwar labour markets that derive from this

perspective have been constructed largely around changes in the organization of (male) blue-collar work in manufacturing.[11] The most
distinctive feature of advanced capitalist labour markets has been the
fact that employment growth occurred in services (where most
women are employed).

Another common metaphor used to describe the new division of
labour is the concept of the "service economy," but it too is limited,
suggesting that manufacturing no longer matters. Manufacturing –
production of goods – does matter as a generator both of wealth and
of employment.[12] The point is rather that manufacturing now generates more information- and data-based occupations (engineers,
lawyers, accountants, designers, clerks), while the "direct producers"
– craftworkers and factory operatives – continue to decline.

The concept of postindustrialism has two reference points. First, it
identifies a transformation in the way goods are produced. This is
manifest in the changing *mix of labour* associated within the goods
sector and the growing importance of producer services (engineering, legal, financial, etc.) that provide inputs for manufacturing and
resource extraction. Second, postindustrialism refers to a dramatic
reduction in the *quantity of labour* required for goods production and
hence the release of labour for other things. The result has been a
spectacular growth of employment in the consumer-oriented services associated with retail, social, and personal service sectors of the
economy.

These shifts in employment patterns have given rise to a large
body of theory and debate over the extent to which such changes in
the *material* division of labour are also consequential for the *social* relations of production.[13] At various times, the postindustrial transition has been implicated in the resurgence of self-employment (the
"old" middle class), the expansion of a new middle class of "knowledge workers," or, as in the work of Mallet, a "new working class" of
technical workers imbued with the capacity to transform capitalism.
Others (such as Braverman) have pointed to postindustrialism's
darker side – the rapid growth of low-wage, unskilled jobs, especially
in the "servant industries" (food and accommodation, cleaning services) – and concluded that postindustrialism is associated with a
process of intensive proletarianization (the degradation of labour).

Most such theories, including those expressed in a non-Marxist
voice (for example, in the works of Clark Kerr and Daniel Bell), im-
plicitly or explicitly proceed from a premise of the primacy of productive forces in shaping class structures. New *forces* of production
erode old *relations* of production, giving rise to new economic structures and new or transformed social classes. It is a view articulated

throughout the writings of Marx and has been defended with unusual intellectual rigour by G.A. Cohen.[14] Writers who take this point of view are often charged with falling into the trap of technological determinism and/or functionalism, a charge sometimes made against Marx as well as against more conventional industrialization theorists.

Intellectual charges and countercharges of this sort reappear with regularity in both Marxist and non-Marxist schools of thought and have their origins in a long-standing debate in the social, and more recently the natural, sciences. The traditional natural-science, or Newtonian, point of view holds that history can be understood by achieving systemic or general knowledge of a system's behaviour. For all their differences, so-called scientific Marxism and neo-classical economics share a common pursuit of "the laws of motion" of capitalist development. More historically minded social scientists, in contrast, have typically been more impressed by the sensitivity of history to "initial conditions."[15] The same general processes can lead to radically different outcomes when inserted into a variety of historical circumstances. Hence the actual seriation of events we call "history" cannot be deduced a priori from general laws or even probabilistic laws since, in the long run, even events with a very low likelihood of occurring can occur. The upshot is considerable scepticism over general theories developed "in one country," a scepticism we consider to be analytically healthy, at least as a starting point.

Our strategy in the chapters that follow is to address these debates by studying the "effects" of postindustrialism under very different national political and economic conditions. Does postindustrialism carry in it a single "logic" leading to similar outcomes in all capitalist economies? Or is it more like an electrical charge, which creates dramatically different effects depending on whether it is used to power a refrigerator or a stove? Should we associate postindustrialism with the ascendancy of a new knowledge class of scientists and technicians, as suggested by Bell? A postindustrial proletariat of fast-food workers? Both? Or do national political and economic circumstances alter the impact of otherwise similar historical processes so that the outcomes of postindustrialism are relatively indeterminate?

Our answers to these questions are of course constrained by the fact we consider only five, not all, advanced capitalist economies. We hasten to point out, however, that *these* five countries are perhaps more appropriate than many others for addressing these questions. On most dimensions related to our understanding of class organization and class politics, Sweden and the United States represent polar contrasts among postwar capitalist countries. Sweden–United States

Table 2.3
Non-Agricultural Labour Force by Industry Sector (percentages)

	United States	Canada	Norway	Sweden	Finland
INDUSTRIAL					
Goods	32	30	32	37	41
Distributive services	11	12	14	11	12
POSTINDUSTRIAL					
Personal & retail	23	21	18	12	15
Business services	11	11	6	4	5
Health, education, & welfare	17	19	23	31	21
Public administration	6	7	7	6	6
	100	100	100	100	100
(N)	(1,407)	(1,982)	(1,609)	(1,148)	(867)

differences with respect to the development of organized labour and labour parties, the impact of classes on the growth and shape of the welfare state, and the way in which women have been incorporated into the paid work-force have long since been staples in the comparative literature about classes. And in broad terms, their adjacent neighbours tend to emulate, if not exactly reproduce, the patterns found in these two nations. As Gösta Esping-Andersen documents, the United States and Canada on the one hand and Sweden, along with its Nordic neighbours, on the other represent two "regime clusters" where classes, class formation, and their effects on social life are the most diverse.[16] In the Nordic countries, organized labour has grown to include most of the labour force, while in North America, and especially in the United States, organized labour is remarkably weak. Political parties representing the working class have played a key, and sometimes dominant, role in postwar Nordic politics; in North America such parties have either been marginal in postwar politics (as in Canada) or non-existent (the United States). But more germane to our purpose, these two clusters differ dramatically in the trajectories followed in their transition from an industrial to a postindustrial economy.

POSTINDUSTRIAL TRAJECTORIES

The argument for diversity – that otherwise similar changes in the material division of labour can lead to substantially different class outcomes – has been suggested by Gösta Esping-Andersen and others, who have highlighted the very different "postindustrial trajectories" followed by different countries.[17] This diversity is illustrated in Table 2.3, where we show the distribution of the non-agricultural

Figure 2.1
Composition of Industrial and Postindustrial Economic Sectors

1 THE INDUSTRIAL SECTOR
   1.1 *Goods Production* is composed of three broad sectors that are usually collapsed
       into a single category because of sample size considerations.
       a *Natural Resource and Natural Resource–Based*: Forestry, Fishing/trapping, Metal
         mines, Mineral fuels, Non-metal mines, Quarries and sand pits, Services to
         mining, Wood industries, Paper and allied, Primary metals, Petroleum and
         coal, Electric power, gas, water
       b *Manufacturing*: Food and beverage, Tobacco products, Rubber and plastics,
         Leather, Textile, Knitting mills, Clothing, Furniture and fixtures, Printing
         and publishing, Metal fabricating, Machinery, Transportation equipment,
         Electrical products, Non-metallic mineral products, Chemical and chemical
         products, Miscellaneous manufacturing
       c *Construction*: General contractors, Special trade contractors, Services to con-
         struction
   1.2 *Distributive Services*: Transportation, Storage, Communications, Wholesale trade
2 THE POSTINDUSTRIAL SECTOR
   2.1 *Personal and Retail Services*: Retail trade, Amusement and recreational services,
       Personal services, Accommodation and food, Miscellaneous services
   2.2 *Business Services*: Finance services, Insurance carriers, Insurance/real estate,
       Services to business management
   2.3 *Health, Education, and Welfare*: Education and related, Health and welfare, Re-
       ligious organizations
   2.4 *Public Administration*: National, Sub-central and Local administration, Other
       government

labour force by the broad industry sectors defined in Figure 2.1.[18]
The industrial-postindustrial division separates the economy into
sectors based both on their historical evolution and on their current
employment profiles. Goods production (e.g., manufacturing) and
distributive services (e.g., railways) have their roots in the nineteenth-century industrial revolution. The postindustrial sector is
composed of both producer and consumer services whose expansion
and current employment patterns were formed in the second half of
the twentieth-century.

   Our results, like those of Elfring and Esping-Andersen,[19] highlight the fact that postindustrial economies come in a variety of sizes
and shapes. The distinctive feature of North American labour markets is the large share of employment in personal, retail, and business
services. The distinctive feature of the Nordic economies (especially
the Swedish) is the large share of employment in health, education,
and social services. As Esping-Andersen shows, the reason for these
differences is to be found in the very different role that class actors,
including unions and political parties, played during the postwar decades.[20] The ability of Swedish labour unions and parties to squeeze

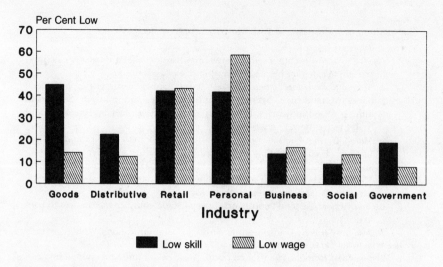

Figure 2.2
Job Skills and Wages by Industry, Canada 1986

out low-wage employers and maintain a strong commitment to full employment and social services has made it difficult, if not impossible, for low-wage personal-service industries to establish a niche in the Swedish economy. In this sense, "politics" – initial conditions – have played a major role in shaping postindustrial employment patterns.

Do these differences in the postindustrial employment mix matter? North American studies of job skills and wages are fairly clear on this matter.[21] Illustrative results on the proportion of low-wage and low-skill jobs (see endnote for definitions) in Canada by industry sector are shown in Figure 2.2.[22] Business services, social services, and public administration have comparatively few low-skill or low-wage jobs; personal and retail services have a large number of both. In terms of "job quality," North America's very large personal- and retail-service sector means a large number of "bad jobs," and the "underdevelopment" of its welfare-state industries implies fewer "good jobs" than would otherwise be the case.

But what of class relations – the relations of ruling that bind employees and their employers together in the workplace? Has postindustrialism brought a new distribution of effective powers over people and productive forces? Do differences in "postindustrial trajectories" matter for the relations of ruling in advanced capitalist

economies? Has postindustrialism brought about a new class structure? Is there a need for us to revise our map of the "relations of
ruling," familiar to us from an industrial economy that we have at-
tempted to capture in the typology elaborated in chapter 1? Or has
the "revolution in the forces of production" in the second half of the
twentieth-century simply brought forward in time "traditional" relations of ruling, inserting them into a new division of labour?

On these matters there is considerable division of opinion. On the
one hand, a whole generation of "new class" theories have emphasized the intensification of the knowledge-skill-credentials component of postindustrial labour markets. The revolution of the forces
of production has diminished the importance of brute manual labour and intensified the importance of the ability to apply abstract
knowledge to deal with concrete problems. The emphasis differs: for
Daniel Bell the issue is control over scientific knowledge; for Alvin
Gouldner, the control of culture. John Goldthorpe highlights the exercise of autonomy and discretion, and Erik Olin Wright, control of
skill and organizational "assets." To some, knowledge, skill, or credentials are constitutive of a "new class" and to others (such as Serge
Mallet) of new class fractions. Among these authors, there is considerable disagreement over the emancipatory effects of this development
but broad consensus that "the relations of ruling" have changed.

Others, notably Harry Braverman and those inspired by him, are
more than sceptical about such conclusions. For Braverman, the logic of
capitalism leads inevitably to processes of capitalist rationalization and
deskilling, processes that have transformed mass white-collar occupations in the past and are now taking their toll on the intermediate
classes as well. Slowly but surely, professionals and managers, precisely
because of their expanding numbers, will find themselves divested of
their "privileges and intermediate characteristics."[23]

The question quite simply is this: to what extent have transformations in the forces of production given rise to processes of proletarianization (or its opposite) within the working and/or new middle
classes of industrial capitalism? And, more importantly, are the consequences of postindustrialism broadly the same across countries, as
is normally assumed in such debates? Or do the changes usually associated with postindustrialism lead to different outcomes because
they occur under radically different "initial conditions"?

"UNPACKING" CLASSES AND ADDING
TEXTURE: AN ANALYTICAL STRATEGY

Our purpose in the following chapters is to provide at least some provisional answers to the sorts of questions posed above, first by unpacking the production relations embedded in the class typology of chapter 1 and, secondly, by adding texture to it. As we indicated in chapter 1, our typology is intended as a heuristic starting point for analysis, one that allows us to ask questions rather than providing, a priori, the answers to such questions.

Efforts to construct class typologies – to define positions in the economic structure – of the sort pursued in chapter 1 represent an attempt to reduce the complexity of production relations – to identify *positions* in the economic structure – in ways that are theoretically and historically meaningful on the one hand and empirically feasible on the other. Such typologies are useful when they are intended to isolate *particular* production relations (or a combination of them) that are theoretically pertinent for the explanation of some other social process, such as class conflict, the formation and distribution of ideologies and beliefs, or even income inequality.[24] But they are decidedly less useful when the purpose is to study production relations themselves. While typologies have the advantage of reducing complexity, they also obscure the underlying components that go into their construction. The reason is that all such typologies are based on theoretical choices to privilege some production relations over others or on the particular way in which a subset of production relations intersect. Some members of the new middle class have administrative duties, while others are mainly responsible for the control of labour. Employees who make decisions over the allocation of capital are classified as managers or executives, and the fact that they are also responsible for the directing and disciplining labour is lost in the process. The result is that any such typology conceals as much as it reveals.

The first prong of our strategy then is to reverse the procedure of chapter 1 by "unpacking" the class typology into its constituent elements: ownership of capital (chapter 3), participation in decision making, and the co-ordination and control of labour (chapter 4). The second prong is to add texture to our typology by considering production relations – effective powers over persons and productive forces – that are not part of our typology. Classes, as we have defined them, are social categories constructed on the basis of the distribution of powers that derive, directly or indirectly, from the ownership and possession of capital. But "the powers of capital" do not exhaust the range of effective powers in a capitalist economy. Over and against these powers are others that derive from the fact that under capitalism, as distinct from slavery, the direct producers own their own labour power. To earn a living they are compelled to sell their labour power, but this does not change the fact that the situation of the proletarian is fundamentally different from that of a slave. The subordination of the proletarian, as Cohen observes, "ensues because, lacking means of production, he [*sic*] can ensure his own survival only by contracting with a capitalist whose bargaining position enables him to impose terms which effect the worker's subordination."[25]

Because they own their own labour power, proletarians can improve their bargaining power (and reduce their subordination) *vis-à-vis* capital in two ways. First, *individual* workers can increase their bargaining power by acquiring scarce skills for which there is no readily available substitute. The historical exemplar is the craft-worker of early industrial capitalism. As the historical record makes clear, such workers were able to exercise considerable power in the workplace and their skills provided protection from both the market and employer coercion.[26] Their modern equivalents are the technical experts and knowledge workers over whom so much analytical ink has been spilled in both mainstream and Marxian debates on class structure.

Second, workers are able to enhance their power with respect to capital because of their capacity to act *collectively* by forming unions, guilds, and associations. Through their ability to deny capital access to labour, organized workers can acquire real powers over economic activity both directly (in the market) and indirectly (through the state). The exercise of these powers, both individual and collective, can alter the capital-labour relation not only with respect to the price of labour (wages) but also with respect to the authority the former is able to exercise over the latter.

Our claim is not that the powers of labour are constitutive of class positions. We will, however, contend that the powers of labour and their level of development require us to qualify our descriptions of the "structure of power in which producing occurs." This means it would be a mistake to presume that when we compare working classes in different countries or at different historical periods, we are comparing equivalents. Some working classes are less proletarianized than others, a theme we take up in chapter 4. Before proceeding, however, we must examine the second, and perhaps more significant, development of the late twentieth century, the feminization of the class structure.

GENDER, CLASS, AND POSTINDUSTRIALISM

There are two reasons why the male blue-collar worker is no longer

Table 2.4
Women's Share of the Labour Force, 1950 and 1982

	1950	1982
United States	28	42
Canada	21	40
Norway	27	42
Sweden	26	46
Finland	41	47

Source: Based upon OECD, *The Integration of Women into the Economy* (Paris: OECD, 1985), 14.

symbolic of the class structure of the advanced capitalist economies. The first is the revolution in the forces of production that makes the direct producer of most goods increasingly redundant. The second, and equally important, reason has been the incorporation of women into the paid labour force. The massive entry of women into paid work in the latter part of the twentieth century has been as dramatic as the changes in industry composition and virtually inseparable from it. As Table 2.4 shows, from about the end of the Second World War until 1982 (about the time of our surveys), women increased their share of employment from approximately one-quarter to over two-fifths of the labour force. Finland is the exception to this pattern. By 1950 women already made up over two-fifths of the Finnish labour force, compared to a quarter or less of the labour force of the other countries.

As Table 2.5 indicates, the labour force participation of women tends to be rather higher in the Nordic countries than in North America. In the mid-1970s, the Norwegian level was closer to the North American pattern than to that of Sweden or Finland. By the early 1980s, however, Norway had drawn closer to the Swedish-Finnish levels.

Almost all of this growth in female employment occurred in services.[27] Indeed, if unpaid domestic labour were counted as an industry in the usual classifications, we might describe postindustrialism more in terms of the shift from unpaid to paid service work and put less emphasis on the "goods to services" metaphor. Most men (56 per cent or more) continue to be employed in the traditional sectors associated with an "industrial" economy: goods and distribution. Most women – approximately two-thirds – are employed in the growing postindustrial sectors of the labour market, especially personal/retail, business, and social services.

As a result, the "new" – postindustrial – working class is predominantly female labour employed in clerical, sales, and service occupations in the service industries (see Table 2.6). And consequently the

Table 2.5
Labour-Force Participation by Sex

	Women		Men	
	1975	1983	1975	1983
United States	53	62	85	85
Canada	50	60	86	85
Norway	53	67	86	86
Sweden	68	77	89	86
Finland	66	74	80	83

Source: Based upon OECD, *The Integration of Women Into the Economy* (Paris: OECD, 1985), 13.

Table 2.6
Selected Characteristics of Working-Class Women

Percentage of Working-Class Women Who Are in:	*United States*	*Canada*	*Norway*	*Sweden*	*Finland*
Clerical, sales, and service occupations	66	64	60	66	66
Goods & distributive industries	34	24	28	26	40
State employment	31	38	55	63	38
Unskilled jobs	86	79	81	77	83

working class now has two prototypes rather than one: the traditional blue-collar male and the postindustrial female service worker. Moreover, variations in postindustrial employment patterns are experienced mainly by women. The large welfare states of Sweden and Norway in particular result in the fact that most women workers are employed by the state in those countries. Half of all employed Swedish women are in social services, compared to only a quarter of American women.

The significant fact about the postindustrial division of labour, then, is not so much that the working class of industrial capitalism has come to an end. Rather, a new working class employed in services has grown up alongside it. And superimposed on this material division of labour is a social division based on gender.

As we show in Figure 2.3, the working class in advanced capitalism has two sexes. In all five countries, women are more likely to be working class than men and less likely to be in any of the other three classes that exercise significant powers over production. In all five countries, women make up 50 per cent or more of the working class and a minority of all other classes, differences that we shall take up in the chapters that follow. But just what historical, social, or political significance should we attach to this fact?

Since the 1970s, it has been commonplace for feminist scholars to

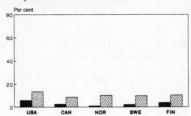

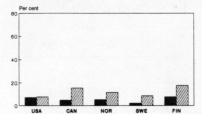

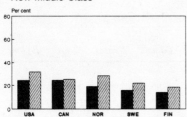

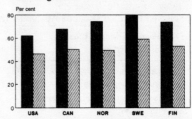

Figure 2.3
Class Distributions by Sex and Nation   ■ Female ▨ Male

comment upon the "gender-blind" character of conventional class theory, but such a charge has had two rather different meanings. Sometimes the charge implies that the "male" preoccupation with class relations results in a disciplinary bias leading to the systematic neglect of gender relations – structured relations of domination and inequality between the sexes. To such a charge, class analysts can plead guilty without necessarily conceding that there are serious flaws in their theories or empirical claims *about* classes. There is no inherent reason why theories about classes must explain all forms of social domination and inequality.

The charge of being gender-blind, on the other hand, can also mean that analyses of classes and processes of class formation which overlook the gendered structure of class relations are both incomplete and incorrect. In short, class analyses that are gender-blind are incomplete on their own terms, not just when measured against the criteria of an alternative problematic. Capitalism and the labour market are not inherently gender-blind, as the conventional wisdom of both neoclassical and Marxian economic theory would have it.

The fact that a "worker" is female rather than male, that she comes to work in a skirt and blouse rather than in overalls, alters the relation between capital and labour in fundamental ways.[28] Two examples will suffice to illustrate.

As we show in chapters 7 and 8, the patriarchal organization of households means that most women sell their labour under very different conditions from those of most men. The burden of the "double day" of paid labour and unpaid domestic labour circumscribes both how much labour power women can sell in the market and the timing of its availability. One result is to transform the conditions under which the capital-labour wage relation is negotiated and the agenda of labour when it confronts capital at the bargaining table. The focus of "class struggle" now expands to include new labour-force practices and state policies such as pay equity and day care. In effect, the struggle over the price of labour and the conditions of its employment is transformed as a result of the conditions and extra-market social relations of the persons (women) who offer their labour for sale in the market. And the upshot is irrevocably to alter the trajectory of class formation in *postindustrial* capitalism. Employers are faced with novel demands about the form of the pay packet, work schedules, and the fringe benefits they must negotiate. The state is faced with new demands for legislation and social programs to protect women against the market. As a result, labour unions and labour parties that fail to take up these demands, to incorporate the material interests of a working class that is predominantly female, become doomed to extinction. Likewise, a *class* analysis that does not take account of the changed conditions of the class struggle is doomed to failure.

Feminist historians, however, have suggested an even stronger version of what it means to say that class relations are "gendered." Their claim is that the organization of relations of ruling in the contemporary workplace is structured not simply by the logic of the market or the imperatives of capital accumulation but also by a logic derived from the patriarchal household.[29] With the decline of the household economy, hierarchically defined gender relations were brought inside the factory gate to become part of a capitalist and, theoretically, universalistic labour market. The subordination of women in the household was reproduced in the relations of power and authority of the capitalist firm. In short, the economic structure of industrial capitalism acquired a social form derived not merely from a logic based on the imperatives of capital accumulation – the logic of the market; it also incorporated social forms derived from the patriarchal household (a term we define in chapter 6). From this perspective, gender subordination in the market is integral to analyses of the relations of ruling in the workplace. Joan Acker, for example, argues that gender is so fundamental to hierarchical structure that alteration of the gender order tends to threaten the hierarchy itself.[30]

Implicit in such arguments is the claim that relations of ruling which at first glance appear to be *class* relations are not class relations at all. On closer inspection, patterns of authority and decision making, the particular way in which powers over capital and labour are allocated, turn out to be *gender* relations, relations of ruling organized to reproduce a structure of power between the sexes, much as slavery in the American South was organized to reproduce a structure of power between the races. Recent history provides numerous examples: the exclusion of women from the practice of medicine; the exclusion of married women from some sectors of the labour force altogether.

But gender relations, like class relations, do not stand still. Many of the formal barriers to *market* equality between the sexes have been eliminated. And under-representation of women in certain occupations, industries, or even classes does not necessarily constitute proof that a patriarchal logic is at work *inside* the market. Such outcomes may be partially or entirely determined by processes that operate prior to or outside of the market: by forms of family organization that prevent or limit women's participation in the market or by patterns of socialization and educational streaming that occur prior to entry into the labour market.

Providing evidence for the claim that patriarchy, as well as class, is at work in organizing relations of ruling inside the market or at the workplace is no easy task. Removing the "blinders" from a gender-blind class analysis involves much more than simply "bringing women in" to the analysis or showing that certain class outcomes differ by sex. In part 1 we adopt such a strategy from time to time, but to leave matters there would be to trivialize the feminist critique. In part 2 we address these matters directly.

In chapter 6 we take up the issue by asking what an economic structure organized on patriarchal principles might actually look like. We then attempt to determine whether contemporary patterns for organizing relations of ruling at the level of the workplace conform to this model. Chapters 7 and 8 turn to the gendered relations of ruling in the household and the manner in which they intersect with women's experience in the labour market. Chapter 9 examines national variations in the "culture of gender" to parallel our discussion of the "culture of class" in chapter 5.

As with class relations, the North American and Nordic nations are particularly apt countries to select for the study of gender relations. They are typically held up as representing polar types of what is possible for women in modern capitalist economies. These differences can be summarized with two broad observations:

1 Wage differences between men and women are significantly lower in Scandinavia than in North America and have been reduced over time,[31] but
2 Sex segregation is considerably higher in Scandinavia than in North America.[32]

Both findings have been replicated with our data by Rachel Rosenfeld and Arne Kalleberg.[33] Among persons employed thirty-five hours a week or more, they report that the income of women relative to men is 58 per cent in the United States, 62 per cent in Canada, 74 per cent in Norway, and 76 per cent in Sweden, ratios that are remarkably close to those found in much larger surveys with much better measures of earnings and income. Conversely, occupational segregation by sex is greater in Norway and Sweden than in Canada and the United States. Using a seven-category occupational classification, Rosenfeld and Kalleberg report an index of dissimilarity that measures the extent of sex-based occupational segregation, ranging from 30 for Canada to 33 for the United States, 40 for Sweden, and 42 for Norway. But does erosion of wage differentials in the Nordic countries reflect an erosion of class differentials? Does greater sex segregation create more work sites where women gain access to positions of power and authority? Do variations in postindustrial trajectories in any way alter gendered relations of ruling in the public sphere? Or, alternatively, have postindustrial economies become the site where public patriarchy has been consolidated? To answer such questions requires filling in the "empty places" constructed in chapter 1. It is to this task that we turn next.

3 Postindustrialism, Small Capital, and the "Old" Middle Class*

As C. Wright Mills observed, the nineteenth-century North American urban worker "was no factory employee: he was a mechanic or journeyman who looked forward to owning his own shop." This was the world of the old middle class – farmers, merchants, craftworkers – in which "four-fifths of the free people who worked owned property."[1] Members of this class did not need to sell their labour power to others to make a living, but rather worked with their own property – whether land, machinery, a store, or other capital – to derive a livelihood. The unity between property and work provided them with a degree of freedom and autonomy unavailable to the growing number of factory workers. While the economic situation of the old middle class was often precarious, the lives of its members were not dictated by the wage contract and time-clock as was the case for paid employees. As Mills also goes on to note, the wide distribution of property in nineteenth-century North America meant that differences in wealth were small and the step into ownership of productive property was not too big. The development of industrial capitalism, however, changed all this.

The historical decline of the old middle class was among the more successful predictions of Marx and Engels. In 1848 they wrote: "The lower strata of the middle class – the small tradespeople, shopkeepers, and retired tradesmen generally, the handicraftsmen and the peasants – all these sink gradually into the proletariat, partly because

*Chapter 3 has been co-authored with Grant Schellenberg.

their diminutive capital does not suffice for the scale on which Modern Industry is carried on, and is swamped in the competition with large capitalists, partly because their specialised skill is rendered worthless by new methods of production."[2]

Through most of the twentieth century, history has proven Marx and Engels correct in this respect. New forces of production and competition among capitalists sounded the death knell of the old middle class and small capitalist alike.[3] In the agricultural sector, new machinery and production techniques led to dramatic increases in productivity and the gradual decline of the family farm. In urban areas, economic and public life became dominated by the multinational corporation, the large labour union, and the state. Against these powerful actors, the old middle class was marginalized as a political and economic force and its membership greatly reduced.[4] Many rearguard political battles were fought against the forces of "big business, big labour, and big government," but these were struggles "against the main drift of a new society; even [their] victories have turned out to be illusory or temporary."[5]

Because of their declining numbers and anticipated demise, the old middle class and small capitalists have been regarded as inherently uninteresting for class analysis. They have been classes in decline, largely irrelevant to considerations of the class character of the advanced societies. In postindustrial society, however, this interpretation is worthy of renewed scrutiny.

In the past two decades, the decline of the old middle class and small capitalists has been reversed, at least in some countries. Two trends demonstrate this fact. The first is a significant rise in self-employment. This trend was first evident in the United States and Canada in the mid-1970s. As shown in Table 3.1, the share of the non-agricultural labour force made up of self-employed individuals increased from 6.9 to 7.5 per cent in the United States and 5.8 to 7.5 per cent in Canada between 1975 and 1985. Between 1985 and 1990 these levels stabilized. Rising levels of self-employment have also been observed in Australia, the United Kingdom, Italy, Belgium, Finland, Portugal, and Ireland.[6]

In Sweden and Norway the pattern has been different. Self-employment in Sweden, which stood at 6.8 per cent in 1967, declined until the 1970s and remained stable at 4.5 per cent until 1985. It is only in the past five years that Swedish self-employment has been increasing. In Norway, self-employment has fallen over the entire period. Similarly, it has continued to decline in Denmark, France, and the Netherlands and has remained steady in Germany.

The second trend illustrating the changing fortunes of small cap-

Table 3.1
Level of Self-Employment in the Non-Agricultural Labour Force,
1975–85 (percentages)

	1975	1980	1985	1990
UNITED STATES				
Total	6.9	7.3	7.5	7.6
Men	8.6	9.0	9.0	9.0
Women	4.4	5.0	5.6	5.9
CANADA				
Total	5.8	6.6	7.5	7.4
Men	6.5	6.9	8.1	8.3
Women	4.8	6.1	6.6	6.4
NORWAY				
Total	7.4	6.5	6.5	6.1
Men	9.5	8.8	9.1	8.4
Women	4.2	3.4	3.3	3.6
SWEDEN				
Total	4.4	4.5	4.5	7.0
Men	6.1	6.2	6.1	10.2
Women	2.2	2.5	2.8	3.8
FINLAND				
Total	5.6	6.0	6.5	8.8
Men	6.5	7.7	8.2	11.9
Women	4.6	4.3	4.6	5.6

Source: Based upon OECD, *Labour Force Statistics: 1970–90* (Paris: OECD, 1992);
calculations by the authors.

ital is the rising share of employment in small firms and the decline in average firm size.[7] The OECD notes declining firm size in Austria, Belgium, France, and Japan and, when only manufacturing is considered, in Denmark, Luxembourg, and the United Kingdom as well.[8] Evidence in the United States suggests a similar pattern.[9] As Wannell has shown for the Canadian case, the 1980s brought a major shift in employment from large firms to companies and establishments[10] employing less than twenty-five workers. The long-term process of the centralization of capital, it would seem, has now gone into reverse.

This resurgence in small-scale capital, particularly the rise in self-employment, contains a significant gender dimension. As the OECD states, "the proportion of females in self-employment has risen almost everywhere over the last decade."[11] The level of female self-employment as a proportion of the total labour force rose by approximately 1.5 percentage points in both the United States and Canada

Table 3.2
Change in Distribution of Private-Sector Employment in Canada, 1983–88
(percentage-point change in shares)

	Number of Employees			
	1–24	25–99	100–499	500+
By company size	+2.6	+1.6	−1.8	−2.5
By establishment size	+2.4	+0.9	−2.8	−0.5

Source: Ted Wannell, "Trends in the Distribution of Employment by Employer Size," Research Paper no. 39, Analytical Studies Branch, Statistics Canada, (Ottawa, 1991), Charts 3 and 7.

between 1975 and 1985, as Table 3.1 demonstrates. The proportion of self-employed women increased by a full percentage point in both Sweden and Finland between 1985 and 1990, although these increases have been smaller than those for self-employed men. In Norway the level of female self-employment, like the overall level, has declined. Taken as a whole, the proportion of female self-employment remains higher in North America compared to the Nordic countries, although the data suggest that the latter may be catching up.

When we examine the composition of the self-employed population, rather than the entire labour force, we can better see the extent of female entry. In Canada the total number of self-employed males increased by 39 per cent between 1975 and 1986; for women this increase was almost three times higher at 117 per cent. Over the same period the number of self-employed males owning incorporated businesses increased by 93 per cent, while their female counterparts increased by 274 per cent.[12] As a result, the female share of all Canadian self-employment increased from 19 to 27 per cent over this period, while the female share of incorporated self-employment almost doubled, rising from 10 to 18 per cent. Similar trends are evident in the United States, and a considerable literature on female business ownership has recently emerged.[13]

This resurgence of self-employment and small capital raises several questions. What are the processes that account for these changes? How can we explain the national variations in these trends? Are these changes a temporary reversal of longer trends or are they economic features of the twenty-first century? What will be the consequences of these changes for relationships within and between classes? In this chapter we begin to address some of these questions, specifically, the national variations in the resurgence of small-scale capitalism, the class character of the burgeoning ranks of the self-employed, and the consequences of the resurgence of small capital for paid workers.

We will argue that the different postindustrial trajectories taken by nations account for the increases in self-employment in some countries and the stable or declining levels in others. In the Nordic countries, a large public sector, particularly in health, education, and social services "squeezed out" small firms throughout most of the 1970s and 1980s; this trend has only recently been reversed with the serious dismantling of the welfare state in Sweden and Finland since the mid-1980s. In the United States and Canada, large shares of employment in personal, retail, and business services have provided more economic space for self-employment and small firms to flourish.

There remains, however, considerable debate over the class character of this resurgent "petite bourgeoisie." The expansion of self-employment is viewed by some as a reversal of historical trends and by others as a new form of proletarianization. Is self-employment a viable escape from the "relations of ruling" of paid work or does it instead represent a shift from the uncertainty of the labour market to a different, equally uncertain, market place? As we will show, the answer depends upon the economic sector in which self-employment occurs. Business services versus personal, household, and related services, two sectors with self-employment growth, stand as very different alternatives to the "relations of ruling" of the labour market.

Rising levels of self-employment and growing employment shares in smaller firms have important consequences for the rest of the labour force as well. Wages, benefits, unionization, and job stability all vary by firm size, and movement towards small-firm employment is generating downward pressure on the working conditions of labour. The resurgence of small capitalism, as we will show in the third section of the chapter, is double-edged, providing a greater number of non-working-class positions for the few while at the same time intensifying the proletarian character of wage labour for the many.

THE RESURGENCE OF SMALL CAPITALISM

In the neo-conservative climate of the eighties, the resurgence of small capital was wildly celebrated as a fresh unleashing of the capitalist spirit. Self-employment and small firms were hailed as symbols of a new "enterprise culture," exemplifying virtues of self-reliance, hard work, and competitive individualism. And in North America, at least, the allure of self-employment – of "being one's own boss" – retains a great deal of popular appeal. As shown in Table 3.3, aspirations to self-employment are particularly prevalent in the United States and Canada, where well over half of all those not currently

Table 3.3
Employees Who Hope to Be Self-Employed, Who Have Been Self-Employed in the Past, and Who Are Self-Employed in their Second Job (per cent)

	United States	Canada	Norway	Sweden	Finland
While growing up, parent mainly self-employed	21	33	21	24	50
Self-employed in the past	16	15	7	8	7
Hope to be self-employed in future	58	53	24	40	29
Have a second job:	10	7	8	10	11
Of those, self-employed in second job	37	33	*	24	28

*In Norway a high proportion of respondents with second jobs did not indicate whether this was paid employment, self-employment, or work without pay. Consequently, a reliable figure cannot be given.

self- employed would like to be so in the future. In comparison, approximately a quarter of all employees in Norway and Finland and, perhaps surprisingly, 40 per cent in Sweden wish to be self-employed in the future.

A distinctive North American pattern also emerges when we examine work biographies of those who do not own capital. American and Canadian employees have more experience with self-employment. In the United States and Canada 15 to 16 per cent of the employed labour force have previously been self-employed compared to only 7 to 8 per cent in the Nordic countries. While most of those who aspire to be self-employed are unlikely to realize their goal, the probability that they will do so has generally been greater in North America than in the Nordic countries. The greater prevalence of self-employment in North America is also evident among employees with second jobs. While similar proportions of employees in the five countries have second jobs (ranging from 7 per cent in Canada to 11 per cent in Finland), the proportion who are self-employed in their second job is highest in the United States and Canada and lowest in Sweden. This raises the question of why attachment to self-employment, and more specifically the resurgence of self-employment and small capital, is more prevalent in North America than in the Nordic countries.

As Goldthorpe suggests, the extent of self-employment in the parental generation can be taken as one indicator of the "maturity" of a nation's working class.[14] He suggests that where self-employment has been low for several generations (as in the United Kingdom), we can expect rather different political and social responses from workers than where links to agriculture and other forms of self-employ-

Table 3.4
Unemployment By Nation (standardized rates)

	United States	Canada	Norway	Sweden	Finland
1979	5.8	7.4	2.0	2.1	5.9
1983	9.5	11.8	3.4	3.5	5.4
1985	7.1	10.4	2.6	2.8	5.0
1987	6.1	8.8	2.1	1.9	5.0

Source: Based upon OECD, Employment Outlook (Paris, September 1988), 24.

ment are still part of the collective experience of most workers. We would be hard pressed, however, to explain national differences in class aspirations with differences in social origins (as shown in the top line of Table 3.3). Bourgeois and petty bourgeois origins still constitute an element in the experience of a significant share of the labour force in all five countries. This is particularly the case in Finland and Canada, where parental linkages to self-employment in agriculture are more recent.

An alternative view is that rising self-employment in the 1980s is simply a short-term cyclical response to recession and high unemployment. In short, workers have undertaken self-employment not as an alternative to employment but to unemployment. National studies suggest that this is the case in some industries, such as construction trades, but overall the counter-cyclical effects of increasing unemployment on self-employment have been declining in recent years.[15] Similarly, the decline in firm size cannot be reduced to the short-term effects of the business cycle.[16] Nevertheless, it is clear that high levels of unemployment are a structural, not a cyclical, feature of North American labour markets. In contrast, full employment has long been a major political commitment of the Nordic governments, especially the Norwegian and Swedish, and they have been remarkably successful in insulating their work-forces from the effects of recession (Table 3.4). Of the three Nordic countries, only Finland has unemployment levels that approximate North American levels (Table 3.4), and of the three, it is the only one where there has been a sustained rise in self-employment since the mid-1970s. These factors may explain, at least in part, national variation in the resurgence of small-scale capitalism.

A second explanation is the rise of the service economy. Through the postwar period the demand for services, both as a final product and as an input into goods production, has risen dramatically, and job creation in the service sector has outpaced the goods sector. Because service-sector firms are typically organized on a smaller scale than firms in goods production, the shift to services may well underlie the increase in small-firm employment shares and levels of self-employment. Evidence indicates, however, that the shift to services explains only a small portion of the change. Ted Wannell's analysis of declining firm size in Canada shows that the shift to services accounts for only one-third of the decline.[17] In other words, while the emergence of a "service economy" accounts for some of the increase in small-firm employment shares, restructuring *within* industries accounts for most of the increase. Steinmetz and Wright's analysis of American trends points in a similar direction. While part of the increase in self-employment in the United States is a consequence of the expanding service sector (where self-employment is relatively high), increasing levels of self-employment *within* "traditional sectors of the industrial economy" also account for a significant portion of this resurgence.[18] Indeed, corporate downsizing in manufacturing became a major feature of the 1980s.

Brynjolfsson and colleagues show that manufacturing firms tend to downsize in response to increased investments in information technologies and that this downsizing takes place through a decrease in vertical integration and greater reliance on market transactions to obtain inputs and distribute outputs. This shift from "hierarchies" to "markets" – and thus an increase in small-scale capitalism – they argue, reflects the reduced transaction and co-ordination costs brought about by new technologies.[19]

Cost reduction and risk avoidance have also fuelled corporate strategies of downsizing and devolvement whereby operations are broken down into smaller units or, alternatively, shifted to smaller firms through franchising, "contracting out," or licensing arrangements. Such arrangements enable larger firms to transfer the costs (and risks) of demand fluctuations and surveillance of labour to smaller firms.

But if such trends underlie the resurgence of self- employment and small-firm employment, how can we explain the cross-national variations discussed above? How might we account for sharp increases in non-agricultural self-employment in the United States, Canada, Australia, and the United Kingdom, but stable or declining levels in many European countries, including Norway and, until recently, Sweden.[20] A major part of the answer lies in the varieties of postindustrial trajectories followed by different nations.

SMALL-SCALE CAPITALISM AND
POSTINDUSTRIAL TRAJECTORIES

As highlighted in chapter 2, there is not a single pathway to postindustrialism but several. These different trajectories impose a hard

Table 3.5
Self-Employment by Total Labour Force and Non-Farm Labour Force
and Sex (per cent)

	United States	Canada	Norway	Sweden	Finland
A. AS A PER CENT					
OF TOTAL					
LABOUR FORCE					
Total	13	14	11	9	15
Men	15	19	15	13	21
Women	10	6	6	3	9
B. AS A PER CENT					
OF NON-FARM					
LABOUR FORCE					
Total	12	9	9	7	10
Men	13	12	11	10	14
Women	10	6	5	3	6

upper limit on the extent to which self-employment can flourish. This upper limit is political in origin and is manifested in the role of the state in determining employment structures.

The levels of non-agricultural self-employment for the five nations in our survey are shown in Table 3.5. These figures are higher than official estimates, such as those of the OECD, because by convention official statistics on self-employment computed for national accounts purposes do not include owners of incorporated businesses who pay themselves a salary. Our sample estimates, which include owners of incorporated firms, are closer to the mark.[21]

The survey results[22] indicate that between 9 and 15 per cent of the labour force in the five countries were working owners of their own businesses in the early 1980s. The proportion was highest in Finland (15 per cent) and Canada (14 per cent) and lowest in Sweden (9 per cent). Higher levels of self-employment in Finland and Canada reflect the greater importance of agriculture in these two countries. In the non-farm sector (Table 3.5, panel B), self-employment is highest in the United States (12 per cent). Despite the recent entry of women into self-employment, capital ownership is still very unevenly distributed by sex.

The vast majority of these capital owners have few or no employees, and, except in the United States, less than 10 per cent have ten or more employees (Table 3.6). Indeed, by no stretch of the imagination can our samples be said to capture what is usually understood as "the capitalist class," the big bourgeoisies who control the commanding heights of their respective national economies.

When we divide the non-farm sector into goods-producing and

Table 3.6
Self-Employed by Number of Employees (per cent)

Number of Employees	United States	Canada	Norway	Sweden	Finland
10 or more	13	5	7	2	5
3 to 9	25	13	12	23	11
0 to 2	62	82	81	75	84
Total	100	100	100	100	100
(N)	(194)	(290)	(196)	(101)	(153)

Table 3.7
Non-Agricultural Labour Force Self-Employed by Sector

Per Cent Self-Employed	United States	Canada	Norway	Sweden	Finland
In goods	9	8	8	8	8
In services	13	10	9	6	11

service industries (Table 3.7), it is evident that virtually all of the cross-national variation in self-employment levels is found in the service sector, ranging from a high of 13 per cent in the United States to a low of 6 per cent in Sweden. Virtually all of these differences in self-employment in services can be attributed to the role of the state in shaping the class structure.

There are two ways the state can influence the overall level of self-employment in the economy. The first is a result of the power of the state to alter the ownership structure *within* economic sectors. By wholly or partially nationalizing particular industries (e.g., steel, health care), governments greatly reduce or eliminate opportunities for self-employment. Throughout the history of *industrial* capitalism, state ownership has been the main mechanism for "socializing" the forces of production.

Nationalization, however, is not the only means the state has for altering the structure of class relations. A second strategy involves public policies that shape the allocation of productive resources *between* sectors, as reflected, for example, in the very different industry mix of employment described in chapter 2. The Nordic tendency to invest disproportionately in health, education, and social services creates higher levels of employment in the welfare state, both directly and by squeezing out low-wage employers in personal and retail services. A large, high-wage public sector makes it difficult for low-wage personal-service industries to compete. When people pay high taxes for comparatively luxurious social services, there is less discretionary income for other things.

Table 3.8
The Effects of Industry Composition and State Employment within Industries on
Self-Employment in the Service Sector, Variations from Sweden (percentages)*

Self-Employment in Services	United States	Canada	Norway	Sweden	Finland
Actual	13	10	9	6	11
Expected	6	6	6	—	7
Welfare-state effect	−4	−2	−1	—	−2
Nationalization effect	−3	−2	−1	—	−2

*For explanation of technique, see endnote 24.

Together these two features of the service economy – the level of
state employment within sectors (a "nationalization" effect) and the
composition of services (what we will call the "welfare state" effect) –
account for all of the national variation in the level of self-employment in the five countries. This is shown in Table 3.8, where we use
standardization procedures to estimate the separate and joint effects
of differences in the sectoral composition of services in the five countries ("the welfare state" effect) and the fact that within each sector,
levels of state employment tend to be somewhat higher in the Nordic
countries than in North America (the "nationalization" effect).[23] The
procedure involves using the Swedish distributions as a base line and
asking counterfactual "what if" questions about the level of self-
employment in the other countries if they had the same mix of services and the same level of state employment within industries as
Sweden.[24] After this adjustment, we see that the *expected* level of self-
employment (Table 3.8, row 2) is virtually identical in the five countries, indicating that most or all of the difference in self-employment
between countries can be explained by these two factors.[25]

Row 1 shows the actual level of self-employment in the service sector. Row 2 shows the expected level of self-employment when both
factors are adjusted simultaneously. Rows 3 and 4 show the relative
importance of each factor. Row 3 (the welfare-state effect) indicates
the expected change in self-employment levels if the other countries
had the same mix of service employment as Sweden and, in particular, its large welfare state. Similarly, row 4 (the nationalization effect)
shows the expected change if the other countries had the same level
of state employment as Sweden within sectors but retained their own
nation-specific mix of services. The results indicate that state ownership and the mix of services share about equally in accounting for
differences in self-employment in services. Not surprisingly, the
magnitudes of these effects are largest for the United States and low-

est for Norway. Finland is the least "Nordic" of the three Nordic countries, a fact consistent with data indicating that, unlike in Sweden and Norway, non-agricultural self-employment has been steadily rising there since the mid-1970s.[26] But what about more recent changes in the Nordic countries?

The rapid increase in Swedish self-employment since 1985, from 4.5 to 7.0 per cent of the non-agricultural labour force, is a remarkable phenomenon, especially the rise of male self-employment from 6.1 to 10.2 per cent. Recent changes in Swedish politics appear to underlie this increase. As Ahrne and Clement document, power relations between capital and labour in Sweden have been shifting throughout the 1980s. The political hegemony of the labour movement, once taken for granted, is now seriously challenged by the political dominance of large capitalist interests. The defeat of the Social Democratic Party in the early 1980s and again in September 1991, the decision by the employers' association (SAF) to withdraw from corporatist arrangements, the pressures to abandon the wage solidarity policy, and other changes attest to the increasing power of employers that has come at the expense of labour.[27] This shifting balance of power and the increasingly contested status of corporatism appear to be altering the previous limitations on small-scale capitalism. Bengt Johanisson points to greater autonomy at regional and local levels of government, the growing emphasis on local employment programs, and increasing pressure for business start-up initiatives as factors that have enhanced the prospects for small-scale capitalism in Sweden.[28] Moreover, under pressure from a mass exodus of capital and a declining tax base, the Swedish state has been decidedly reduced. Many tasks previously performed by government employees are now being "contracted out" with the result that many former employees, particularly men, have been transformed into self-employed workers. The same process has been underway in Finland.

These changes have resulted in the rapid growth of self-employment within finance and business services in both Sweden and Finland, as well as in distributive services in Sweden. While growth in finance and business services has also been experienced in the United States and Canada, the rate of growth has been much lower than in Sweden and Finland (see Table 3.9, panel A). In occupational terms, growth in Swedish self-employment has occurred in several occupational categories. Nonetheless, the proportion of self-employment comprised of clerical workers is higher in Sweden than any other OECD country. While 2 to 4 per cent of non-agricultural self-employment in the United States, Canada, and Finland is comprised

Table 3.9
Growth of Self-Employment by Selected Industries and Occupations (annual averages in percentages)

	United States (1983–90)	Canada (1983–90)	Sweden (1987–90)	Norway (1983–90)	Finland (1983–90)
PANEL A: INDUSTRY					
FIRE[a] & business services	6	9	13	−1	16
Other services[b]	4	4	2	3	na
Manufacturing	2	na	−4	−4	4
Distribution[c]	−1	2	5	0	0
PANEL B: OCCUPATION					
Professional & technical	3	6	7	2	−9
Administrative & management	4	12	7	−6	22
Clerical	5	1	4	0	0
Services	5	1	7	1	0

Source: Based upon OECD, *Employment Outlook* (Paris: OECD, July 1992), 188–9, Tables 4.A.3 and 4.A.6.

[a] FIRE includes financing, insurance, and real estate.

[b] Other services includes community, social, personal, and household services.

[c] Distribution includes transport, storage and communications.

"na" indicates that figures are not included in the OECD publication.

of clerical workers, this figure is 15 per cent in Sweden.[29] In Finland, self-employment growth has been located predominantly within administrative and management occupations; again, the proportion of self-employment comprised of such workers is higher than almost every other OECD country.[30] Norway is becoming somewhat distinct from its Nordic neighbours, since self-employment has declined in almost every industry since 1983.[31] Whether this represents increasing diversity within the Nordic countries or merely a delayed response to political changes remains to be seen.

In short, while the politics of postindustrialism have placed limitations on self-employment in the Nordic countries throughout much of the postwar period, this limitation is now being rapidly eroded. Paid workers are being transformed into self-employed individuals. In Sweden they are in clerical occupations; in Finland they are in administrative and management positions. But what are the consequences of these trends? Does self-employment represent a viable alternative to paid employment for North American or Nordic workers? Can we expect labour markets to be reshaped as a growing proportion of Canadians, Americans, and Swedes either own small firms or work in such firms? It is to these questions that we now turn.

THE CLASS CHARACTER OF SMALL-SCALE CAPITALISM

The recent increases in self-employment and small-firm employment point to potentially momentous changes in both the structure of labour markets and, for Marxian theorists, their understanding of the history of class structures and the economic forces that shape them. These developments suggest nothing less than a reversal of the long-term trend toward the centralization of capital and a resurgence of the old middle class and small capitalists. Not surprisingly, reactions to these developments have been cautious. At the heart of the matter is whether the resurgence in self-employment represents a process of de-proletarianization, an expansion in the number of people who own and control their own means of production, or simply a new form of proletarian subordination to capital.

In their critique of Steinmetz and Wright, Marc Linder and John Houghton point to a number of reasons for pausing before rushing to conclude that the old middle class is on the rise again.[32] Rather than a process of de-proletarianization, much of the observed rise in self-employment, they argue, simply represents employer strategies to reduce some of the marginal employment costs associated with social security and other fringe benefits. Rather than selling commodities or services in the market, many newly self-employed persons are selling their labour to their traditional employers under new, less favourable conditions. Homeworking and freelancing are examples of the growth of new forms of marginal, semiproletarian, and poorly paid self-employment. Many observers, including the Economic Council of Canada, note that the average earnings of the self-employed without employees are lower in most industries and occupations than those of comparable paid workers and, as a result, the council includes self-employment together with other forms of "nonstandard" jobs, such as part-time work.[33]

Others have pointed to the loss of autonomy and control exercised by small capitalists and members of the old middle class as these individuals fall under the domination of large business interests.[34] While maintaining legal ownership of their businesses, small firms may be dependent upon a single purchaser of their products or bound to a large organization through legal agreements. The widespread emergence of subcontracting and franchising relationships illustrates the point. In such cases, the economic activities of the old middle class may be far from the image of the independent, self-directed owner-operator. Instead, small-firm operations may represent little more than nominally autonomous enterprises taking on the risks and uncertainties shed by larger firms.

While such observations capture part of the change, the evidence indicates that matters are more complex. Steinmetz and Wright point out that growth in incorporated small businesses – the most likely site of *real* petty bourgeois expansion – has been more rapid than in unincorporated business, where the marginal self-employed are likely to be found.[35] Evidence indicates that the same pattern exists in Canada.[36] The growth of small firms also attests to the resurgence of small-scale capitalism. Wannell's analysis of Canadian data and ongoing research at Statistics Canada show that the trend towards smaller firm size is robust, irrespective of whether it is measured at the establishment, company, or enterprise level and that these trends are not reducible to short-term effects of the business cycle.[37] Johnson's cautious treatment of the British data suggests similar conclusions.[38] The assumption of old-middle-class and small-capitalist subservience to large corporations has also been challenged, and several writers have underscored the independence maintained by small firms, even by many of those engaged in subcontracting relations.[39]

The empirical question that remains is the degree to which new positions of self-employment offer de-proletarianized, as opposed to proletarianized, forms of work. Neither our data nor official statistics provide evidence that can be used to adjudicate this debate decisively. Data on earnings, hours of work, incorporation, and employment of labour can be used, however, to document the dramatic variation in the forms and profitability of self-employment, particularly in those sectors where it is growing most rapidly. For illustrative purposes we will focus on the Canadian experience.

The sectoral distributions of the Canadian self-employed population in 1975 and 1986 are shown in Table 3.10. The most notable change over this period is the continued decline of self-employment in agriculture. In 1976, 26 per cent of the Canadian self-employed were in the agricultural sector. By 1986 this proportion had dropped to 17 per cent. The share of the self-employed in natural resources, manufacturing, construction, and distributive services remained relatively constant over this period. In contrast, the proportion of the self-employed in services rose dramatically, growing by almost 3 per cent in consumer services and 4 per cent in business services. Within consumer services, self-employment in retail trade, as well as in

Table 3.10
Self-Employed Population by Sector, Canada 1975–86 (per cent)

	1975	1986	% Point Change
Agriculture	26.3	17.0	−9.3
Natural resources*	1.7	2.3	+0.6
Manufacturing	4.8	4.7	−0.1
Construction	11.7	11.5	−0.2
Distributive services⁺	8.6	9.6	+1.0
Consumer services	35.0	37.8	+2.8
Business services	7.1	11.3	+4.2
Social services	4.6	4.9	+0.3

Source: Gary Cohen, *Enterprising Canadians: The Self-Employed in Canada*, Statistics Canada, Cat. #71–536 (Ottawa: Supply and Services Canada, October 1988), 118–9, 124–5, Tables 6A & 6D.

*Mining, quarrying, and oil wells are excluded since estimates were not published for 1975.
⁺ Communications and utilities have been excluded for the same reason.
Columns 1 and 2 do not total 100 per cent because of these exclusions; the positive and negative changes do not balance to 0 for the same reason.

accommodation, food, and beverage services, actually dropped between 1975 and 1986 (both by .4 per cent). In contrast, self-employment in "other services," mainly personal, household, and related services, rose by 3.6 per cent. In business services, self-employment shares in the finance, insurance, and real estate sectors have remained relatively constant, while business services increased by 3.9 per cent. In sum, business services, along with personal, household, and related services, have been the major growth poles of self-employment in Canada through the 1980s.

While both of these major growth sectors have been expanding, they differ considerably along a number of dimensions (see Table 3.11, panel A). Self-employment in personal, household, and related services is undertaken primarily by women (65 per cent) and is most frequently in the form of own-account work; that is, by self-employed individuals who work alone and do not employ paid labour. In contrast, business services are dominated by men (78 per cent) and the employment of paid workers is much more prevalent (54 per cent). The rate of incorporated self-employment stands at only 15 per cent in personal, household, and related services, while this figure is almost three times higher in business services (41 per cent). Finally, almost 90 per cent of self-employment in business services is undertaken on a full-time basis, compared to 61 per cent in personal, household, and related services. These differences result in very different earnings profiles for these two sectors (Table 3.11, panel B). Self-employed earnings in personal, household, and

Table 3.11
Self-Employment in Personal, Household, and Related Services and Business
Services by Selected Characteristics, Canada 1985

Panel A (per cent)	Personal, Household & Related Services	Business Services
Males	35	78
Females	65	22
Own-account workers	80	46
Self-employed with paid employees	20	54
Incorporated	15	41
Unincorporated	85	59
Full-time	61	87
Part-time	39	13
Panel B		
ALL SELF-EMPLOYED		
Median earnings	$ 5,100	$29,700
Average earnings	$10,700	$37,200
OWN-ACCOUNT WORKERS		
Median earnings	$ 3,300	$19,600
Average earnings	$ 8,600	$27,200
SELF-EMPLOYED WITH PAID WORKERS		
Median earnings	$17,600	$37,400
Average earnings	$19,600	$43,400

Source: Gary Cohen, Enterprising Canadians: The Self-Employed in Canada, Statistics Canada, Cat.
#71–536, (Ottawa: Supply and Services Canada, October 1988), Tables 6A, 15, 26.

related services are only a fraction of those in business services. This
is the case for both own-account workers and those with paid employees, but as 4 of every 5 self-employed individuals in personal,
household, and related services are own-account workers, the financial profile of this sector is particularly poor.

These data for business services and personal, household, and related services do not provide direct evidence about the (de)proletar-
ianized nature of self-employment. For this we require information
on the relations between the self-employed and the firms with which
they do business. The data presented here, however, do highlight the
extensive differences in these rapidly growing sectors. The low earnings and marginal forms of self-employment prevalent in personal,
household, and related services suggest that this is not a viable *economic* escape from the "relations of ruling" of paid labour. "Becoming one's own boss" in this context means a shift from the uncertain-

ties of the labour market and paid employment to a different, equally uncertain market place. Comparing the earnings of paid workers in personal, household, and related services (the mean earnings were $12,800 in 1985; the median earnings were $10,400) to the earnings of self-employed individuals shown in Table 3.11, we see that this shift is likely to mean a drop in pay. Whether the economic limitations of self-employment in this sector are off-set by non-monetary rewards, such as independence, is a question that remains unanswered.

For the self-employed in business services, the situation is quite different. Self-employment, at least for those that survive the perils of business start-up, is a much more viable escape from the "relations of ruling" of paid employment. Self-employment is generally undertaken in more stable forms and, on average, earnings from self-employment exceed those of paid workers in this sector (mean earnings of paid workers were $20,400 in 1985; median earnings were $16,800). The heterogeneity in this comparison is not a new characteristic of self-employment. The changes brought about by postindustrialism, however, are adding new dimensions to traditional heterogeneity. Comparing sectoral changes we find two new paths of self-employment, each characterized by dramatic differences. Heterogeneity based on sex is a second new dimension. Although an increasing number of women have entered the ranks of the self-employed, they remain concentrated in a few industry sectors and generally earn less than their male counterparts. Whether these differences are diminished as more women become self-employed and own older, more established businesses remains to be seen.

SMALL CAPITAL AND THE FUTURE OF THE WORKING CLASS

As Marx observed, processes of capital concentration and centralization were important not just because of the resulting concentration of economic power in fewer hands. The other side of the dialectic was the concentration of workers in fewer and larger workplaces, making it possible for them to communicate with one another and mobilize their own power resources through collective organization. On this, too, Marx was correct. The potential for workers to form unions and increase their bargaining power has always been greater in large, than in small, firms. For example, in Canadian firms with fewer than 20 employees, only 10 per cent of work hours are filled by unionized workers; this figure is double (20 per cent) for firms with 20 to 99 workers, triple (33 per cent) for firms with 100 to 499 work-

Table 3.12
Wages by Firm Size (average wages compared to largest firms[a])

	1–19	20–99	100–499	500+
Canada (1986)	65	79	89	100
United States (1983)		57	74	100

Source: René Morissette, "Canadian Jobs and Firm Size: Do Small Firms Pay Less?" Research Paper no. 35, Analytical Studies Branch, Statistics Canada (Ottawa, 1991), 26; calculations by authors; based upon OECD, Employment Outlook (Paris, 1985), 78.

[a] Per cent of average wages paid compared to firms with 500 or more employees. Canadian figures include full-time jobs only; American figures exclude agriculture.

ers, and quadruple (44 per cent) for firms with more than 500 workers.[40] American research shows a similar pattern.[41]

Wage differences across firm size are equally striking (Table 3.12). Average wages in firms in Canada with less than 20 employees, for example, are only 65 per cent of those paid by firms with 500 or more workers. In firms with 20 to 99 workers, this figure is 79 per cent. Again, American data show a similar pattern. These differences reflect higher rates of unionization and higher "worker quality" in larger firms, but even when these factors are held constant the firm size–wage rate relationship remains.[42] Wage differentials are reinforced by large differentials in fringe benefits. In Canada only 14 per cent of work hours in firms employing fewer than 20 workers are covered by a pension plan, compared to 30 per cent and 49 per cent in firms employing 20 to 99 and 100 to 499 workers respectively (see Table 3.13). The proportion of work hours covered by a pension plan is five times higher in large firms (more than 500 workers) compared to small firms (less than 20 workers). In the United States, workers in small firms are also much less likely to have a pension plan or health insurance coverage than workers in larger firms.

The consequences of small-firm employment are also apparent when job stability is considered. Garnett Picot and John Baldwin's study of quits and layoffs in Canada shows that workers in small firms face a much higher probability of permanent separation from their employer than workers in larger firms. The probability of permanent separation from a small firm (those employing less than 20 workers) is 60 per cent higher than from a firm with more than 500 workers.[43] These differences can be partially explained by the lower wages paid by small firms, by the higher proportion of young (less stable) workers in these firms, and by the industry sectors where small firms are located (in services where labour turnover is high).

Table 3.13
Pension and Health Plans Coverage by Firm Size (per cent)

Canada (1986)	1–19	20–99	100–499	500+	
Pension coverage[a]	14	30	49	73	

United States	1–24	25–99	100–499	500–999	1000+
Health insurance coverage[b]	35	65	75	79	86
Pension retirement coverage[b]	17	41	64	74	88

Source: René Morissette, "Canadian Jobs and Firm Size: Do Small Firms Pay Less?" Research Paper no. 35 Analytical Studies Branch, Statistics Canada (Ottawa, 1991), 32; calculations by authors; based upon OECD, Employment Outlook (Paris, 1985), 79.
[a] Per cent of work hours covered by a pension plan.
[b] Per cent of workers with health insurance or pension/retirement coverage.

However, even when these factors are held constant, a greater degree of job instability in small firms remains.

In sum, workers in smaller firms are less likely to be unionized, to receive health and pension benefits, and to receive high wages, and they are more likely to face permanent separation from their employer. The correlates of corporate downsizing and the increase in small-firm employment, then, are not difficult to anticipate: lower wages, greater insecurity of employment, and, potentially, a decline in the strength of organized labour. Hence, if Marx's "law of large numbers" is still operative, the real significance of the resurgence of small-scale capitalism lies less in the rising numbers of the old middle class and small capitalists and more in the negative effects it generates in the rest of the labour market.

There is, however, another interpretation of these developments. In the now abundant literature on post-Fordism, corporate downsizing is associated with the end of the Fordist model of "mass production," in which semi-skilled, but well-paid, workers are combined with product-specific machinery to produce a large volume of standardized goods for homogeneous markets. The emergent and increasingly successful technologies, it is argued, combine skilled labour with general-purpose machinery to produce small batches for specialized markets. Economies of scope, not of scale, are now the order of the day, so the argument goes, resulting in smaller production units and more craftlike working conditions. The shift from Fordist mass production to systems of "flexible specialization" denotes a period of "craft revival" rather than an intensified proletarianization of labour.[44]

Both interpretations are, of course, theoretically and empirically plausible. And indeed, both sorts of processes may be occurring simultaneously, leading to de-proletarianization of the labour process in some parts of the labour market and re-proletarianization in others. The hard empirical question concerns the relative mix and balance among these (potentially) offsetting developments. North American research on the "declining middle" and wage polarization during the 1980s suggests both views have merit but that on balance the more pessimistic scenario is closer to the mark.[45] There has been disproportionate growth at both the top and the bottom of the labour market (and a "declining middle"), but the latter changes have been substantially larger than the former.[46] Are these results related to corporate downsizing and the return of small-scale capitalism? Canadian evidence indicates a direct link. Wannell's analysis at Statistics Canada shows that during the 1980s the increase in small-firm employment depressed average earnings by 1.5 per cent, and the effect was stronger in goods-producing industries (1.6 per cent) than in services (1.1 per cent).[47] Patterns in wages and earnings are, of course, not direct measures of "proletarianization" or its opposite; they do, however, directly reflect changes in the distribution of labour's bargaining power *vis-à-vis* capital and so provide indirect evidence of the effects of the processes at work.

When taken together, these results on the growth in self-employment and small-scale capitalism on the one hand and polarization in wages and earnings on the other suggest the following. Postindustrialism and the economic restructuring associated with it in North America have indeed created more room for the expansion of the old middle class and small capitalists. The expansion of non-working-class places for some, however, has simultaneously intensified the proletarian character of other places in the class structure. While the high wages and skills characteristic of small-firm workers in industries such as business services provide a case for optimism, the weight of the evidence suggests that a greater share of employment in smaller firms will lead to a decrease in remuneration, unionization, and job stability within the labour force.

IMPLICATIONS: THE FUTURE OF THE OLD
MIDDLE CLASS

The claim that new *forces* of production erode old *relations* of production has long been a first principle of Marxist theory. There is precious little, however, in either Marxist or other traditional sociological perspectives that would have allowed us to anticipate the return of the old middle class and small-scale capitalism in the late twentieth century. In the short run at least, the old middle class and small employers have reversed their historical decline and become an "ascendant class." For some, this renewed vitality of the small capitalist sector provides new avenues of exit from waged work and unpaid domestic labour. For others, it represents new semi-proletarian employment relations, increased insecurity, and lower wages.

The return of small-scale capitalism is clearly a contingent, rather than a necessary, consequence of postindustrialism, however. Thus far politics, not technological determinism, have made the difference. Until the mid-1980s, truly dramatic growth rates in self-employment levels were limited to the Anglo-American democracies – Australia, Canada, the United States, and the United Kingdom – all countries that Esping-Andersen groups together as "liberal" welfare-state regimes where market forces are privileged and social regulation of market-driven processes and outcomes is weak. This political course has been particularly evident through the 1980s as the Anglo American democracies embarked on ambitious programs of neo-liberal economic restructuring that favoured the growth of small enterprise. Deregulation, privatization, and "contracting out" removed barriers to entry and created new opportunities for small business to flourish. And during the period of recovery following the recession of the early 1980s, small business was publicly celebrated for its role in generating employment. This celebration was congruent with the political cultures of Canada and the United States. In both countries the social culture of classes continues to bear the imprint of populism, the main cultural repertoire for articulating popular protest and class conflict in North American political history (see chapter 5). The hero of the populist narrative is not the worker but the independent producer whose livelihood and traditional way of life are threatened by capitalist modernization, including "big business" and "big labour." The return of small-scale capitalism to postindustrial North America provides both fuel and vindication to the carriers of these populist residues inherited from the past.

What of the Nordic countries? Throughout the period of social democratic dominance, the direction of resources and consumption into health, education, and social services limited the scope for small-scale capitalist growth. Such limitations are not, however, etched in stone as postindustrial trajectories change. Recent developments in Sweden and Finland dramatically underscore this point. The restructuring of the welfare state and the changing balance of power between capital and labour have provided the space for self-employment to flourish.

But if "politics matters" in shaping postindustrial trajectories, so does technology. New technologies – new forces of production – are leading to corporate downsizing and the growth of smaller units of production. The results of Brynjolfsson and colleagues that show how firms shift from "hierarchies" to "markets" as a result of reduced transaction costs brought about by new technologies are a case in point. And while the theoreticians of post-Fordism may exaggerate the competitive advantage of "economies of scope" over "economies of scale," there is little question that the emergent production models they point to are real. The assembly lines and white-collar factories of the Fordist era are unlikely to disappear. But they will be complemented by the subcontractor and small consulting firms required to service them. Whether or not this resurgence of small-scale capital will bring intensified proletarianization for the many or the craft revival anticipated by the theoreticians of post-Fordism remains to be seen and to be *determined*. Flexible specialization, as Piore and Sabel admit, could well flourish in a regime that resembles "the old Bourbon Kingdom of Naples, where an island of craftsmen, producing for the court, was surrounded by a sub-proletarian sea of misery." [48]

Emergent patterns in North America point in the direction of a "Naples" model. But it would be premature for anyone to predict the inevitability of such an outcome. In the 1980s, downwardly flexible labour markets allowed both North American economies to generate large numbers of new jobs, jobs that were disproportionately generated by small firms. It remains to be seen, however, how long this strategy can be pursued before its potential for further growth is exhausted or its negative effects on workers and their families resisted. A key element in the equation will be the capacity of labour to shape the transition, a topic to which we return in chapter 4.

4 Postindustrialism and the Regulation of Labour

Since the seventies, debates over postindustrialism's class structure have revolved around two questions. The first question is *historical*: Does postindustrialism contribute to the "degradation of labour" and the rise of a new service proletariat, as many scholars since Harry Braverman have argued?[1] Or does postindustrialism de-proletarianize labour by eliminating less skilled occupations and generating a "knowledge economy," as argued by Daniel Bell?[2]

The second set of questions, those that concern us here,[3] are *comparative* and emerge from a body of research that has noted some remarkable differences in postindustrial employment structures. These comparative differences are, of course, pertinent to the historical question since they suggest that debate was misformulated. Postindustrialism may have a variety of outcomes rather than just one. The challenge is to document this variety and then explain it.

In the United States, Gösta Esping-Andersen concludes, postindustrialism has brought a new managerial revolution, not a knowledge revolution.[4] The upper reaches of America's occupational structure, it seems, are dominated by managers and administrators, while Sweden's is characterized by a large number of professionals and technical (knowledge) workers.[5] According to the International Labour Organization (ILO), administrative and related occupations made up over 11 per cent of the American labour force and only 2.2 per cent of Sweden's at about the time our surveys were conducted. In contrast, 27 per cent of the Swedish work-force was in professional and related occupations compared to 16 per cent in the United States.[6]

Esping-Andersen attributes these differences to the welfare state. Sweden's large cadre of professional and technical workers, he argues, is a result of the high level of employment in health, education, and welfare services. In the United States, more managers are required to administer the complex system of corporate welfare created to compensate for an underdeveloped public system. Others have advanced competing explanations for these differences. Sam Bowles, David Gordon, and Tom Weisskopf argue that the larger administrative component of the American economy reflects greater intensity of supervision over American workers, a response by employers to growing resistance on the shop floor.[7] Yet others have claimed that America has more managers because of its central position within the international economy.[8]

All of these interpretations are theoretically and historically plausible, but they have remained just that – interpretations without evidence. The classification of jobs according to conventional occupational typologies on which these conclusions rest are simply not up to the task of answering the questions they raise. As we will see, debate over why the American economy is overmanaged hinges mainly on assumptions concerning what managers really do when they manage. Occupational data cannot adddress this question. Once created, occupational typologies cannot be "unpacked" into their constituent elements. Our class typology suffers from no such constraint.

In the first part of this chapter, we show that the American class structure is different. Its distinguishing feature is the large amount of administrative overhead that goes into the control and surveillance of labour. American firms are not "overmanaged," but American workers are "oversupervised." Since more employees are required for the control and surveillance of labour, the American new middle class is larger and its working class smaller than elsewhere. The imprint of the "American way" for organizing workplace relations is also evident in Canada. In those sectors of the Canadian economy traditionally dominated by American capital, Canadian practices are identical to American ones.

The result, as we show in the second part, is that American workers are more "proletarianized" than in the Nordic countries, less likely to have conceptual autonomy and discretion in carrying out their jobs. And while the American new middle class is larger, it is also more "proletarianized" than elsewhere.

Does postindustrialism matter? Past studies on the long-term effects of the shift to services have uniformly concluded that postindustrialism raises the skill content of jobs, and our results provide no exception to these conclusions.[9] On average, postindustrial service jobs are more likely than jobs in the industrial core to require employees to think on the job and exercise discretion. However, the scope of this development is limited both by the mix of postindustrial services (as Esping-Andersen argues) and by country-specific methods for regulating labour. Not all postindustrial economies are the same.

Despite this diversity, the project of building classes faces similar challenges in all postindustrial economies. Within the working class, new cleavages based on sex, job skills, industry, and occupation must be confronted. The "new middle class" must be embraced or attacked. Here too, as we review in the final part, the comparative experience proves instructive.

DECONSTRUCTING CLASSES: WHAT DO THE MANAGERS DO?

Though the most recent, Esping-Andersen's analysis was not the first to observe the apparent "overmanagement" of the American economy. In an earlier generation of comparative studies, Val Burris, Carlo Carboni, and David Livingstone each highlighted the apparent overdevelopment of the managerial strata in the United States.[10] They concluded that the American pattern should be understood as a product of the unique position of the United States within the world economy. Drawing on Stephen Hymer's classic essay, Burris argued that the large number of managers in the United States reflects the concentration of the administrative, planning, and research functions in the metropolitan centre of an American-dominated multi-national economy.[11] For Livingstone, the fact that Canada has fewer managers than the United States reflects its position as a "secondary imperialist formation" and net importer of foreign capital.[12] Consistent with this conclusion, Burris and Carboni also showed that the United Kingdom has a relatively large managerial strata, a residue, presumably, of its imperial past and continued importance as an international financial centre.

A second, more recent account of American distinctiveness points instead to indigenous and idiosyncratic features of the American industrial-relations system. For Bowles, Gordon, and Weisskopf, America's high administrative overhead is largely a result of American forms of labour control that emphasize intensive supervision and regulation of workers.[13] In addition to developing complex organizational forms for the administration of capital, America led the way in developing the systems of internal labour control associated with Taylorism and the rise of mass production.[14] This model was successfully exported to the majority of advanced capitalist countries, but usually with important modifications depending in part on the relative power position of labour. In the United States, they argue, the accelerated growth of administration since the Second World War reflects increasing intensity of supervision over American workers, a response by employers to growing resistance on the shop floor.[15]

Esping-Andersen adds a distinct "postindustrial" twist to these views.[16] Because the public welfare state is so underdeveloped in the United States, the corporate welfare system must compensate. More managers are required to administer the huge and complex fringe-benefit programs that constitute America's private "welfare state." And because the United States lacks a well-developed system of labour exchanges and worker-training institutions, American firms require very large personnel departments to recruit and train labour. In contrast, Sweden's large cadre of professional and technical workers is a result of the high level of employment in health, education, and welfare services.

The critical difference between these views concerns what "managers" actually do when they manage. The verb "to manage" has a double meaning in the corporate world. Most commonly, management refers to positions in which incumbents participate in decision making over the *allocation* of the forces of production to their various uses – where and when to invest, what products will be produced, what mix of capital and labour will be used in production, and the like. But as Braverman notes, the "verb *to manage*, from *manus*, the Latin for hand, originally meant to train a horse in his paces, to cause him to do the exercises of the *manège*."[17] And as he documents, the growth of modern management had as much to do with developing a cadre of employees to regulate labour as with delegating powers to allocate and decide on the uses of capital.

Ajudication of the competing views of why the managerial strata is larger in the United States than elsewhere hinges in part upon the relative mix of these two functions. In the "labour-control" thesis of Bowles and his colleagues, the presumption is made that "management" is mainly required for the regulation of labour. When Burris argues that the United States has more managers because of its location in the international economy or when Esping-Andersen concludes that more managers are required to administer America's private welfare state, the presumption is that managers mainly do the work of planning, co-ordination, and administration.

All of these studies, however, are unable to distinguish between

Table 4.1
Labour Force Involved in Decision Making (percentage)

	United States	Canada	Norway	Sweden	Finland
EXECUTIVES	6	4	5	4	6
ALL DECISION-MAKERS BY TYPE OF PARTICIPATION					
Decides	17	18	20	15	23
Advises	9	7	6	8	5
All	26	25	26	23	28
ALL DECISION-MAKERS BY TYPE OF DECISIONS					
Budget	8	10	15	10	16
Investment	21	21	25	21	27
Organization	22	21	24	23	25
(N)	(1267)	(1808)	(1470)	(983)	(785)

the functions of management because of their reliance on standard occupational classifications. Occupational typologies do distinguish between "managers" and "supervisors," but this is a hierarchical, not a functional, division. Almost one-half of all employees classified as managers according to the usual occupational criteria in our surveys have no policy-setting function. Instead, their main function is the control and surveillance of labour. The measures of decision making and authority used to construct our class typology enable us to determine this division directly.

We turn first to the policy-setting function. In Table 4.1 we show the percentage of employees classified as executives in our class typology, those who have any involvment in decision making of any sort, and, finally, by the types of decisions made. If either the Burris or Esping-Andersen theses is correct, we would expect the United States to lead on some or all of these measures. The percentage of employees with executive powers scarcely differs among countries, and the differences are not statistically significant. This is a rather demanding test of the argument, however, since, by design, executives do not include most mid-level employees who participate in corporate planning.[18]

When we include all decision-makers and those who advise decision-makers, the numbers change but the conclusions do not. The percentage of all employees who participate in some way in the policy-setting process ranges from 23 per cent in Sweden to almost 28 per cent in Finland. The highest level of participation in policy set-

Table 4.2
Participation in Decision Making by Industry Sector

Percentage Decision-Makers in:	United States	Canada	Norway	Sweden	Finland
Goods & distributive services	14	14	17	12	16
Postindustrial services[a]	20	21	23	18	30

[a] Postindustrial services include personal and retail services, business services, health, education, and welfare, and public administration. Differences between industrial sectors within countries are all significant at the .05 level of confidence or better.

ting is in Norway and Finland, not in the United States. Nor are there large differences across policy domains, whether with respect investment decisions,[19] budgetary decisions,[20] or decisions affecting overall work organization.[21] Where differences are present, they systematically contradict the claim of American distinctiveness.

In Table 4.2 we show the proportion of decision-makers by two broad sectors – in the industrial core (goods production and distribution) and in postindustrial services. The shift to services has been the source of a "new managerial revolution," but the size of this revolution is virtually an international constant. There is significantly more policy-making participation in postindustrial services than in the industrial core, but the magnitude of differences (6 to 7 percentage points) is virtually identical among countries. The exception is Finland, where the difference is 14 percentage points.

These results cast considerable doubt on conventional interpretations that attribute the large number of managers in the United States to its centrality in the structure of international capital. Nor do they support Esping-Anderson's conclusion that the United States bears high administrative overhead costs because of its underdeveloped welfare state. Quite simply, there is little or no difference in the share of employees involved in corporate planning and administration in the five countries.

This conclusion changes dramatically, however, when we turn to the second function of management – the control and surveillance of labour. The class-structure survey distinguishes between two broad types of authority in the workplace – that involving co-ordinating the work of others[22] (task authority) and the ability to discipline subordinates[23] (sanctioning authority), corresponding to the distinctions drawn in chapter 1 between the work of "co-ordination and unity" and that of "control and surveillance." The United States is exceptional by either standard (Table 4.3). It takes approximately a third of the American labour force to oversee the work of others, compared to about a fifth of all employees in Sweden and Finland. Canada and Norway fall between these extremes. It is also comparatively

Table 4.3
The Co-ordination and Control of Labour

Per Cent of Employees with:	United States	Canada	Norway	Sweden	Finland
Task authority	32	26	26	20	19
Sanctioning authority	28	21	20	15	13
Task supervisors with					
sanctioning authority	83	78	73	68	69

All four countries are different from the United States at the .05 level of confidence or better
for all three dimensions.

rare in the United States to find a separation between the work of
"co-ordination and unity" on the one hand and "control and surveillance" on the other (Table 4.3, panel 2). In sum, America does have
more "managers" but only if the work of management is expanded
to include the regulation of labour.

We can take advantage of another feature of the North American
labour markets to add yet greater weight to this conclusion. Canadian economic development has been controlled by American capital
to an extent unparalleled in any other developed economy. American capital developed, and continues to control, large sectors of the
Canadian economy associated with manufacturing and resource extraction, while Canadian capital was historically confined to areas of
circulation and distribution – finance, transportation, and utilities.[24]

The American branch plant brought not only investment capital
but also American methods for organizing the labour process and an
identical industrial-relations system.[25] In an earlier article, we show
in considerable detail how Canada's history of dependent industrialization has affected class relations in Canada.[26] In sectors of the Canadian economy where American branch-plant capital has been
dominant, American methods for organizing production relations
are also prevalent. We provide some illustrative results in Table 4.4.
American ownership has been concentrated in privately owned
goods-producing firms. In postindustrial services, it has been minimal. As the results indicate, in the goods-producing sector the
amount of administrative labour used for the control and surveillance of workers is virtually identical in Canada and the United
States. In postindustrial services, where Canadian capital and the
Canadian state are the main employers, Canada fits neatly into the
Nordic pattern.

The results in Table 4.4 also highlight the fact that high levels of
labour control are characteristic of all sectors of the American economy, industrial and postindustrial alike. The pattern is consistent
even at the most detailed levels of disaggregation. In the health,

Table 4.4
Employees with Task and Sanctioning Authority by Sector[a]

Percentage of Employees with:	United States	Canada	Norway	Sweden	Finland
TASK AUTHORITY					
Private goods	32	30	25	17	14
Postindustrial services	32	24	26	21	22
SANCTIONING AUTHORITY					
Private goods	27	25	19	13	12
Postindustrial services	29	19	21	16	14

[a] Private goods includes non-agricultural goods-producing firms not owned by government. Postindustrial services include personal, retail, and business services, health, education, and welfare, and public administration.
All differences from the United States are significant at the .05 level of confidence or better, except Canadian private goods for both types of authority.

education, and welfare sector, for example, 25 per cent of American and only 11 per cent of Swedish employees have sanctioning authority. That the administrative overhead of American firms is high by international standards is a result of the high proportion of employees given over to the control and discipline of labour.

What accounts for these patterns? Without detailed historical evidence, any interpretation is necessarily tentative. There is, however, sufficient secondary evidence to suggest that our findings are broadly consistent with what has been identified as the "American way" for organizing work relations and the labour process. The growth of Taylorist principles for organizing the labour process in the early part of this century and their elaboration after the Second World War are now a well documented feature of American economic development.[27] As Braverman pointed out, the intensification of supervision and the rise of a complex apparatus for controlling labour was part and parcel of Taylorism. The point of the strategy was to remove control of the labour process from workers and to put it in the hands of management. Taylor's formula for a division of labour carried out by unskilled workers brings with it a requirement for large supervisory structures both to co-ordinate the labour process (task supervision) and to discipline workers (sanctioning supervisors). In the 1950s and 1960s this system evolved into a complex pattern of shop-floor regulation characterized by elaborate rules and classification procedures defining job boundaries and wage rates and a rigidly codified set of grievance procedures. The result, as Piore and Sabel remark, is an industrial-relations system marked by constant disputes, any one of which might provoke a strike. To mitigate this threat required a judicial system capable of assessing the details of particular disputes.[28] Under the "American way," the shop floor becomes the site of a complex system of industrial jurisprudence, what Michael Burawoy has called the "internal state."[29] In effect, the United States has so many supervisors for much the same reason it has so many lawyers: the oft-noted litigiousness of American public life (the "external state") is reproduced by the "internal state" at the workplace.

Variants of American shop-floor methods were exported abroad but always subject to modification and change, a result of differences in timing, economic and political arrangements, and the organization of labour.[30] Our results suggest that the Nordic evolution was rather different from the American one. Nordic unions tend to take responsibility for administering workplace benefits and entitlements with less discretionary (i.e., arbitrary administration) privileges. In Canada, by contrast, the impact of American practice was more immediate and direct and hence more pronounced. The social forces that organized the industrialization process in Canada were not merely similar to the American ones but in large measure identical – American capitalists and "international" branches of American labour unions.

Let us recapitulate what we have established thus far. Past studies, using conventional occupational categories, have identified a surprising amount of national diversity in the relative importance of these twin developments. America, it seems, has become dominated by the managerial side of the professional-managerial couplet, while other countries, such as Sweden, appear headed towards the "knowledge society" celebrated by Daniel Bell.

Our analysis thus far has allowed us to settle some aspects of the debate that has flowed from earlier studies. First, there is a remarkable degree of similarity and convergence in the amount of labour required in all five countries for the work of "management" as conventionally understood – policy setting and administrative decision making associated with resource allocation and control over the means of production. This result casts considerable doubt on claims that the American class structure is "different" because of its position within the international economy (Burris) or as a result of the high level of administration required because of an underdeveloped welfare state (Esping-Andersen). Postindustrial services do indeed appear to be the source of a "new managerial revolution" (see Table 4.2), but the size and scope of the additional managerial overhead required by the service sector is virtually identical across countries.

In contrast, the United States and those sectors of the Canadian economy traditionally dependent on U.S. capital have much higher levels of administrative overhead for the regulation of labour. In the language of chapter 1, *Taylorism* (the creation of complex hierarchies for the regulation of labour), not *Sloanism* (the creation of managerial structures for the allocation of capital), has left the most distinctive imprint on the American class structure and its Canadian offspring. Further, there is no evidence that traditional practices developed for the regulation of an industrial work-force have been altered in the modern, postindustrial service industries in the United States.

It would be premature, however, to conclude that the modern, postindustrial sectors of the economy are simply clones of their industrial predecessors. The main focus of the postindustrial literature has not been directed toward new practices of management or control of labour but on the rapid expansion of "knowledge work," especially in the high-end business and social services (see chapter 2). We now take up this issue.

THE CLASS ORGANIZATION OF KNOWLEDGE WORK

Since the 1970s, the *historical* question of postindustrialism's effects on the skill content of work has dominated social-science debate to the point where reference to the contrasting views of Daniel Bell and Harry Braverman on this matter have become social-science ritual. This attraction to the Bell-Braverman couplet arises from the stark contrast they seem to represent between alternative visions of our postindustrial future. Both agree that *industrial* capitalism relies largely on brute labour and obedience to routine, but they part ways on where things will go from there. In the now-conventional representation of this debate, we face either a postindustrial Nirvana of knowldege where everyone will be a brain surgeon, artist, or philospher (Bell) or, alternatively, a postindustrial Hades where we shall be doomed to labour mindlessly in the service of capital (Braverman).

When drawn in *these* terms, the historical debate is now no debate at all. Bell is the clear winner. Although much less than a knowledge revolution, the net result of the shift to services has been to increase the requirements for people to think on the job.[31] The service economy has brought a mix of both unskilled employment in retail and personal services and high-skill employment in business and public services, but on balance the effects of the latter outweigh the former. Where unskilled service jobs have grown most rapidly – in Canada and the United States – they mainly serve as "ports of entry" to the labour market for new workers rather than as a site for the formation of a new "postindustrial" proletariat.[32]

As these issues have been resolved, attention has shifted from skill *levels* to their social *form*. Esping-Andersen's discussion of "postindustrial trajectories" points in this direction, as do popular debates over differences among German, Japanese, and American production methods. The American mass-production model based on a combination of specialized machinery and semi-skilled labour, it is argued, is now exhausted.[33] The new, and ascendant, production models rely more on combining general-purpose tools with "flexible" workers who are able, like the craftworkers of old, to apply general knowledge to solving specific problems. To put matters another way, the question is no longer one of skill levels but their distribution and, more pointedly, their distribution among *classes*. The "American way" of concentrating knowledge in the planning department of giant corporations will no longer do.

Ironically, this shift of attention from skill levels to its social form returns us to the concerns that were at the heart of Braverman's analysis. He did not in fact claim that the knowledge embedded in the labour process of the advanced economies had fallen. On the contrary, "since the development of technology and the application to it of the fundamental sciences," he concludes, "the labor processes of society have come to embody a greater amount of scientific knowledge ... and ... *the 'skill' content of these labour processes is much greater now than in the past*."[34] The question that preoccupied Braverman was not the *average* skill level of the labour force but its distribution among classes. His claim was that knowledge and science had been appropriated by the expanding administrative cadres of the modern enterprise (managers) and that the "degradation" (deskilling) of *labour* (workers) was the result.

As we shall see, it is in the comparative, not the historical, context that Braverman's analysis acquires leverage. His observations concerning the distinctive character of the *American* labour process, with its systemic bias towards unskilled labour and intensive supervision, was essentially correct. His error lay not in his description of the systemic bias of American capitalism but rather in his theoretical leap to conclude that a *particular* expression of capitalist organization – the American way – was indicative of a *general* logic of capitalist development.

Our analysis proceeds as follows. We begin by examining national differences in postindustrialism's effects on job skills and their class determinants. Here there is precious little support for a Braverman-like thesis. Postindustrialism is not a zero-sum game in which the managerial classes grow at the expense of the working class. The knowledge-intensive character of postindustrial work sites is evident across the whole of the class structure. But if postindustrialism matters, it matters more in some countries than in others. Consistent with Esping-Andersen's conclusions, the "knowledge revolution" is more advanced in some countries than others, with Sweden and the United States providing the extremes. The reasons for these differences, however, have more to do with nation-specific forms for organizing the labour process of both workers and managers than with variations in postindustrial trajectories. In this comparative context, Braverman's description of *American* methods for organizing the "relations of ruling" come closer to the mark. Before proceeding, however, we must pause briefly to alert the reader to our procedure for distinguishing "skilled" from "unskilled" jobs. A more extensive discusssion and empirical analysis is presented as appendix 2 to this volume.

IDENTIFYING KNOWLEDGE WORK

How would we know a "skilled" job if we saw one? For Braverman, what distinguishes skilled from unskilled work is the unity of conception and execution – purposive work in which the directing mechanism is the power of conceptual thought.[35] As with Aristotle, Aquinas, and Marx, the unity of conception and execution (or of cognition and will, to use Aristotle's language) defines the essence of *human* activity and distinguishes human labour from that of animals. When this unity is dissolved, the activity of humans becomes, if you will, non-human. This occurs in a social division of labour in which conceptual work is appropriated by management and returned to the worker in the form of detailed prescriptions or embedded in machinery. Because *knowledge* (cognition) is made redundant, *control* (volition) passes from workers to their employers.

The concept of "skill," then, as Ken Spenner writes, has a double referent: skill as *job complexity* – "the level, scope, and integration of mental, interpersonal, and manipulative tasks on a job" – and skill as *autonomy-control* (or self-direction) – the notion that "the structure of work roles provides more or less room for the worker to initiate and conclude action, to control the content, manner and speed with which a task is done."[36]

Of the five national surveys, only the Canadian made an effort to measure job skills extensively. Based on the work of Melvin Kohn, these measures included a battery of items to distinguish jobs in terms of both the "cognitive complexity" of work and "occupational self-direction" (autonomy).[37] Though these measures are not available for other countries, we were able to use the Canadian evidence to validate the one skill measure included in all surveys and, at the same time, to address an unresolved debate within the Comparative Class Structure Project. In all five surveys, respondents were asked whether their jobs required them to design important aspects of their work and to put their own ideas into practice (conceptual *autonomy*). They were then asked to provide typical examples of such work, which were subsequently coded to establish the level of conceptual *complexity* required in the position.[38]

Subsequently, both Wright and his critics expressed concern that this measurement procedure was flawed.[39] The main concern was that the procedure did not adequately differentiate jobs that allow for discretion and initiative (say, a janitor or house cleaner) and those that also require a significant level of analytical complexity (scientists, technicians). The presumption was that the measurement procedure allowed for too many "false positives" – autonomous employees in comparatively routine jobs. As we show in appendix 2, these concerns were misplaced. Rather than being too inclusive, the Canadian skill measures indicate that Wright's classification of "semiautonomous" employees provides a fairly rigorous criterion for identifying employees whose jobs require both initiative (self-direction) and high levels of cognitive complexity.

In the sections that follow, we use this measure to distinguish skilled from unskilled workers and skilled managers (executives and the new middle class) from managers who serve as mere "transmission belts" (Braverman's phrase) for orders communicated from above.[40]

POSTINDUSTRIALISM, CLASSES, AND KNOWLEDGE WORK

The shift of employment from the production of goods to the production of services is among the defining features for postwar economic history in all advanced capitalist economies. And despite the gloomy scenarios associated with Braverman and the "deindustrialization" theorists of the 1980s, the service economy has not resulted in the deskilling of the labour force. The 1980s did bring polarization in the structure of wages and earnings, as Robert Kuttner and other deindustrialization theorists predicted.[41] But the forces driving this change had little to do with "deindustrialization" and the shift to services.[42] As the results in Table 4.5 show, postindustrial services provide significantly more skilled jobs than jobs in the traditional industrial core. On average, 42 per cent of postindustrial service employees are in skilled jobs, compared to 26 per cent per cent

Table 4.5
Percentage of Employees in Skilled Jobs within Sectors and Classes

	United States	Canada	Norway	Sweden	Finland
BY SECTOR					
Goods & distribution	25	26	31	23	25
Postindustrial services	38	42	47	43	46
Difference[a]	+13	+16	+16	+20	+21
BY CLASS					
Executives	83	91	87	78	96
New middle class	52	55	66	64	70
Working class	17	23	24	23	19

[a] Differences between sectors significant at .05 level or better in all five countries.

of employees in goods and distribution (+16). The smallest difference between the industrial and postindustrial sectors (+13) is in the United States and the largest (+20) in Finland and Sweden. Such differences are hardly surprising and vary little from what is generally well known from conventional studies based on more refined skill measures.

As Braverman warned, however, the "unity of conception and execution" is not randomly distributed in class societies. Almost all executives and the majority of the new middle class, but less than a quarter of the working class, are in jobs that require significant initiative and conceptual input (Table 4.5). And as indicated by the same table, postindustrial services employ more managers (executives plus new middle class) than do goods and distributive industries. Hence, higher average skill levels in postindustrial services may simply reflect differences in class structure *between* sectors (more managers and fewer workers), rather than differences in skill levels *within* classes. As we show in Table 4.6, however, this is not the case. The presence of a larger managerial stratum in postindustrial services accounts for only a small share of the total difference in skill levels between sectors.

The "shift-share" analysis in Table 4.7 divides the total difference in skill levels between sectors into three components: (a) the share due to differences in the distribution of classes between sectors (a "class effect"); (b) the share due to differences in skill levels within classes (a "labour-process effect"); and (c) their interaction. A Braverman-like scenario of postindustrialism's effects on the labour process would be indicated by a positively signed class effect and a negatively signed labour-process effect. In fact, both signs are positive and everywhere small class effects are overwhelmed by sectoral differences in the organization of the labour process. The shift in class structure

Table 4.6
Percentage of Employees in Managerial Positions within Sectors[a]

	United States	Canada	Norway	Sweden	Finland
Goods & distribution	36	32	32	23	21
Postindustrial services	41	35	35	28	34
Difference	+5	+3	+3	+5[b]	+13[b]

[a] Managers = executives + new middle class.
[b] Difference between sectors significant at .05 level or better.

associated with postindustrialism (more managers, fewer workers) matters, but differences in skill level *within* classes matter much more. The knowledge-intensive character of postindustrial service work is no artifact of yet another "managerial revolution" that transfers knowledge and job skills from labour to capital.

If postindustrialism matters, however, it clearly matters more in some countries than in others. The largest labour-process effect (+17.5) is found in Sweden and the lowest (+10.8) in the United States. What accounts for these differences and of what consequence are they? In the section that follows, we turn our attention to the working class.

POSTINDUSTRIAL TRAJECTORIES AND THE NEW LABOUR ARISTOCRACY

As a description of the skill content of *industrial* capitalism, Braverman's depiction of a "degraded" working class in which the unity of conception and execution have been broken is close to the mark. In the United States, only 11 per cent of workers engaged in goods production and distribution have significant control of their own labour process (Table 4.8). And only in Norway is there a significant difference from the American pattern. Clearly, however, postindustrial services are different. The new labour aristocracy of skilled "knowledge workers" ranges from 22 per cent of service workers in the United States to almost a third in Sweden and Canada. But what accounts for the variability among countries? The extremes are provided by Sweden on the one hand and the United States on the other. These are also two of the countries central to Esping-Andersen's "postindustrial trajectories" thesis, so we shall begin there.

Esping-Anderson's claim is that differences in postindustrial class structures are a function of differences in the postindustrial service mix. The welfare-state bias of the Swedish economy, he argues, creates a highly professionalized social-welfare employment structure. In contrast, the American preference for "food, fun, and wine" industries (personal services) results in a comparatively unskilled

Table 4.7
Decomposition of Sector Differences in Skill Levels

Goods & Distribution – Postindustrial Services Contrast	(1) = Total Difference	(2) + Class Effect	(3) + Labour-Process Effect	(4) Inter-action*
United States	+13	+2.5	+10.8	−0.4
Canada	+16	+1.0	+15.0	−0.1
Norway	+16	+1.5	+14.6	−0.2
Sweden	+20	+2.5	+17.5	−0.1
Finland	+21	+2.5	+13.7	−4.4

*See text for discussion of this term.

employment structure. Aggregate differences in postindustrial skill levels, however, may also result from differences in the way the work of otherwise similar (e.g., welfare-state) workers is organized. America may be different not as a result of pecularities in the "postindustrial trajectory" it has followed but because of pecularities in American methods for regulating the work-force.

The shift-share analysis in Table 4.9 provides a test of these claims. Quite simply, the question is whether postindustrialism produces fewer knowledge workers in the United States than Sweden because of (a) differences in the mix of postindustrial services between countries (an "industry effect") or (b) differences in the proportion of knowledge workers within industries (a "labour-process effect"). If Esping-Andersen is correct, the size of the *industry effect* should be substantial in the U.S.–Sweden contrast, where the gap in welfare-state employment is largest, and should decline as a function of the share of welfare-state employment in postindustrial services. Accordingly, we have arranged the country contrasts in Table 4.9 to reflect between-country differences in the share of postindustrial service employment in health, education, and social services.[43] In the U.S.–Sweden contrast, for example, the difference in the share of service workers employed in health, education, and social services is 27 percentage points; in the U.S.–Canada contrast, the difference is close to zero. To estimate industry effects, postindustrial service workers are divided into the four sub-sectors defined in chapter 2: personal and retail services; business services; health, education, and welfare services; and public administration.

In the U.S.–Sweden contrast, the industry effect (−6.3) is substantial and outweighs differences that result from the organization of the labour process. This finding confirms Esping-Andersen's conclusion that U.S.–Swedish differences in the mix of skilled and unskilled service workers are a result of a Swedish bias toward high-level social

Table 4.8
Skilled Workers as a Percentage of All Workers by Sector

Skilled Workers in:	United States	Canada	Norway	Sweden	Finland
Goods & distribution	11	14	19*	13	12
Postindustrial services	22	31*	29*	32*	29*
Difference[a]	+11	+17	+10	+19	+17

* Significantly different from the United States at the .05 level of confidence or better.
[a] Differences between sectors significant at the .05 level or better for all five countries.

services and an American bias toward low-level personal services. Moreover, the size-of-the-industry effect declines, as expected, as a function of the size of the welfare-state employment gap between countries. The presence of a rather large interaction term in the U.S.–Swedish contrast indicates caution in assessing the magnitude of these effects but, as indicated in the footnote, not the conclusions we have drawn.[44]

It also shows, however, that differences in "postindustrial trajectories" tell only part of the story. There are substantial labour-process effects in all four contrasts with the United States. The magnitude of this effect is similar for the U.S.–Nordic contrasts and even larger in the Canada–U.S. contrast. The implication is that a more routinized labour process characterized by fewer workers with significant control over their own labour process is a *generic* feature of American service industries, not simply a result of its underlying *mix* of services. The United States has fewer welfare-state workers than Sweden and fewer skilled workers as a result. But the American welfare state also employs a less skilled labour force than other countries.

Together these results simultaneously sustain Esping-Andersen's "postindustrial trajectory" thesis and highlight its limits, empirical and analytical. Empirically, the "social democratic" way through the postindustrial transition relies on Sweden as the major exemplar. It has been an exception among nations in the growth of welfare-state employment, which may well have reached its zenith even there. Analytically, the substantial labour-process effects highlight the fact that the relation between a specific material division of labour and the organization of the labour process is a contingent, rather than a necessary one. The same material activities (caring for children, designing software) can be organized within very different systems for structuring the labour process. Sweden provides a striking contrast to the United States, and this is substantially due to Sweden's highly developed welfare state. But Canada's service economy provides an equally striking contrast to the U.S. experience, and this has nothing

Table 4.9
Decomposition of Skill Level in the Working Class by Sector

Contrast	(1) = Total Difference	(2) + Industry Effect	(3) + Labour- Process Effect	(4) Inter- action*
U.S.–Sweden	−9.5	−6.3	−5.6	2.4
U.S.–Norway	−6.9	−2.8	−4.3	0.2
U.S.–Finland	−7.1	−2.9	−4.5	0.3
U.S.–Canada	−8.5	−0.1	−8.1	−0.3

* See text for discussion of this term.

to do with differences in welfare-state or any other type of employment. Rather, it is a result of divergent paths in the social organization of otherwise similar postindustrial services: the same outcome can be reached through a variety of postindustrial pathways.

POSTINDUSTRIAL MANAGERS

Postindustrial managers are different from their industrial predecessors. Postindustrial services employ only slightly more managers (Table 4.10) than firms engaged in the production and distribution of goods. But their managers are more likely to be involved in decision making and less likely to be involved in the control and surveillance of workers. These postindustrial differences in what managers do are evident not only in the cross-section but also in patterns of change over time. In Table 4.11 we use occupational data from the Canadian census to show changes in the composition of administrative occupations between 1971 and 1986. During this period there was a dramatic decline in the per cent of administrative occupations with only supervisory responsibilities and a corresponding rise in middle- and upper-level management positions.[45] The industry-specific patterns also make clear that the growth in management occupations has little to do with expansion of pseudo-managerial positions in fast-food restaurants and video stores. In the low-end personal and retail services, there are few middle or senior management positions.

In view of all this, it is hardly surprising to find that postindustrial managers are more likely to be required to think on the job. Postindustrial services employ more skilled managers than firms in goods and distribution (Table 4.12), and the number of such managers is virtually an international constant. The results for unskilled managers, however, are equally instructive. The United States has more managers than other countries and, as a result, a larger middle class.

Table 4.10
The Powers of Management[a] by Sector

	United States	Canada	Norway	Sweden	Finland
PER CENT OF EMPLOYEES WHO ARE MANAGERS IN:					
Goods & distribution	36	32	32	23	21
Postindustrial services	41	35	35	28	34
Difference	+5	+3	+3	+5[b]	+13[b]
PER CENT OF MANAGERS WHO HAVE DECISION-MAKING POWERS IN:					
Goods & distribution	39	42	53	52	78
Postindustrial services	49	59	67	69	87
Difference[c]	+10	+17	+14	+17	+9
PER CENT OF MANAGERS WHO HAVE SANCTIONING AUTHORITY IN:					
Goods & distribution	76	77	68	62	62
Postindustrial services	70	53	56	53	41
Difference	−6	−24[b]	−12[b]	−9	−21[b]

[a] Managers = executives + new middle class.
[b] Difference between sectors significant at .05 level or better.
[c] Difference in decision-making powers between sectors significant at .05 level or better for all countries except Finland.

But this difference is entirely due to the size of the managerial strata with little control over how they manage. Deskilled labour, it appears, requires a superstructure of deskilled administratrors. The structural complement to high levels of control over workers (as in the United States) is a large administrative apparatus that serves as a "transmission belt" between labour and management. Moreover, this large strata of deskilled administrators characterizes postindustrial services as well as the industrial core. This is a generic feature of postindustrial services in both the United States and Canada, not a product of the North American bias towards low-skilled personal and retail services.[46]

These results, like those of part 1, highlight the *contingent* character of postindustrialism's consequences: *new forces of production can be embedded in old relations of production.* The "American way," which results in a large number of relatively unskilled workers regulated by an overdeveloped administrative apparatus, is a generic feature of

Table 4.11
The Distribution of Management and Supervisory Occupations, Total
and Selected Industries, Canada 1971–86

	High-Level Managers	Middle-Level Managers	Supervisory	Total
All industries				
1971	11	17	72	100
1986	20	29	51	100
Goods				
1971	8	15	7	100
1986	16	29	55	100
Social services				
1971	49	16	34	100
1986	53	29	18	100
Business services				
1971	17	24	59	100
1986	32	33	35	100
Personal services				
1971	2	12	86	100
1986	4	19	77	100
Retail services				
1971	3	4	92	100
1986	10	8	82	100

Source: Census of Canada, Special Tabulations.

the American industrial-relations system, one that permeates the
postindustrial world much as it did its industrial predecessor.

In this comparative context, Braverman's insight into the history
of American work organization regains its cutting edge. His obser-
vational skills did capture the systemic bias of *American* labour practices. His error lay not in his *description* of the bias of American capitalism but rather in his *theoretical* leap to conclude that this particular
expression of capitalist organization was indicative of a general logic
of capitalist development.

POSTINDUSTRIALISM AND LABOUR'S FUTURES

The *generic* features of postindustrial class structures can now be
summarized in a few stylized facts. First, the class structure of postindustrial economies is characterized by a substantial and growing
cadre of managers and administrators who exercise the traditional
functions of investment and control over production and the con-

Table 4.12
Skilled and Unskilled Managers[a] as a Percentage of the Employed Labour Force by
Industry Sector (per cent of all employees)

	United States	Canada	Norway	Sweden	Finland
SKILLED MANAGERS					
BY SECTOR					
Goods & distribution	18	16	18	13*	15
Postindustrial services	25	23	28	21	26
Difference[b]	+7	+7	+10	+8	+11
UNSKILLED MANAGERS					
BY SECTOR					
Goods & distribution	18	15	13*	9*	5*
Postindustrial services	16	13	7*	7*	8*
Difference	−2	−2	−6[c]	−2	−3

* Significantly different from the United States at the .05 level of confidence or better.
[a] Managers = executives + new middle class.
[b] Differences between sectors significant at the .05 level or better for all five countries.
[c] Difference between sectors significant at the .05 level or better.

trol and surveillance of labour. Of these, only a small fraction exercise "real economic ownership" – the *executive* powers of investment and resource allocation associated with the traditional owner-entrepreneur. The vast majority – the new middle class – are engaged in day-to-day administration of labour and the means of production.

The working class of the postindustrial world includes an important, but declining male, blue-collar core employed in the production and distribution of goods. They have been joined by a predominantly female postindustrial working class employed in the provision of services and clerical labour (Table 4.13). Unlike the industrial working class, postindustrial service workers tend to be employed by the state. Postindustrial services are also where the new labour aristocracy of knowledge workers are employed.

Taken together, these postindustrial tendencies have diminished the working class numerically and thrown up new divisions within it. The new middle class expands as the working class declines; the knowledge-intensive character of postindustrial work creates a new labour aristocracy; and new cleavages of sex, occupation, and public/private divisions must be addressed.

For labour militants and party activists, such postindustrial diversity must be experienced as a sort of postindustrial hell. Life was surely more simple and the class project more straightforward when the world was divided between men carring lunch pails and other

Table 4.13
Characteristics of the Working Class by Sector

	United States	Canada	Norway	Sweden	Finland
WORKERS IN GOODS AND DISTRIBUTION WHO ARE:					
Male	61	73	70	72	61
Blue-collar	68	69	64	72	70
Private sector	91	87	74	78	83
Skilled workers	11	14	19	13	12
WORKERS IN POSTINDUSTRIAL SERVICES WHO ARE:					
Female	67	66	67	75	88
White-collar	83	89	91	96	91
State employees	43	48	63	77	63
Skilled workers	22	31	29	31	29

men wearing bowler hats. But here again the comparative experience is instructive.

Through most of the postwar era, Swedish labour has demonstrated a remarkable capacity to absorb these postindustrial developments. The initial success of Swedish social democracy during the 1930s was based on a political coalition between the industrial working class and agricultural producers. Then, in the 1950s and 1960s, Swedish labour successfully adapted this coalition strategy to strike alliances with the new middle class, service-sector workers, and women, a pattern emulated more or less successfully throughout the Nordic region.[47] The result is reflected in the high levels of union membership in all sectors of Nordic society (Table 4.14). What the Nordic experience demonstrates is that there is nothing intrinsic to postindustrialism's class structure and class divisions to mute the strength of the labour movement.

American and Canadian labour movements have faced a rather different fate. By the early fifties, union membership had risen to about a third of the non-agricultural labour force in both countries and then hovered around 30 per cent until the early sixties. Thereafter, American labour began its decline, moderately through the end of the seventies and precipitously in the eighties. By 1990 only 16 per cent of the non-agricultural labour force in the United States was unionized. In contrast, union density in Canada began rising in the sixties, from approximately 30 per cent of the non-agricultural labour force in 1965 to 40 per cent in 1983, falling back to 36

Table 4.14
Union Membership by Sex, Class, and Sector

Per Cent Unionized by:	United States	Canada	Norway	Sweden	Finland
SEX					
Female	15	31	60	80	80
Male	27	44	66	86	84
CLASS					
New middle	19	36	70	86	86
Working	29	41	62	84	83
SECTOR					
Goods & distribution	35	47	62	87	81
Postindustrial services	12	33	65	80	83

per cent by 1990.[48] The result of labour's decline in the United States is apparent in low levels of union membership in all parts of the labour market and in a substantial membership gap between sexes, classes, and industrial sectors (Table 4.14). Similar gaps but higher levels of union membership characterize the Canadian labour force.

At first glance, the implications of postindustrialism for North American labour would appear obvious: while labour has maintained a foothold in the industrial core, the growing postindustrial service sector (and by implication women, the new labour aristocracy, and the new middle class) has been, if not a wasteland for labour, at least an impediment to growth. As Pradeep Kumar shows, however, the reality is more complex.[49] *Private* sector services (business, personal, retail) where 10 per cent of workers or fewer are union members do fit the wasteland metaphor. In contrast, the major – indeed, only – source of union growth in both countries has been in postindustrial *public* services. In the United States, union density rates grew from 18 to 36 per cent between 1968 and 1988 and in Canada from 50 to 90 per cent. In both countries, organized labour in the industrial core has been either stagnant or in decline. Between 1968 and 1988 union density in manufacturing fell from 43 to 23 per cent in the United States and from 46 to 40 per cent in Canada. Where the Nordic data demonstrate that there are no automatic effects of postindustrial divisions on organized labour, the American experience shows that the industrial working class is not the eternal font of militancy and working-class strength.

The major challenge of postindustrialism to the labour movement, we would contend, arises from the fact that the postindustrial working class is predominantly female. The feminization of the working class changes the capital-labour relation since the conditions under which women supply their labour differ so radically from that of men (see chapter 8). With the feminization of the labour force, issues related to care giving and domestic labour emerge from the household and become issues for employers concerned with absenteeism, turnover, and worker motivation on the one hand and for unions concerned with building and maintaining their constituency on the other. The struggle for pay equity in wages and benefits are symptomatic of the feminization of the wage relation and the postindustrial "class struggle." Such struggles not only demand new strategies but also provide the occasion for new divisions within the working class. Recent Swedish experience is a case in point.

Postindustrial divisions based on sex and sector are embedded in the very structure of the Swedish labour movement. The Swedish Trade Union Confederation (LO) is the main representative of industrial workers, and 57 per cent of its members are men. The Confederation of Salaried Employees (TCO) represents clerical workers, teachers, and civil servants, 60 per cent of whom are women. A third organization, the Swedish Confederation of Professional Associations (SACO), represents Sweden's new labour aristrocracy, but labour solidarity has traditonally depended on co-operation between the LO and TCO, which account for the majority of workers. During the eighties, the traditional alliance between these two large unions began to unravel.

The Swedish welfare state is the major employer of Swedish women, but welfare-state employment has hinged on a wage strategy that limits gains in the more productive goods sector in order to maintain employment levels and wage rates in public services. Maintaining wage solidarity became increasingly difficult in the eighties as (mainly male) workers in the private sector demanded wage increases in line with productivity growth in their own industries and firms. As a result, "the most serious conflicts (including major strikes) in the Swedish labour market have, throughout the 1980s, occurred between public and private-sector trade unions. In this sense, one might easily imagine a war between (largely) male workers in the private sector and (largely) female workers in the welfare state."[50]

The implication, as Esping-Andersen concludes, is that the future of Swedish social democracy may depend on whether the bonds that bring men and women together in households will be strong enough to weather public-private divisions in the labour market. Postindustrial divisions do not bring an end to the class struggle; they do, however, drastically alter the terrain on which it is fought.

CONCLUSION: DO NATIONAL DIFFERENCES MATTER?

The first revolution to transform industrial capitalism in this century gave rise to a new cadre of executives whose powers to administer capital are virtually indistinguishable from those of the traditional owner-entrepreneur. But as our results indicate, capitalism remains a form of rule of the many by the few. The relative size (4 to 6 per cent) of this "new capitalist class" differs little, if at all, among the five countries.

In contrast, national differences in the way the work of "the many" is regulated are more pronounced. The supervision of American labour requires a larger "middle class" and a more disciplined working class than elsewhere, a pattern replicated in sectors of the Canadian economy where American capital has traditionally been dominant. For what, if anything, are these national differences consequential?

The "American way" is associated with a more complex pattern of shop floor regulation – detailed job classification and seniority rules – along with a larger administrative superstructure to regulate it. While both features lead to "structural rigidities" in the *organization* of production, more complex systems of job classification and longer hierarchies also create greater opportunity for *individual* "flexibility" and job mobility. Burawoy's description of the internal labour market at Allied, a Chicago manufacturing enterprise, highlights the ease with which workers could exit from undesirable situations by bidding on other jobs within the firm as they became vacant.[51] The internal labour market is characterized not only by horizontal, but also by vertical movement through a hierarchy of jobs based on the seniority principle. In Sweden, he notes, these extensive rewards to seniority are absent.[52] The result is that in the United States "the possessive individualism associated with the external labor market is imported into the factory."[53]

Burawoy's claim is that the complex hierarchies characteristic of the American industrial-relations system produce individual, rather than collective, strategies of resistance and change. Or to use, Hirschmann's language, the possibility of *exit* from undesirable situations makes it less likely that grievances will give rise to *voice* – political efforts to change existing circumstances.[54] This, of course, is a classical thesis found in Marx, as well as in the current generation of social-mobility studies.[55]

But is it true? Do North American and Nordic workers differ by virtue of the degree to which they see real possibilities to exercise the exit option and move up the job hierarchy? The results presented in

Table 4.15
Promotion Prospects by Sex, Employed Labour Force

Promotion Prospects for:	United States	Canada	Norway	Sweden
EMPLOYED WOMEN				
More than half	33	20	7	6
Some	15	15	5	13
Few	28	29	29	37
None	24	36	59	44
	100	100	100	100
(N)	(577)	(645)	(600)	(456)
EMPLOYED MEN				
More than half	38	27	12	8
Some	19	17	8	10
Few	25	30	37	49
None	17	25	43	33
	100	100	100	100
(N)	(649)	(770)	(856)	(540)

Promotion Question: Do people in positions like yours eventually get significant promotions? that is, a change in job title that brings a significant increase in pay or responsibilities?

Table 4.15 indicate that the answer is yes. Respondents in four of the five countries were asked about the promotion prospects they could expect on the job – the proportion of people at their place of work in positions like theirs who could expect to be promoted. (A promotion was defined as a change of job title that brings a significant increase in pay and responsibilities.) The possible responses included "more than half," "some," "few," and "none at all." The Nordic–North American contrast could not be more striking for both men and women. Less than 20 per cent of Nordic men and women assess promotion prospects as good ("more than half") or even fair ("some"). In the United States, in contrast, over half the men and almost half the women fall into these categories. And Canadian men and women fall only slightly behind their U.S. counterparts. Nordic–North American differences within the working class (Table 4.16) are equally strong.

This perceived fluidity in North American labour markets has long been a theme in the comparative literature on class politics and class formation. Both Marx and Sombart remarked on the mobility of labour as a factor inhibiting class formation in the United States, a theme taken up most forcefully in the recent writings of John Goldthorpe on social mobility.[56] Frequently, these structural accounts of the "individualism" of the North American worker have stumbled

Table 4.16
Working-Class Promotion Prospects

Promotion Prospects for:	United States	Canada	Norway	Sweden
WORKING-CLASS WOMEN				
More than half	30	19	5	6
Some	15	15	5	14
Few	29	27	28	35
None	26	39	62	46
	100	100	100	100
(N)	(399)	(468)	(476)	(371)
WORKING-CLASS MEN				
More than half	32	25	10	7
Some	19	17	7	10
Few	27	29	37	46
None	22	30	45	37
	100	100	100	100
(N)	(351)	(770)	(498)	(375)

over the fact that national differences in mobility regimes are not especially large or in the expected direction. But typically these studies only consider long leaps across occupational groups or classes. As a result, they are unable to capture differences that result from the complex hierarchies of internal labour markets described by Burawoy that produce no "long leaps" across broad occupational or class boundaries but may produce many "short leaps." Short leaps, however, may be quite as effective in producing the individualistic strategies imputed to job mobility.

As Hirschmann, and many others, has pointed out, "exit has been accorded an extraordinarily privileged position in the American tradition,"[57] and many have puzzled over this fact. Some, such as Hartz, have traced the individualism of Americans to the original foundations of the settler societies built, as they were, not only by a "liberal fragment" but also by migrant populations who chose exit (emigration) over political confrontation and collective action in their home societies.[58] The puzzle, of course, is how this "preference" gets transmitted and reproduced across the generations and even centuries. Our results suggest that at least part of the answer to the puzzle lies in the elaborate hierarchies that offer North American workers greater opportunity for exit – to change jobs as a way of improving their life situation.

We suspect, however, that there is more underlying the career aspirations and petty capitalist dreams (see chapter 3) of North American workers than objective possibility and material conditions. It would be difficult to argue, for example, that the Nordic preference for voice over exit can be reduced to promotion opportunities on the shop floor. People not only face objective class possibilities; they filter these possibilities through their beliefs, understandings, and values about class alternatives. They develop strategies for struggle and resistance that reflect not only immediate circumstance but also a collective wisdom shaped by past struggles, successes, and failures. If the immediate experience of class is shaped by the postindustrial present, the cultural repertoire through which these experiences are filtered, as we show in the following chapter, bears the imprint of the industrial, and even preindustrial, past.

5 The Political Culture of Class

At least since Sombart, the apparent absence of class-based and, specifically, socialist political parties in the United States has bemused and troubled social scientists. Contrary to the predictions of Kautsky and other early Marxist theoreticians, America did not lead the way in the development of a class-based political system or in the formation of a political party organically linked to organized labour.[1] The subsequent debate over "American exceptionalism" – the fact that electoral politics in the United States did not assume the shape of the "democratic class struggle" presumed to be normal for industrial capitalist societies – has been a long one.

Class-based forms of political behaviour of the sort associated with the European experience have, of course, never been completely absent from the North American experience.[2] The point is rather that neither class-based organizations nor class-based political identities have ever acquired the axial importance in social and political life in the same way as in many, though not all, European societies. But what are we to make of this fact? Should we follow convention and conclude that because North American patterns of class formation do not live up to the theoretically expected (European) model(s) that North American political life is "classless"? Does the (relative) failure of North American workers to develop European-like repertoires of political critique, collective organization, or political protest mean they lack "a critical political consciousness"?[3] Underlying the conventional view of North American class politics is a curiously linear, unidimensional, and even teleological understanding of class formation and working-class history. All working classes, as it were, have a single destiny to be realized, and all can be located according to the level or stage of class consciousness they have achieved. Class consciousness becomes a continuum, or set of stages, along which working classes at different times and places can be ranked as high or low. Such a strategy precludes the possibility of identifying historical diversity in processes of class formation. The question of "North American exceptionalism" is defined negatively, as something that did not happen, rather than as an historical variant requiring explanation. As Ira Katznelson observes, the North American experience of class has been different; the analytical task is "to specify how and in what ways?"[4]

Our first claim in this chapter is that Americans and Canadians do display a distinctive class orientation and a "critical political consciousness," one that is readily interpretable against the background of the history of political protest and class alliances that shaped both nations in the twentieth century. From the end of the nineteenth century and well into the twentieth, small agricultural producers occupied the strategic "centre" in North American politics. The family farm, not the factory, was where most North Americans made their living. From these agrarian roots emerged the modal form of popular protest in both countries: populist movements of both the left and the right. Where agrarian movements made common cause with urban workers, the result was to produce populist movements of the left. But unlike in Sweden, where organized labour was the dominant partner in a farm-labour alliance that brought the Social Democrats to power in the 1930s, in Canada and the United States organized labour remained a subordinate, and often hesitant, ally. The result was not a "classless politics" but a particular form of class politics whose residues have provided the cultural repertoire from which movements of resistance and protest have continued to draw well into the second half of the century.

What of differences within North America? A long tradition in Canadian social science, bolstered over the years by the writings of American sociologist Seymour Martin Lipset, has insisted that Canadian politics do differ from American.[5] Mention is usually made of the existence and periodic success of a nominally socialist party in Canada, the New Democratic Party (NDP), more developed welfare-state institutions, and more extensive state ownership of industry. The view that Canada has a more leftist political culture than the United States has been further reinforced over the past several decades by the erosion of union membership in the United States and its corresponding rise in Canada.[6] The upshot is that, despite major differences in theoretical orientation and explanatory emphases, the starting point for a great deal of Canadian political analysis begins and ends with the presumption that "Canada is more receptive than the us, but less receptive than Western Europe" to a social-democratic form of politics.[7]

Others have challenged this view. When placed against a broader comparative backdrop, the mid-Atlantic imagery of Canadian class politics begins to break down. Aggregate levels of class voting in the two countries are indistinguishable.[8] Historical differences in social spending, unemployment, and income inequality have been a matter of degree rather than kind.[9] As Jane Jenson has argued, the collective identities around which postwar Canadian politics were built were based on a "politics of place" not a "politics of class."[10] Whereas welfare-state reforms elsewhere were often seen as a strategy for breaking down class divisions, Canadian reforms were justified as a means of eliminating regional disparities in benefits and living standards.

Our second claim in this chapter is that the latter view is closer to the mark than the former. The way in which Canadians and Americans think *about* classes and evaluate class actors is more similar than different. Rather than bobbing about in the mid-Atlantic, Canadian class culture is anchored in full view of the American shoreline.

FROM CLASS STRUCTURE TO CLASS
FORMATION: HOW PEOPLE THINK
ABOUT CLASSES

At issue in the debate over the distinctiveness of class politics in Canada and the United States is the nature of the linkage between class structure and class formation, the process by which relations of production provide the basis for collective action and the formation of group identities. Class identities and political organizations based on production relations do not emerge mechanically from class relations any more than identities and organizations based on gender, region, race, or ethnicity. As Adam Przeworski observes of conventional writings on class formation and class consciousness: "If everyone who is a manual worker in industry is expected to behave politically qua worker then the theory is simply false ... Social cleavages, the experience of social differentiations are never given directly to our consciousness. Social differences acquire the status of cleavages as an outcome of ideological and political struggles."[11] If workers (or farmers or capitalists) acquire their identities in the process of ideological and political struggles, this also means that a potential outcome of such struggles is an identity clearly differentiated from the class-based communities and organizations associated with an individual's class location. While there may be a "natural" affinity between the working class and the institutions of organized labour or left-wing political parties, affinity is not necessity. Class identities, loyalties, and interests not only intersect but also compete with identities, loyalties, and material interests based on race, gender, language, religion, region, and nation. And the result of actual historical struggles may be overt hostility towards organized labour and/or its political representatives within the working class itself. As Przeworski emphasizes, "Political class struggle is a struggle *about* class before it is a struggle among classes."[12]

How then do people think *about* classes? Our concern is not with how people think about classes as abstractions (as in "the working class" or "the middle class"). Especially in North America, the language of class is used, as often as not, to refer to consumption, not production, relations. A "middle-class" identity more likely reflects a family income sufficient to maintain a "middle class" life-style than the subject's position in a set of production relations. One consequence is that traditional measures of class identification – asking respondents to locate themselves in the class structure as members of the "working" or "middle" classes or "lower" or "upper" classes – are ambiguous with respect to the underlying conceptual construct being measured.

Nevertheless, people do hold definite opinions about the institutional expressions of class interests defined by production relations, about the cleavages created by those relations, and about the legitimacy of the claims advanced by groups (bosses-workers, employers-employees) identified by these cleavages. In a strike situation, for example, few people even in North America have difficulty identifying who the "workers" are or whose side they are on in a conflict between "bosses" and "workers." Similarly, even high-wage workers have little difficulty shedding "middle class" identities when they leave their suburban homes and commute to their place of work. When they pass through the factory gates, "middle class" identities are left behind. On the shop floor, they become workers, both to themselves and to others.

If this sharp differentiation between workplace and community identities is, as Katznelson argues,[13] the analytical key to understanding American exceptionalism, it also provides the methodological key to study how people think about classes. If measures of class identification are inadequate because of the ambiguity inherent in the vocabulary of class, we should turn to measures and methods rooted in the context of the workplace and the ways people experience the capital-labour conflict directly.

Survey respondents in four of the five countries (the United States, Canada, Norway, and Sweden) were asked a series of questions concerning their attitudes towards workers and their employers. The first set focused on workers in the context of a strike situation:

1 "Striking workers are generally justified in physically preventing workers from entering the place of work."[14]
2 "During a strike, management should be prohibited by law from hiring workers to take the place of strikers."

The response set to these questions was a four-level Likert scale ranging from strongly agree to strongly disagree.

3 A third question asked respondents to consider a hypothetical situation where workers are out on strike over wages and working conditions and to indicate which of the following outcomes they would like to see occur:
   a the workers win their most important demands;
   b the workers win some of their demands and make some concessions;
   c the workers win only a few of their demands and make major concessions;
   d the workers go back to work without winning any of their demands.

This question was not asked in the Finnish and Norwegian surveys and so is reported only for Canada, the United States, and Sweden.

The second set of questions asked for views on the role of business corporations in society. Respondents were asked to agree or disagree with two statements:

4 "Corporations benefit owners at the expense of workers and consumers."
5 "Big corporations have far too much power in Canadian (or American/Swedish/Norwegian) society today."

Finally, they were asked whether they thought an alternative to market capitalism is possible by agreeing or disagreeing with the statement:

6 "It is possible for a modern society to run effectively without the profit motive."

As with items one and two, the response set to these questions was a four-level Likert scale ranging from strongly agree to strongly disagree. For ease of presentation, we dichotomize the responses to show the percentages adopting pro-labour and anti-corporate sentiments respectively.

As shown in Tables 5.1 and 5.2, the Nordic response profile is characterized by strong pro-labour and anti-corporate attitudes and, especially in Norway, a view that alternatives to the profit motive are feasible. The North American patterns indicate a culture much less optimistic about alternatives to the profit motive and less supportive of organized labour but, surprisingly, even more hostile to business corporations.

The extent of pro-labour solidarity in Sweden and Norway is evidenced by the fact that four-fifths of Swedish and Norwegian respondents think that striking workers are justified in preventing strikebreakers from entering the workplace. In Canada and the United States less than a third share this view. Three-fifths of Canadians and about half the Americans agree that laws should be established to prevent such situations from arising, however. Norwegians show a curious pattern, for which we have no ready explanation. Most think that strikers should be able to prevent strikebreakers from crossing a picket line, but only about half believe the state should outlaw the use of strikebreakers.

The strongest evidence of sharp differences between Swedish and North American attitudes is found in the outcomes respondents would like to see in a strike situation. The majority of North Americans (75 per cent) opt for a compromise solution in which both sides – workers and their employers – make important concessions. Among Swedes, the modal preference (51 per cent) is for a clear victory by labour, a position taken by only 11 per cent of Canadians and 16 per cent of Americans.

Attitudes towards business corporations are a different matter (Table 5.2). Like the Swedes, four-fifths of Canadian and American respondents believe corporations have too much power in society. Two-thirds of Canadian and Swedish respondents, 56 per cent of Americans, and only half the Norwegians think corporations benefit owners at the expense of workers and consumers. This deep anti-corporate sentiment in Canada and the United States does not translate into anti-capitalist sentiment, however. Less than a third of Canadians and Americans think it is possible to organize an economy

Table 5.1
Attitudes toward Strikebreakers by Country

	United States	Canada	Norway	Sweden
PRO-LABOUR (PER CENT AGREE):				
Workers are justified to prevent strikebreakers from crossing picket lines	31	27	78	84
Strikebreakers should be prohibited by law	49	60	51	82
IN A STRIKE SITUATION RESPONDENT WOULD LIKE TO SEE WORKERS:				
Win their most important demands	16	11	na	51
Win some demands and make some concessions	75	74	na	44
Win few or no demands	13	15	na	5
	100	100	na	100
(N)	(1,286)	(2,044)	na	(1,085)

Table 5.2
Attitudes towards Business and Profits by Country

Anti-Business (per cent agree):	United States	Canada	Norway	Sweden
Corporations have too much power	79	81	66	79
Corporations benefit owners at the expense of workers and consumers	56	66	50	67
It is possible for society to run effectively without the profit motive	27	32	69	46

without the profit motive, compared to almost half the Swedish respondents and over two-thirds in Norway. There is a strong Nordic history of co-operatives as alternatives to profit-seeking corporations.

What should we conclude from all this? We might well surmise that North Americans lack a "critical political consciousness" if this were defined in only one dimension at a time – by their attitudes towards labour. But being for or against "labour" tells us nothing about whether people are also for or against "capital." By adding just this single dimension of complexity, the picture changes considerably. If North Americans are critical of organized labour, they are equally or more critical of big business. The way North Americans think *about* classes is distinctive relative to the Nordic pattern. But it is distinctive in a particular *way*. It is a way, moreover, that is readily interpretable against the background of how popular resistance to capital has been structured in twentieth-century North America.

THE POPULIST LEGACY

When compared to Sweden and Norway, Canada and the United States do display a distinctive class orientation, one familiar to most North Americans and, we will argue, one that is readily interpretable against the history of political protest in Canada and the United States. It is individualistic, but the source of this individualism is not a classical liberal view of the world. It has a critical stance towards capitalism, but the critique is not one that stems from a labour-centric class analysis. Rather, the stance taken by North Americans against "big business" and "big labour" – a pattern found over and over in public opinion polls[15] – reflects the populist legacy that arguably has provided the dominant form of political rhetoric and social mobilization during struggles of resistance and change throughout the century. The signal importance of populism in shaping class struggles in the United States and Canada in the first half of the twentieth century has been highlighted in an important essay by John Conway.[16] Our claim is that this populist legacy has also been critical in shaping the way North Americans think about classes in the second half of the century.

Populism is an expression of the "radical democratic tradition" that Bowles and Gintis trace to the seventeenth-century levellers, the eighteenth-century *sans culottes*, and the nineteenth-century chartists and agrarian populists.[17] Its distinguishing feature is the line drawn between the organized few and the unorganized many. Within this tradition, as Stedman Jones writes, "the dividing line between classes was not between the employer and employed, but that between the represented and the unrepresented."[18]

The origins of populism are to be found among those who initially bear the costs of capitalist development: small, independent commodity producers in agriculture and craft production. Such protest is directed against "big business" that threatens to destroy the livelihood and traditional way of life of small producers. It advocates the use of state power to resist the destructive power of capitalist market domination, but it is not anti-capitalist. The goal is not so much to seize state power in order to establish a new social and economic order but to defend the past against the encroaching influence of new forms of monopolizing corporate power in industry, finance, and circulation. It is prepared to use state power to combat this development, but it is not statist; "big government" is as abhorrent as "big business." As Lenin wrote in his discussion of Narodism, populism is "a theory of the mass petit-bourgeois struggle of democratic capitalism against liberal-landlord capitalism."[19]

But small producers are not the only ones who bear the costs of capitalist modernization. The emergent industrial working class also bears these costs, with the result that there is common ground for a potential alliance between these two classes. Such alliances, especially farm-labour alliances, have been common during the development of corporate capitalism. In Sweden a farm-labour alliance brought the Swedish Social Democrats to power in the thirties and sustained them into the fifties.[20] In Canada a similar alliance brought the first avowedly socialist government in North America – the Co-operative Commonwealth Federation (CCF) – to power in the province of Saskatchewan in 1944. As Conway documents, the CCF depended on the long tradition of agrarian populism for both its rhetoric and its forms of organization.[21]

Farm-labour alliances had even a longer history and greater importance in the United States. With the support of farmers and workers, Robert LaFollette won 17 per cent of the national vote in the 1924 presidential elections.[22] And during the thirties, groups calling themselves the Co-operative Commonwealth Federation contested Democratic primaries in Washington and Oregon, electing a number of members to the United States Congress.[23]

Farm-labour alliances were not merely the result of a common enemy. In the early stages of capitalist development, the two classes were often composed of the same people. The first generations of industrial workers incorporated the farmers and artisans (and their sons and daughters) displaced by industrialization. With the advent of mass democracy, alliance formation was encouraged by the imperative of winning electoral majorities, since democracy requires numbers if political protest is to be transformed into political power.

The critical ingredient shaping the outcome of such alliances was the relative balance of power between the two sides. In Sweden, labour was dominant from the beginning and as the electoral importance of farmers declined, the social democrats were able to abandon their agrarian allies. In contrast, the CCF first came to power in 1944 in a predominantly agrarian province. The successor to the CCF, the New Democratic Party, was careful to maintain its distance from organized labour until the sixties. And even in recent elections, the New Democrats have emphasized their role as defender of "ordinary

Canadians," not of the "working class" or of organized labour.[24] From the time of the New Deal, American workers found a home in the Democratic Party, at least until the seventies. But with its multi-factional party structure, Democratic leaders were compelled to avoid becoming too closely identified with any one "special interest" group. And since the seventies, the party has actively distanced itself from its relationship with organized labour.[25]

The immediate reason for this reticence of North American parties to become too closely identified with labour is not difficult to discern. In North America, populist opposition to the organized "few" includes opposition to organized labour, a fact repeatedly demonstrated in both Canadian and American surveys.[26] As Paul Stevenson and Michael Ornstein show, Canadians are generally satisfied with the current distribution of power in Canada, with two exceptions: corporations and unions are seen as having too much of it; farmers and small business people have too little.[27] In Tom Langford's community study of Guelph workers, 78 per cent of the respondents agreed that unions are responsible for the gains made by *workers*, but only 44 per cent agreed that these gains help *most Canadians*. To the majority of these workers, organized labour is part of the problem, not part of the solution. Seventy-eight per cent believed that Canadian unions have become too big and too powerful.[28]

Our thesis then is that the repertoire of protest and resistance in North American political culture continues to bear the imprint of this populist past. Or, more correctly, there are two forms of oppositional discourse available for popular movements to seize on: a *minority* discourse of the left that pits "labour" against "capital" and a popular, populist discourse that pits the unorganized many against "big business," "big government," *and* "big labour."

	Pro-Labour	
Pro-Business	Yes	No
Yes	Corporatist	Conservative
No	Left-Labour	Populist

Figure 5.1
How People Think about Classes

Figure 5.1 highlights the possible range of attitude configurations ("class orientations") people may hold towards the two fundamental classes of capitalist societies – labour and capital:

1 *Left-Labour* represents the perspective of the classical labour militant, supportive of organized labour and critical of big business.

Table 5.3
Class Orientation by Country

Class Orientation	United States	Canada	Norway	Sweden
PRO-LABOUR				
Left-labour	22	24	30	60
Corporatist	6	8	21	19
ANTI-LABOUR				
Populist	42	42	17	7
Conservative	30	26	32	14
	100	100	100	100
(N)	(1,349)	(2,094)	(1,565)	(1,057)

2 *Conservatives* are the main antagonists of labour, hostile to unions and supportive of business interests.
3 *Corporatists* are sympathetic to labour but also hold positive views of the role of business interests in shaping society.
4 *Populists* are equally sceptical of both "big business" and "big labour."

The "corporatist" label is drawn from the Scandinavian experience, where a system of corporatist regulation has shaped postwar relations between labour and capital. Under this arrangement, labour, social, and many other issues are decided upon through a co-operative relation between highly organized employers and unions in a centralized bargaining system and in a variety of agencies and boards.[29]

Table 5.3 presents national profiles of the distribution of these attitude configurations ("class orientations") about the role of corporations and unions in society. To operationalize the typology, we first constructed two composite indices of respondent attitudes towards labour and business and then cross-classified the indices. The details of the index construction are reported in the endnote.[30]

Swedish attitudes are characterized by what John Logue has called "a kind of Social Democratic ethical hegemony."[31] Three-fifths of the Swedish labour force hold left-labour views, and together anti-labour populists and conservatives are only a fifth of the work-force. In Canada and the United States, there is no single hegemonic group, but populists clearly occupy the strategic centre, with two-fifths of the labour force. Both the "left" (left-labour) and the "right" (conservatives) constitute significant minorities (between 20 and 30 per cent), but both must turn to the populist centre to form a majority. Corporatists are relatively common in Norway and Sweden (a fifth) but rare in North America (6 to 8 per cent). In Norway, corporatists occupy a place of special strategic importance for labour: the left-labour faction is only 30 per cent of the work-force and an alliance with corporatists is necessary to form even a narrow pro-labour majority.

CLASS CLEAVAGES

Since Robert Alford's classic study of class voting in the Anglo-American democracies, whether or not a nation's politics could be described as "class politics" or "classless politics" has been measured in terms of the size of class *cleavages* found in voting, popular attitudes, and other forms of behaviour.[32] In essence, the answer to the question of whether "class matters" has been predicated on the discovery of significant class divisions in society.

In Table 5.4 we present indices of class cleavage between the working class and the three other major classes on the class-orientation typology and for the underlying pro-labour and anti-business indices that go into its construction. The index of class cleavage for the class-orientation typology is measured with the index of dissimilarity.[33] For the two components, the measure of cleavage is simply the percentage difference between the working class and each other class adopting a pro-labour or anti-business position.[34] In all cases, the index of class cleavage can be interpreted as the magnitude of difference between the reference class in the table and the working class.

Consistent with its image of a country where "class matters," Sweden has the highest level of class division on all measures. But the United States and especially Canada can hardly be considered "classless," at least by this standard. Indeed, class divisions on labour issues are even stronger in the two North American countries than they are in Norway. In all countries, the divisions are especially sharp between workers and the capitalist-executive class. In no country are there large differences between workers and the new middle class, least of all in the Nordic countries, where the new middle class is highly unionized.

But what should we conclude from these divisions? That Sweden stood on the verge of class warfare in the early eighties? That we need to revise our classless view of social relations in North America and especially in Canada, where class divisions are decidedly more pronounced than in Norway? Does the fact that divisions between workers and the old middle class are sharper in Sweden than elsewhere tell us that coalitions across these boundaries are less likely in Sweden? As we show in the following section, just the reverse is true.

Table 5.4
Indices of Class Cleavage by Country

	United States	Canada	Norway	Sweden
Class Cleavage between the Working Class and the:		Class Orientation		
Capitalist-executive class	−23	−38	−32	−44
Old middle class	−17	−19	−13	−37
New middle class	−11	−8	−9	−15
		Pro-Labour		
Capitalist-executive class	−25	−26	−17	−39
Old middle class	−17	−19	−12	−17
New middle class	−12	−7	−5	−5
		Anti-Business		
Capitalist-executive class	−19	−33	−32	−43
Old middle class	−4	−4	−13	−37
New middle class	−3	−2	−8	−14

More important than size of class divisions are the underlying levels of *intra-class* solidarity that generate these cleavages.

CLASS SOLIDARITY, CLASS ALLIANCES
AND CLASS CONFLICT

As we will demonstrate, similar, even identical, levels of class cleavage can be produced from very different underlying patterns of class solidarity. As a result, national differences in the size of class cleavages tell us rather little about national differences in the way people think about classes, the likelihood of class conflict, or the potential for forging alliances between classes. In Sweden, class cleavages are the product of a united working class that commands the sympathies of both the old and new classes and even a significant share of the capitalist-executive class. In North America the reverse situation exists. The working class is divided within itself, commands few supporters in other classes, and faces a cohesive "ruling class" of capitalists and corporate executives.

Consider first the distribution of class orientations in the capitalist-executive class (Table 5.5). In the Nordic countries the "ruling class" is a house divided against itself, while in North America capitalist and executive solidarity is virtually complete. The largest fraction of the capitalist-executive class in all four countries is resolutely conservative. But where North American capitalists and executives are to-

Table 5.5
Class Orientation of the Capitalist-Executive Class by Country

Capitalist-Executive Class Orientation	United States	Canada	Norway	Sweden
PRO-LABOUR				
Left-labour	8	8	10	24
Corporatist	4	4	26	22
ANTI-LABOUR				
Populist	39	29	10	7
Conservative	49	60	54	47
	100	100	100	100
(N)	(135)	(130)	(107)	(69)

Table 5.6
Class Orientation of the Working Class by Country

Working-Class Orientation	United States	Canada	Norway	Sweden
PRO-LABOUR				
Left-labour	27	29	35	68
Corporatist	8	9	19	16
ANTI-LABOUR				
Populist	40	41	17	7
Conservative	26	22	29	9
	100	100	100	100
(N)	(716)	(1,205)	(913)	(711)

tally united in their opposition to labour, in Norway and especially in Sweden there is little solidarity on labour issues. Fully 46 per cent of Swedish capitalists and executives express support for organized labour. About half of these do so from a corporatist point of view, but the other half appear to be labour militants. If there is a crack in the upper reaches of the North American class structure, it is due to populist scepticism over the role of big business, especially in the United States.

Patterns of class solidarity in the working class (Table 5.6) are the mirror image of those in the "ruling class." Support for organized labour is virtually universal among Swedish workers. Eighty-four per cent are pro-labour, including 68 per cent who are left-labour militants and an additional 16 per cent who are corporatists. North American workers, in contrast, are sharply divided among themselves. Only about a third are labour supporters, two-fifths are populists, sceptical of both labour and business, and a quarter are conservatives. Norwegian workers are considerably more supportive of

Table 5.7
Class Orientation of the New Middle Class by Country

New-Middle-Class Orientation	United States	Canada	Norway	Sweden
PRO-LABOUR				
Left-labour	18	24	26	53
Corporatist	6	7	24	25
ANTI-LABOUR				
Populist	47	44	18	8
Conservative	30	26	32	15
	100	100	100	100
(N)	(391)	(524)	(403)	(208)

Table 5.8
Class Orientation of the Old Middle Class by Country

Old-Middle-Class Orientation	United States	Canada	Norway	Sweden
PRO-LABOUR				
Left-labour	15	15	24	32
Corporatist	3	3	18	34
ANTI-LABOUR				
Populist	46	51	16	6
Conservative	36	31	42	28
	100	100	100	100
(N)	(105)	(236)	(142)	(64)

labour (54 per cent) than North American workers, but there too division prevails, including a significant conservative minority (29 per cent).

Class attitudes in the new middle class (Table 5.7) are virtually indistinguishable from those of the working class. In Sweden and Norway the majority are labour supporters, and in Canada and the United States they tend to be populist. Like capitalists and executives, the old middle class (Table 5.8) in North America is anti-labour but predominantly populist. In Sweden, two-thirds of the old middle class are labour supporters.

In sum, while there are sharp capital-labour divisions in all four countries, these divisions are not what distinguish underlying national cultures *about* classes. Swedish class divisions are the result of a militant and cohesive working class, a middle class that is broadly supportive of labour, and a sharply divided bourgeoisie. In Canada and the United States the reverse is true. The working class is sharply divided within itself, there is only modest support for labour within the intermediate strata, and the bourgeoisie is united in its opposition to organized labour. If there is a "mid-Atlantic" pattern to be found, it is in Norway rather than in Canada. Norwegians in all classes are less favourable towards labour than Swedes and more favourable towards business than North Americans.

But what cuts across these divisions are two quite distinctive cultural configurations. In the Nordic countries, a corporatist culture of business-labour co-operation plays a decisive role by muting anti-labour sentiment among the new middle class, the old middle class, and capitalists and executives. Especially in Sweden, a decidedly militant working class can find numerous allies across the entire class spectrum so long as militancy stops short of revolution and can accommodate some degree of co-operation with capital.

In North America, labour militants face a dilemma even within the working class. The barons of "Wall Street" (in the United States) or of "Bay Street" (in Canada) are always available as targets for popular protest. But protest *against* "big business" must be carefully separated from overt support *for* "big labour" if the populist centre is to be mobilized. Unlike in Sweden and other European nations, opposition to capital is not a currency that can be converted into support for labour. On the contrary, the populist centre is ripe for mobilization from both the left (against big business) and the right (against labour). Canadian populism has produced successful parties of the left (the CCF/NDP) and the right (Social Credit). During the eighties, so-called Reagan Democrats provided the mass base necessary for America's neo-conservative revolution against "big government" and "big labour."

To emphasize the strong similarity between the class cultures of Canada and the United States is not to dispute the oft-noted differences between Canadian and American social and economic life. The trajectory of welfare-state development in Canada, for example, has differed from the American one since the sixties as a result of the racialization of social politics in the United States.[35] During the same period, organized labour in the United States went into a precipitous decline, while union density levels continued to rise in Canada. Such differences clearly call for explanation. Our concern, rather, is with a long theoretical tradition that would attempt to construct such an explanation in terms of fundamental differences in national cultures *about* class.

THE LONG ARM OF HISTORY?

Our claim that Canada and the United States share a common political culture *about* classes has two theoretical targets. The first of these emerged during the sixties and claimed that Canada–U.S. differences in social and economic life were a result of fundamental differences in values and ideology that could be traced to the values and ideologies of the founders of these two "new nations." Others have sharply disagreed with the conventional *explanation* for Canada–U.S. cultural differences while maintaining that the facts of the matter are essentially correct: "Canada is more receptive than the US, but less receptive than Western Europe" to a social-democratic form of politics.[36] Our sights are targeted on both points of view.

The roots of these debates can be traced to Louis Hartz's well-known "fragment" theory of American exceptionalism.[37] Hartz argued that the political cultures of the new nations are the product of the beliefs and ideologies brought by the founding generations to the New World. Carriers of liberalism, they created societies with neither the privileged aristocracy nor the deferential peasantry of the European "whole." They were "fragment" cultures without an old order against which to rebel. In the absence of a feudal tradition emphasizing class and status, class-based identities failed to evolve – hence, no socialism in America.

Taking up the Hartz thesis, Seymour Martin Lipset, Gad Horowitz, and virtually all leading Canadian social scientists of the sixties argued that Canada was different. The "liberal fragment" model fit the United States but not its northern neighbour. Especially after the American Revolution, Canada became the site where a paternalistic, élitist Tory "fragment" of British society consolidated its world. Toryism represents the classical conservative strain of European politics: society is a hierarchical corporate entity composed of estates and classes, not merely an agglomeration of individuals pursuing their self-interest. The result is a social order where both élites and masses are more given to collective solutions – more state ownership, more social programs, more labour unions. There is more protection for group rights in Canada and less for individual and property rights. The élitism of the Tory fragment creates more deference for authority, a more law-abiding citizenry, and less crime. But its organic model of society leaves a place for social classes and for "socialism."

Nowhere, according to Lipset, are these cultural differences more evident than in the decline of American organized labour since the 1960s and its continued growth in Canada.[38] Until the sixties, organized labour in the two countries grew in tandem, with Canada lagging somewhat behind U.S. levels. By 1986 union density in the United States had declined to about 18 per cent of paid non-agricultural workers, while in Canada it had risen to almost 40 per cent.[39] The facts of the matter are indisputable. But our evidence strongly suggests that we should look to something other than political culture to account for the facts.[40] Canadian labour has been more successful in organizing workers since the sixties, but the reasons for this divergence in Canada–U.S. labour history are not to be found in greater Canadian affection for organized labour.

Our results have shown only marginal differences in Canadian and American attitudes towards organized labour. Gary Bowden's careful analysis of Canadian and American attitudes towards labour over the postwar period is even more persuasive because of his ability to trace these attitudes across time.[41] He shows that in both absolute and relative terms Canadians have consistently perceived organized labour as *more* threatening than Americans, not less. As Bowden concludes: "Lipset's analysis implies Canadian public opinion should be more favourable to unions than American public opinion. The data, however, show the reverse: more Canadians than Americans view unions as too powerful; more Canadians than Americans perceive labour as the greatest threat; fewer Canadians than Americans have confidence in labour as an institution; more Canadians than Americans blame unions for inflation."[42] That Canadians see organized labour as a more powerful force in society than do Americans is hardly surprising in light of the facts. American unions have been in decline since the sixties. In Canada, organized labour has grown in strength, reinforcing the imagery of "big labour" as a powerful force shaping Canadian society. Moreover, growth has mainly occurred among public sector employees – teachers, nurses, postal workers – who, when they strike, disrupt the lives of "ordinary" Canadians more than do strikes by industrial workers.

The similarity in attitudes and the antipathy of many workers towards organized labour reflect historical experiences closer in time than those identified by Lipset. As highlighted in chapter 4, Canada's history of "dependent industrialization" meant that class relations in the two nations have been organized not merely by *similar* social institutions but, as often as not, by the *same* social institutions. American unions brought Gomperism and a tradition of "business" unionism to Canada, a tradition that dictated the pursuit of narrow self-interest – of union, not working-class, solidarity. Gains won at the bargaining table, such as better pensions, were confined to those represented at the table. The unorganized working class went without. Not until the end of the seventies did a new kind of "social unionism" – an effort to use labour's (albeit limited) power to win gains for the whole of the working class – begin to emerge in Canada.[43] It has yet to appear in the United States.

In postwar Sweden, organized industrial workers began to forge new bonds with the expanding white-collar strata. In contrast, industrial unions in postwar North America were engaged in what Mike Davis has called "labour's civil war" between the communist and noncommunist left.[44] As a result, industrial workers were in no position to establish an alliance among themselves, much less with anyone else.[45] New, emergent fractions of the working class remained outside labour's ranks and even large sectors of the industrial working class were left unorganized. As the opinion polls and our results show, for these workers the labour movement was often perceived as part of the problem, not part of the solution. A labour-centric vision of society in which unions and labour parties become symbols of the collective good and social transformation did not emerge at a mass level. As Robert Brym and his colleagues have shown, European-like patterns of political class behaviour did emerge in some regions where the "power resources" of labour made a left strategy a plausible alternative for Canadian workers.[46] But in the absence of such an alternative, the majority of those who came to adulthood in the postwar decades returned to the populist sentiments of their youth.

THE FUTURE OF CLASS POLITICS: POSTINDUSTRIAL CLEAVAGES

To highlight the populist core of both Canadian and American political discourse provides what is arguably a more plausible historical account of contemporary political culture in North America than one which appeals to the legacy of events that occurred two centuries ago. The populist experience is a proximate one that many of those currently living have experienced and the institutional expressions of which are still active. But what of the future?

By the time our surveys were conducted in the early 1980s, the cohorts whose experience formed the basis of the postwar period were beginning to leave the labour force, to be replaced by younger workers whose links to the 1930s or even the 1950s were limited or nonexistent. Male, blue-collar, industrial workers no longer held pride of place in the class structure. New divisions based on sex and skill, new occupations, and postindustrial work sites had changed all this. How has the legacy of populism fared under these new, postindustrial conditions? Is there any evidence of a shift to the left or, as the politics of the 1980s would indicate, a more conservative mood among workers who are younger, more likely to be female, more educated, and with limited experience of the factory floor?

What of the Nordic countries? The union density rates shown in chapter 4 indicate little difference among men and women, the new middle class and the working class, or across economic sectors. But as we reported in chapter 4, during the eighties cracks began to appear in the Swedish labour movement between industrial workers and public-sector workers, between men and women, and between the representatives of the new labour aristocracy of professional and technical workers (SACO) and other unions. Were these postindustrial divisions foreshadowed in the class attitudes of Swedish workers at the beginning of the eighties when these surveys were conducted?

To answer these questions requires us to turn our attention to differences *within* countries, rather than differences *between* countries, and we will discuss the evidence for each country in turn. Our conclusions are based on the results of a multivariate logistic regression analysis presented in the appendix to this chapter. The highlights are summarized in the text, and the reader is referred to the appendix for details. Readers who wish to check our conclusions against the tables should pause to spend a few moments reading the textual introduction to the appendix.

For reasons of both parsimony and sample size, we focus our discussion on the class attitudes of workers and the new middle class. We report the results with a degree of caution. Although our survey questions provide a powerful tool for identifying rather dramatic differences between countries, they are less satisfactory for capturing subtle differences of meaning within countries where there are commonly understood meanings associated with symbol-laden terms such as "workers," "corporations," and "unions."

POPULISM IN NORTH AMERICA

In the United States, postindustrialism has brought a consolidation of the populist centre at the expense of both the left and the right, but predominantly of the latter. The new middle class is more populist than the working class; women are more populist than men; and service-sector employees are more populist than people employed in goods production. Younger workers and even the middle-aged tend to be more populist then people over fifty. For the most part, this "postindustrial populism" is not a result of more negative attitudes towards labour but rather a more critical stance towards American business. American women, for example, are more populist than men not because they are more likely to be anti-labour but because they are less likely to be conservative. (Readers can verify this conclusion against the results in the appendix by noting the sign and significance level of the coefficient for women across equations.) There are two important exceptions to this generalization. The populism of the new middle class does reflect more negative attitudes to labour. And the populism of public-sector employees draws upon greater scepticism of both business and labour.

This postindustrial populism is mitigated, however, by the conservatism of knowledge workers. We included two indicators in our regressions: the measure distinguishing autonomous from non-autonomous jobs and another indicating whether the respondent had a post-secondary degree or not. The skilled and the educated are decidedly more conservative than other employees – more critical of labour and more favourable to business.

In Canada the differences are less sharp. As in the United States, women are more populist than men but mainly because they are less likely to support labour. And as in the United States, knowledge workers in Canada are more conservative than other employees. The most dramatic finding concerns the class attitudes of public-sector employees, who are decidedly more conservative and anti-labour than expected, given their high levels of unionization. The greater strength of public-sector unions in Canada is not reflected in the political attitudes of public-sector employees, a finding that confirms our earlier conclusions about the limits of cultural explanations of Canada–U.S. differences in unionization rates. The young, in contrast, are somewhat more supportive of labour than older workers despite lower rates of union membership.

Together these results suggest that in both Canada and the United States, postindustrial patterns of labour organization have strengthened the populist centre and, to a lesser extent, the right at the expense of the left. Knowledge workers are less favourable to organized labour and more supportive of big business. In Canada, organized labour has been more successful in organizing public-sector employees, but this success has not been translated into a corresponding shift in their support for labour. In both countries, women have tended to concentrate in the populist centre: 48 per cent of Canadian women and 49 per cent of American women (Table 5.9). The weaker attachment of women to the labour movement is not a result of lower rates of union membership. In Canada, over half of the unionized men (52 per cent) are strong labour supporters, compared to 39 per cent of unionized women. In the United States, 62 per cent of the unionized men are strongly pro-labour, compared to 44 per cent of unionized women.

Concepts, we should point out, are not innocent. When we refer to the class attitudes of contemporary working women as *populist*, we impute a causal process or at least an implicit understanding of meanings to what the simultaneous rejection of both capital and

Table 5.9
Class Orientation by Sex in Canada and the United States (percentage)

| | Pro-Labour | | Anti-Labour | |
	Left-Labour	Corporatist	Populist	Conservative
UNITED STATES				
Men	27	7	36	30
Women	21	6	49	24
Difference	−6	−1	+13	−6
CANADA				
Men	31	9	37	23
Women	22	7	48	23
Difference	−9	−2	+11	0

labour *means* to these women. Historically, as we have seen, populism emerged as an expression of the *class* interests of independent commodity producers (farmers, craftworkers) against the encroachment of big business. Despite the resurgence of self-employment in postindustrial labour markets (see chapter 3), we would be hard pressed to sustain such an interpretation for the majority of working women in the present period. How then to account for this and other expressions of postindustrial populism? In the conclusion, we will offer some speculations on this question.

NORDIC SOCIAL DEMOCRACY

What of Sweden and Norway? As we have seen earlier, the hegemony of labour is evident among the whole of the Swedish labour force, and the logistic regressions give no indication of the erosion one might have anticipated in light of developments during the eighties. If there are cultural cracks in Swedish social democracy, they are not evident here. The new middle class tends to be more corporatist than workers but not anti-labour. There are no significant differences between men and women or across age groups. As in North America, however, knowledge workers in both Nordic countries are more conservative than other employees despite high levels of union membership. However, unlike in Sweden, postindustrial cleavages in Norway give some indication of an emergent neo-populism, both among the young and among public-sector employees. As with its class structure, Norwegian class attitudes display a distinctively mid-Atlantic quality.

In general, our results show that nation-specific class attitudes have either been resilient in the face of, or reinforced by, postindus-

trialism. The exception is worth noting, however. In all four countries, "knowledge workers" – those with more education, autonomy,
and skill – differ significantly from their respective national patterns.
And in all four cases, they are more conservative than other members of the working or new middle classes. The new labour aristocracy, like the old, poses a problem for labour. Those who possess "human capital" are closer to the world-view of those who possess other
forms of capital than they are to less skilled workers. These results
confirm the insight of a great deal of theoretical literature which argues that knowledge workers are different. They belie the main thesis of that literature, however: the new labour aristocracy has not become the "grave-digger" of capitalism.[47]

CONCLUSION

The experience of class in North America has been different. Our
main purpose in this chapter has been to take up Katznelson's challenge to specify how and in what ways, to reconstruct what is to be
explained. In the past, "American exceptionalism" has been defined
largely in terms of a liberal legacy emphasizing individualism and
achievement. Earlier in this volume we saw evidence of this individualism: American and Canadian workers are more anxious to own
their own business, they have higher expectations of individual mobility by moving up promotion ladders, and they are clearly less favourable to collective solutions of the sort offered by the labour
movement. Our challenge, then, is not to conventional claims about
American individualism but to conventional claims about its origins
and import. Its roots derive not from Locke but from the radical
democratic tradition articulated and reproduced in the populist social movements that provided the major vehicles of popular resistance, protest, and change from the late nineteenth century on-
wards.

Debates over the Canadian experience have revolved around
whether or not Canadian political culture deviates from the model of
liberal individualism traditionally imputed to the United States. Did
the Tory ethos make more room for "socialism" in Canada? In light
of our results, the question needs reformulation. Does Canadian political culture deviate significantly from the legacy of populism that
has played such a determining role in American politics during the
twentieth century? Our answer is no. We have no doubt that Canadians and Americans differ from one another in many subtle ways
and on a variety of issues, just as New Englanders differ from Americans raised in the South or people in Western Canada differ from

French-speaking Québécois (see chapter 9). Rather, our claim is that to search for the roots of such differences within the framework of a hypothetical continuum between the "class-based" political cultures of Western Europe and the liberal individualism of North America is misguided.

Socialists, social democrats, labour militants, and even communists have been an important and sometimes determining force in shaping North American political life during the twentieth century. Socialists and social democrats have maintained a viable "third party" in Canadian politics since the forties and played a similar role as the left wing of the Democratic Party in the United States.[48] Earlier in the century, communists were elected to municipal office in both Milwaukee and Winnipeg. From the thirties to the fifties, they controlled important labour unions in both countries. But in neither country did a European-like class politics, even of the social-democratic variety, provide the axial principle of political cleavage.

As our results have shown, North American corporate leaders have a clear vision of their class interests and since the seventies have articulated these interests in an especially forceful way.[49] But the majority of North Americans do not view public life through the prism of the capital-labour divide. Rather, the "critical political consciousness" of North Americans, their cultural repertoire of protest and resistance, was forged in the crucible of a radical democratic populism.

Would-be reformers from both the left and the right have recognized these populist residues in North American political culture and appeal to them regularly. In their electoral campaigns of the early seventies, both George McGovern in the United States and David Lewis in Canada were clearly recognizable as the heirs of the populist tradition. Lewis, then leader of the NDP, won broad support, if not electoral victory, with his attack on big business – "corporate welfare bums," as he described them. However, his strategy was a clear rejection of the socialist vision of the Waffle group, left nationalists he had earlier ejected from the party.

But if North American populism has proven resilient, it also faces a conundrum. In an earlier era, populists looked to the state and sought electoral office to protect themselves against powerful organized interest groups. As the state has grown in power and become more intrusive in the daily lives of "ordinary" Canadians and Americans, it too has become a target for populist resentment. As Bowden shows, during the sixties and seventies, "big government" rather than big labour or big business became identified as "the main threat to the future of the country" in public-opinion polls.[50] Both Ronald Reagan and Brian Mulroney played upon these sentiments in their electoral sweeps of the 1980s. The rapid growth of the state during the postwar decades means that now "big government" is among the "organized interests" from which the unorganized many seek protection. But from whence will this protection come?

For many, the answer of choice is to be found in the "new social movements" – in the environmental, peace, and women's movements, in the movement for gay rights, and in the voices of cultural and racial minorities. The residues of populism are common to all of these movements: a refusal to define group interests as class interests, or the social order in terms of the division between capital and labour. Traditional populism was not a "classless" politics. It found its roots in the class interests of small landholders, artisans, and shopkeepers threatened by "big business." When workers did not see themselves protected *by* unions but, instead, requiring protection *from* unions, they too turned to populism. The dynamic that has sustained the neo-populism of the new social movements is similar. Since the sixties, minorities and women in both Canada and the United States have had to struggle not only against the practices of "big business" but, as often as not, against the exclusionary practices of organized labour as well. As we show in chapter 9, where women's struggles did not become labour's struggles, this rift was accentuated. But we run ahead of our story. First we must turn to consider the focus of these struggles: the "relations of ruling" that organize the social world of men and women, the subject of part 2.

APPENDIX:
LOGISTIC REGRESSIONS PREDICTING
CLASS ORIENTATION AMONG THE
WORKING AND NEW MIDDLE CLASSES

The logistic regressions in this appendix allow us to identify the independent effect of the many factors that are or could be associated with class orientation discussed in this chapter. The models were estimated with a view to answering questions about the potential consequences of patterns of postindustrial labour-market organization on class orientation. Is there an indication, for example, that women, younger workers, or employees with post-secondary degrees differ from the modal pattern characteristic of each country – populism in North America or a left-labour orientation in Sweden.

All of the independent variables will be familiar from earlier chapters, although we adjust our industry categories to reflect our substantive concerns in this chapter. We divide services into commercial services (personal, retail, and business) and public services (public administration and health, education, and social services) because of our particular interest in the class attitudes of public-sector workers, who not only work for the state but are also highly unionized.

For simplicity, only those class orientations relevant to a particular country are included. In Canada and the United States, corporatism is a residual category in which few cases are found and for which our results showed no significant effects for any of the variables included. Thus corporatists were added together with "left-labour" to create a more inclusive "pro-labour" category. For Canada and the United States, we are concerned with whether there are significant deviations from the populist centre in any of our subgroups and if so, whether the shift is towards a more conservative or pro-labour stance. There were too few populists in Sweden to estimate reliable parameters, so they are excluded altogether. In Sweden we want to know whether left-labour dominance may be eroding (say, among younger people) and if so, whether the difference is in the direction of a more conservative or more corporatist position. Only in Norway, are all four possible orientations relevant.

Logistic regression allows us to estimate effect parameters for a binary dependent variable – in this case, a particular class orientation such as populist/not populist – from a set of independent variables. Logistic coefficients can be interpreted as the change in the log odds associated with a one-unit change in the independent variable, although they can readily be expressed in more conventional probability form.[51] Here all independent variables were treated as categorical variables, and coefficients are expressed as a deviation from the reference category indicated by the square brackets. The coefficient for the new middle class, for example, is the difference between workers and the new middle class. A positively signed coefficient for the new middle class means its members are more likely than workers to adopt a particular class orientation.

A separate equation is estimated for each possible configuration of class attitudes. To interpret the results, consider the row for sex in Table 5A.1. As indicated by the square brackets, men are the reference category, and the coefficient for women indicates the difference between men and women. We see that women are less likely to be pro-labour than men (−.302). This does not mean they are more conservative than men. The coefficient (−.178) is negative and not statistically significant. Rather they are much more likely to be populists, as indicated by the positive and significant coefficient.

Table 5A.1
Logistic Regression Estimates Predicting Class Orientation among Working and
New Middle Classes, United States

	Pro-Labour B (s.e.)	Populist B (s.e.)	Conservative B (s.e.)
Constant	−.937** (.170)	−.669* (.309)	−.934** (.338)
Class [Working]			
New middle	−.444** (.170)	.386** (.148)	.035 (.168)
Sex [Men]			
Women	−.100 (.158)	.296* (.139)	−.327* (.159)
Age [50+]			
16–29	.294 (.199)	.305+ (.179)	−.467* (.197)
30–49	−.050 (.202)	.349* (.178)	−.300 (.195)
Industry [Goods]			
Commercial services	.148 (.172)	.346* (.161)	−.570** (.178)
Public services	−.471* (.219)	.996*** (.138)	−.812*** (.214)
Education [High school or less]			
Post-secondary	−.424* (.169)	.107 (.148)	.304+ (.169)
Autonomy [No autonomy]			
Autonomous	−.293 (.195)	−.228 (.167)	.592** (.182)
Union Status [Not union]			
Union member	1.438*** (.169)	−.448** (.168)	−1.387*** (.234)
Chi2	139.39***	69.93***	88.29***
N	979	1026	1026

Significance levels: + .051 − .100; * .011 − .050; ** .001 − .010; *** better than .001.

Table 5A.2
Logistic Regression Estimates Predicting Class Orientation among Working and New Middle Classes, Canada

	Pro-Labour B (s.e.)	Populist B (s.e.)	Conservative B (s.e.)
Constant	−.555*	−.229	−1.51
	(.252)	(.233)	(.272)
Class [Working]			
New middle	−.193	.144	.041
	(.123)	(.113)	(.131)
Sex [Men]			
Women	−.302**	.4000***	−.178
	(.115)	(.109)	(.127)
Age [50+]			
16–29	.292*	−.174	−.103
	(.149)	(.139)	(.166)
30–49	.145	−.121	−.012
	(.147)	(.139)	(.162)
Industry [Goods]			
Commercial services	.019	−.074	.086
	(.132)	(.147)	(.150)
Public services	−.315*	.080	.300+
	(.156)	(.148)	(.174)
Education [High school or less]			
Post-secondary	−.190	.025	.233+
	(.119)	(.112)	(.131)
Autonomy [No autonomy]			
Autonomous	−.327*	.029	.341*
	(.130)	(.120)	(.136)
Union Status [Not union]			
Union member	.883***	−.366**	−.700***
	(.119)	(.114)	(.134)
Chi2	113.02***	35.45***	51.61***
N	1674	1687	1687

Significance levels: + .051 − .100; * .011 − .050; ** .001 − .010; *** better than .001.

Table 5A.3
Logistic Regression Estimates Predicting Class Orientation among Working and New Middle Classes, Norway

	Left-Labour B (s.e.)	Corporatist B (s.e.)	Populist B (s.e.)	Conservative B (s.e.)
Constant	−.582+	−1.049**	−2.02***	−1.519***
	(.306)	(.350)	(.389)	(.316)
Class [Working]				
New middle	−.181	+.173	+.153	+.072
	(.153)	(.176)	(.187)	(.152)
Sex [Men]				
Women	.010	.061	−.095	−.175
	(.134)	(.159)	(.167)	(.139)
Age [50+]				
16–29	−.075	−.492*	.689**	−.076
	(.174)	(.210)	(.234)	(.188)
30–49	−.125	−.137	.391+	.128
	(.153)	(.174)	(.213)	(.164)
Industry [Goods]				
Commercial services	−.032	−.259	.053	.342*
	(.148)	(.175)	(.196)	(.157)
Public services	−.100	−.333+	.555**	.033
	(.169)	(.197)	(.209)	(.178)
Education [High school or less]				
Post-secondary	−.403**	−.069	−.034	.657***
	(.153)	(.176)	(.178)	(.146)
Autonomy [No autonomy]				
Autonomous	−.300*	.116	.024	.267+
	(.150)	(.172)	(.182)	(.145)
Union status [Not union]				
Union member	.385*	−.148	−.194	−.150
	(.132)	(.153)	(.161)	(.136)
Chi2	31.90***	14.07	19.18*	44.37***
N	1330	1330	1330	1330

Significance levels: + .051 − .100; * .011 − .050; ** .001 − .010; *** better than .001.

Table 5A.4
Logistic Regression Estimates Predicting Class Orientation among Working and New Middle Classes, Sweden

	Left-Labour B (s.e.)	Corporatist B (s.e.)	Conservative B (s.e.)
Constant	.234	−1.999***	−1.791**
	(.397)	(.506)	(.645)
Class [Working]			
New middle	−.220	.392+	.021
	(.185)	(.225)	(.308)
Sex [Men]			
Women	−.129	.108	−.405
	(.160)	(.211)	(.287)
Age [50+]			
16–29	.072	−.315	−.157
	(.210)	(.293)	(.375)
30–49	−.033	.221	−.145
	(.186)	(.246)	(.342)
Industry [Goods]			
Commercial services	−.413*	.367	−.517
	(.191)	(.262)	(.351)
Public services	−.219	.359	−.116
	(.191)	(.258)	(.332)
Education [High school or less]			
Post-secondary	−.321+	.151	.428
	(.176)	(.223)	(.290)
Autonomy [No autonomy]			
Autonomous	−.451*	.577**	.653*
	(.175)	(.222)	(.292)
Union status [Not union]			
Union member	1.072***	−.644**	−1.544***
	(.201)	(.234)	(.277)
Chi2	68.90***	39.99***	46.64***
N	835	835	835

Significance levels: + .051 − .100; * .011 − .050; ** .001 − .010; *** better than .001.

PART TWO

Gender Relations
in Postindustrial Societies

6 Bringing In Gender: Postindustrialism and Patriarchy[*]

We began our analysis in part 1 by highlighting two major changes that have irrevocably altered contemporary capitalist economies: changes in the material division of labour and in the composition of the people employed by capital. The astute reader will have noted that despite the importance we attached to the second of these developments – the feminization of the labour force – we have been rather silent on this topic until now. This strategy has been deliberate. As our work proceeded, it became apparent that to address the implications of this development would require us not simply to "add gender on" but rather to reorient our analysis fundamentally.

Since the seventies, the observation that class relations are gendered and the charge that conventional class theory is "gender-blind" have been commonplace. In the real world, structures of inequality, relations of domination and exploitation, are shaped by the complex interaction of divisions based on sex as well as class, to which one might add divisions of race, ethnicity, immigrant status, age, or disability. But what exactly does it mean to say that a particular analysis of classes and class relations is blind to divisions based on sex, race, age, or any other social cleavage, for that matter?

One implication is that we simply become attentive to *differences*, recognizing that class experiences, class effects, and class processes can and do differ depending on one's sex, race, age, or even the region of the country in which one lives. We have identified some

*Chapter 6 has been co-authored with Clarence Lochhead.

important gender differences in earlier chapters and will examine more as this chapter proceeds. But class analysis can plead guilty to remaining silent on "differences" without necessarily conceding that there are serious flaws in its theories or empirical claims *about* classes. There is no inherent reason why theories about classes must explain all forms of social domination and inequality.

The more serious charge in our view is that the conventional problematic of class analysis precludes posing (and answering) fundamental questions *about* gender relations. We can illustrate this point with an example from the field of political sociology. Recent studies of the welfare state formulated within a class perspective have asked questions about whether and to what extent the welfare state has transformed relations *between classes.*[1] Has the welfare state strengthened labour when it encounters capital? Do social programs reduce the compulsion of workers to sell their labour to any employer at any price? Are workers able to use "politics" to alter market forces? These *questions* have generated a small industry of theory and research in the social sciences, most of which had little or nothing to say about women, the major clients of the welfare state. To overcome this silence, it is not sufficient simply to *add* gender – to be attentive to differences – but we must change the question itself: To what extent has the welfare state transformed relations between the sexes?[2] Have welfare states augmented or reduced women's dependence on and their subordination to men? Have new social programs produced new and different forms of organizing social relations between the sexes or merely reproduced and reinforced traditional gender relations?

Changing the question does not alter the data or the historical record. Rather, the same data and events must be examined from a fundamentally different point of view. Had Weber or Durkheim, like Marx, produced a treatise on the revolutions of 1848 in Europe, their accounts would have differed from those of Marx not because of the events but because of the questions they would have posed about those events. Marx's concerns with class struggle and the fate of capitalism would have given way to Durkheim's concerns with the possibility of social integration in a complex industrializing society.

In the same way, we will have occasion in part 2 to return to some of the data already reviewed in part 1, but we do so to answer a different question, a question about gender relations rather than class relations. Our particular question concerns "relations of ruling" – about the effective powers of men and women in both the public and domestic spheres, about the relations of ruling *between* men and women, and about the attitudes men and women hold about these relations. In this chapter, we examine relations between men and women at their place of employment. In chapters 7 and 8 we turn our attention to the household.

To study such issues in a meaningful way requires a model, a benchmark against which actually existing gender relations can be measured and assessed. Just as we develop our understanding of postindustrialism by using class relations under industrial capitalism as our benchmark, to situate relations of ruling between men and women in the present requires an understanding of the relations between them in the past.

Throughout most of recorded history, patriarchy – rule by male heads of households – has been the dominant form of social organization that has regulated relations between men and women. A useful starting point is Michael Mann's description of "traditional patriarchy," a form of social organization characteristic of most societies for which we have written records up to the eighteenth century in Western Europe. In such societies, Mann writes,

power is held by male heads of households. There is also clear separation between the "public" and the "private" spheres of life. In the "private" sphere of the household, the patriarch enjoys arbitrary power over all junior males, all females and all children. In the "public" sphere, power is shared between male patriarchs according to whatever other principles of stratification operate. No female holds any formal public position of economic, ideological, military or political power. Indeed, females are not allowed into this "public" realm of power.[3]

Mann's description has the form of a Weberian ideal type, subject to numerous variations and historical qualifications, but sharply drawn to separate the "present" from the "past." According to Mann, this "traditional" patriarchal society no longer exists, if only "because the particularistic distinction between the public and the private sphere has been eroded, first by employment trends and the emergence of more universal classes, secondly by universal citizenship by all persons in the nation, and thirdly by the nation-state's welfare interventions in the 'private' household/family."[4]

The likely erosion of patriarchal social relations by the impersonal forces of the market has been anticipated by observers of capitalism from Friedrich Engels down to contemporary neo-classical economists. In *The Origins of the Family, Private Property and the State*, published in 1884, Engels argued that breaking down the public-private divide through "the reintroduction of the entire female sex into public industry" was the first step towards eliminating the "domestic enslavement of women." Once women are "in the market," as the neo-classical economists would say, rational capitalists seeking to maximize profits would treat all labour – male or female – as abstract commodities, and differences based on the sex of the seller of labour power would disappear. Relations of ruling based on sex – gendered relations of ruling – would be replaced by relations of ruling based on property; capitalist powers would replace patriarchal powers.

As Mann and many others have pointed out, however, traditional patriarchy proved to be more resilient than expected. Concurring with Heidi Hartmann, he writes:

Male workers and employers together contrived to create a labour-market in which priority was given to males. Patriarchy acquired a new colouration: almost all men worked in the public sphere, at least half the women looked after the private household. The remaining women did work in the public sphere. But their wages could barely support a household; their occupations could be regarded as extensions of their private domestic roles ...; they would fit employment around their family life cycles; and even if they worked they also undertook most domestic labour.[5]

Mann's analysis illustrates how relations of ruling based on gender *may* be eroded by relations of ruling based on property, but the outcome of the historical intersection of patriarchy and class is indeterminate, creating at least two distinct historical possibilities. One is the potential for the elimination of all relations of ruling based on gender – the "genderless" world of class relations based on labour as a wholly abstract commodity. Power, domination, and inequality would not disappear but would be entirely organized around the class principle, that is, by rights attached to property rather than to ascriptive statuses.

The second historical possibility – the one actually realized, according to Mann – is that the relations of ruling based on property would themselves be transformed by relations of ruling based on gender. Mann calls these revised employment relations "neo-patriarchy," a subtle transformation of traditional forms involving gender segregation cross-cutting both the public and private spheres.

But what exactly is patriarchal about neo-patriarchy? What conditions warrant the continued use of the language of patriarchy to describe contemporary social relations between the sexes? The concept of neo-patriarchy implies both a break with the past and the reconstitution of male authority in a new form. It implies, by way of negation, that some features of traditional patriarchy are no longer operative. With the advent of industrial capitalism, the walls dividing the private from the public sphere were breached. Now, under postindustrialism, what was once a trickle of women into public life has become a river.

But the concept of neo-patriarchy also implies a link between past and present that warrants the continued use of the term "patriarchy" to describe contemporary gender relations. In the *domestic sphere*, a sufficient condition for retaining the language of patriarchy to describe relations among household members would be the exclusive, or almost exclusive, exercise of executive power over household resources by a senior male (see chapter 7). The residues of traditional patriarchy are also evident in domestic practices that privilege men's participation in public life over that of their female partners. This occurs, for example, when women, but not men, turn down opportunities for employment or career advancement because of family responsibilities (see chapter 8).[6]

The question of whether the language of patriarchy also provides an appropriate metaphor to describe gender relations in the *public sphere* is more complex. It is not sufficient for this purpose simply to demonstrate *differences* between men and women, whether in earnings or in their access to positions of power. Rather, it is necessary to demonstrate that such differences are the *effects* of *processes* to which the language of patriarchy can be meaningfully attached. In Joan Acker's words, the term "gendered institution" means that gender is "present in the processes" that create differential outcomes for men and women.[7]

A *weak version* of the claim that patriarchy has pertinent effects in organizing economic activity is captured by what Wally Seccombe has called the "labour supply thesis."[8] Women's subordination in the labour market – the public sphere – is an *effect* of their subordination within the household. Women's inferior performance in the labour market is a result of domestic patriarchy, the privileging of men's participation in public life and the specialization of women as unpaid homemakers and family care-givers. Because of domestic patriarchy, women sell their labour under market conditions subordinate to those of men. Domestic labour and child rearing limit the amount of labour time women can sell in the market and when they are available for paid work. Many women must work part time, and there are periods when they must be absent from the labour market altogether. These work patterns affect their earnings, their accumulation of labour-market experience, and their career prospects for promotion. Because of anticipated labour-force interruptions, employers engage in "statistical discrimination" against women. We have shown elsewhere, for example, that women tend to be excluded entirely from jobs for which training costs are born by the employer.[9] Given a choice, "rational" employers will prefer to invest in workers with the highest expected rate of return on that investment. Accordingly, they are reluctant to make such investments in their female employees so long as they anticipate that women will leave the firm for child rearing or other family obligations.

The labour-supply thesis is a "weak version" of the claim that patriarchy shapes the public sphere, since it does not argue that relations of ruling *within* the capitalist workplace are themselves patriarchal. Gender differences in public life are *effects* of domestic patriarchy, hence exogenous to the labour market. When women do enter the public sphere, the logic of the market prevails. Employers may discriminate against women, but they do so because "discrimination is profitable under most circumstances, and hence is rational conduct for profit maximizers."[10]

The *strong version* of the thesis is rather more serious both for class theory and for neo-classical economics. It argues nothing less than that existing relations of ruling in the "capitalist" workplace are determined not simply by the "logic of the market" or by considerations of technical efficiency but by a "logic of patriarchy." Relations of ruling in the public sphere are as they are in order to reproduce men's control over women's labour and/or to prevent women's control of men's labour. Gender differences are the result of processes that are endogenous to the market, not merely the exogenous effects of domestic patriarchy.

This is a dramatic claim since it implies nothing less than the assertion that class theorists are wrong when they *name* relations of ruling *class* relations. The process structuring relations of ruling in the workplace is a gender, not a class, process. As Cynthia Cockburn shows, women are absent from positions of power and privilege in the workplace not merely as a result of market forces and the pursuit of profit but because of "men's resistance."[11] Like the Pope, men in the corporation and the union hall cling to St Paul's teaching that women should not exercise authority over men.

Adjudicating among these claims is difficult since the outcomes we observe in the real world are simultaneously the results of all these processes. The task is made doubly difficult in a study designed to answer questions in class, not gender, analysis.[12] Consider the results in Table 6.1, where we show the proportion of positions in each class held by women and the level of women's representation in each class. The index of representation measures the difference between women's share of employment within a class and their share of total employment. In the United States, for example, women make up 47 per cent of the employed labour force in our sample but account for only

Table 6.1
Sex Composition of Classes and Index of Women's Representation, Employed
Labour Force

Women's Representation[a]	United States	Canada	Norway	Sweden	Finland
Female share of labour force	47	45	41	47	50
EXECUTIVES					
Per cent female	28	16	4	(19)	26
Representation	−19	−29	−37	−28	−24
NEW MIDDLE CLASS					
Per cent female	40	41	30	36	42
Representation	−8	−4	−11	−11	−8
WORKING CLASS					
Per cent female	53	49	49	52	55
Representation	+6	+4	+8	+5	+5

[a] Calculation of representation is simply per cent female within a class subtracted from the female share of the total labour force. Calculated scores may show slight discrepancies, these are the result of rounding procedures.

( ) = 41 cases. All other figures based on 50 or more cases.

28 per cent of all executives. The result is an index value of −19 (28 − 47 = −19). Conversely, women are *over*-represented in the working class relative to their share of employment (hence the + sign).

The results in Table 6.1 point to some rather striking national differences, notably the much lower level of representation of women in the upper levels of the Swedish and especially the Norwegian class structures. The nature of these differences become more apparent when we "unpack" the class typology into its constituent elements. Recall from chapter 1 that respondents are allocated to the executive and new middle classes on the basis of four criteria: whether the respondent is involved in policy setting (decision making); whether the respondent is a member of the management hierarchy; and whether the respondent exercises task or sanctioning authority over other employees. Table 6.2 presents indices of women's representation for each dimension, distinguishing, as in previous chapters, between sanctioning authority and task authority.

The results highlight a very pronounced North American–Nordic difference. Relative to North America and especially the United States, women in Sweden, Norway, and Finland find it very difficult to make their way into positions that involve the exercise of authority over other employees and especially into middle- and upper-management positions. These results are consistent with the now-familiar finding reported in chapter 2 that sex segregation among occupa-

Table 6.2
Index of Women's Representation in Decision-Making and Authority Positions[a]

Positions	United States	Canada	Norway	Sweden	Finland
Middle & upper management	−11	−15	−32	−29	−24
Decision-makers	−12	−11	−16	−15	−12
Sanctioning authority	−10	−13	−23	−22	−23
Task authority	−11	−11	−19	−18	−19

[a] See note, Table 6.1.

tions is also much sharper in the Nordic countries than in North America, while wage differentials between men and women are lower in the Nordic countries than in North America.

Since the sixties, the American strategy for addressing differences based on gender or minority status has emphasized affirmative action and anti-discrimination legislation requiring employers to increase the chances for women and minorities to compete within broad occupational groups. Gender politics in North America has made it symbolically important for women to be seen to be represented at all levels of the corporate hierarchy. In contrast, Swedish strategy has emphasized making it "easy" for women to enter the labour market and a policy of wage compression that reduces wage differentials between typically male and female jobs. [13]

As others have noted, these diverse policies have yielded some paradoxical results. The experience of Norwegian and Swedish women is the result of a Nordic strategy to erode the *boundary* between the public and private spheres without a corresponding transformation in the patriarchal organization of domestic life. Swedish tax legislation provides strong incentives for women to enter the labour market, and widely accessible day care makes it possible for them to do so. Because of the welfare state, there is high demand for women's labour in traditional female occupations in health, education, and social services.[14] These policies have been reflected in considerably higher rates of female labour-force participation in the Nordic countries (see chapter 2).

But as we show in chapter 7, progressive labour-market policies have done little to challenge *domestic* patriarchy. As elsewhere, married women and mothers in the Nordic countries still bear the burden of caring for children and of most domestic labour. As a result, the high labour-force participation of Nordic women mainly takes the form of additional part-time employment, which offers little in the way of on-the-job training or opportunity for career advancement. The economic returns to part-time employment in Norway and Sweden are higher than in North America, and more women are

Tables 6.3
Women's Representation in Decision-Making and Authority Positions by
Employment Status[a]

Positions	United States	Canada	Norway	Sweden	Finland
MIDDLE & UPPER MANAGEMENT					
All	−11	−15	−32	−29	−24
Full-time[b]	−12	−11	−18	−18	−24
DECISION-MAKERS					
All	−12	−11	−16	−15	−12
Full-time[b]	−11	−10	−11	−7	−13
SANCTIONING AUTHORITY					
All	−10	−13	−23	−22	−23
Full-time[b]	−8	−11	−13	−14	−22
TASK AUTHORITY					
All	−11	−11	−19	−18	−19
Full-time[b]	−9	−8	−10	−11	−17

[a] See note, Table 6.1. Calculation of representation is per cent female within a class minus
female share of the full-time labour force.
[b] Full-time defined as 35 hours or more per week.

in the labour force as a result. [15] But as Gisele Asplund notes, "Part-
time work can ... hinder a woman's career, since managerial positions
call for all her time, while the part-timer is also excluded from further training and other important activities that would help her to
mount the career ladder."[16]

As we show in Table 6.3, Asplund is right. A major factor accounting for the comparative under-representation of women at the upper levels of the Nordic class structure is their high level of part-time
employment. In our samples, almost half of all employed women in
Norway and Sweden are part-timers, compared to approximately
one-quarter of employed women in the United States and Canada,
figures that correspond very closely to official estimates.[17] When we
remove part-timers from the analysis, the indices of representation
for the United States, Canada, Norway, and Sweden converge considerably. For example, Norwegian–U.S. differences in women's representation in management positions, declines from 21 to only 6 percentage points, and the difference in women's representation in
positions with authority virtually disappears. Finland, where part-
time employment is comparatively low, remains an unexplained out-
lier.[18]

These effects of part-time employment on gender differences in
class location are illustrative of what we have called the "weak version" of the thesis that class structures are "gendered institutions,"
that domestic patriarchy – the privileging of men's participation in

public life and the specialization of women as unpaid homemakers and family care-givers – has pertinent effects in the public sphere. In chapters 7 and 8 we return to consider this link between domestic patriarchy and public life in some detail.

Few would dispute the claim that domestic arrangements have real consequences for women's labour-force experience. More contentious and more difficult to demonstrate are the claims of the "strong version" of the thesis. How might we establish whether the workplace itself is a "gendered institution" not in the sense of merely producing gender differences but gender differences created as a result of a patriarchal, rather than a class or market, logic? Let us recall the main features of "traditional patriarchy."

1 *Rule by senior males*: in traditional patriarchy, ultimate authority in the household is vested in the hands of senior males and in the public sphere power is shared among male patriarchs. Note that the necessary condition to satisfy this definition of traditional patriarchy is not that all men are patriarchs (heads of households), since junior males are subordinate to senior males and there is no guarantee that all men will eventually become patriarchs. Rather, the point is that all patriarchs are men.
2 The second distinguishing feature of traditional patriarchy is *the iron law of anti-matriarchy* (our phrase, not Mann's). Women are not denied all power and authority under traditional patriarchy. In multi-family and polygamous households, women could and did rule over other women based on seniority and/or their relation to the patriarch. Rather, under traditional patriarchy, women's powers and authority are limited by the fact *that they do not rule over men*, the iron law of anti-matriarchy.

Traditional patriarchy of this sort prevailed in advanced agrarian societies, where most economic activity, production as well as reproduction, took place in the household. It continues intact in the modern era in small family-owned firms. The family farm, for example, is almost always transmitted through the male line, and farm daughters remain in farming only by becoming "farm wives." With industrial capitalism, however, the locus of economic activity shifts from the household to the firm. The question is whether the patriarchal form for organizing relations of ruling moves with it?

Neil Smelser, among others, describes early experiments to transfer the family form directly from the household to the factory.[19] In the Lancashire cotton mills of early-nineteenth-century England, families were brought in as the basic units of work organization, with the male head in charge of regulating the work of women and children and co-ordinating production with other male heads. Such efforts to superimpose *traditional* patriarchy on factory life organized around kinship units soon became the exception rather than the rule. But the failure of the family variant, traditional patriarchy, to become the modal form of industrial organization does not mean the *principles* of patriarchy were also abandoned. Neo-patriarchy – the extension of patriarchal rules for organizing relations of ruling to social units other than kinship groups – was adopted instead.

An economy may be said to be organized on patriarchal principles to the extent that the basic units of economic activity, whether households or firms, are ruled by senior males; where power to regulate relations among economic units is held by senior males; and where relations within economic units conform to the law of anti-matriarchy, that is, where women are excluded from exercising authority over men. Where members of these economic units are not related by kinship, the term patriarchy applies only by way of analogy, hence neo-patriarchy.

Prima facie evidence for the existence of neo-patriarchy in the modern firm comes from several generations of élite studies which show that the executive office and the corporate boardroom continue to be almost exclusively male domains.[20] The peaks of the corporate world (executives) and relations between firms (board directors) are typically ruled by men. In family-held firms, rule by senior males is perpetuated by the practice of transmitting ownership between generations from fathers to sons and only rarely to daughters. As a result, "rule by senior males" is still the norm rather than the exception.

It could be objected, of course, that women now hold positions of power in considerable numbers (see below) and increasingly have become independent proprietors of their own businesses as well (see chapter 3). But as we have pointed out, traditional patriarchy did not exclude women from the exercise of power but rather from the exercise of power *over men*. Production relations in the household were organized not merely for reasons of technical efficiency but to preserve a power ordering between the sexes. The challenge to the "strong version" of the thesis is to find evidence of a comparable pattern in the modern firm. Here, the work of Bill Bielby and James Baron on sex segregation has been insightful.[21] Their analyses have highlighted two important points about the gendered structure of organizations. Many studies have shown a long-term trend toward desegregation of work when occupations or industries are taken as the unit of analysis. There are many more women in traditional

Table 6.4
The Gendered Structure of Authority Relations,
Canada (percentages)

| | Sex of Respondent | |
Per Cent Who Report to:	Women	Men
A male superior	55	93
A female superior	44	6
Both*	1	1
Total	100	100

* Respondents with more than one immediate superior of
whom one was male and one female.

male-dominated occupations than in the past and more men in traditional female occupations. But when one shifts the unit of analysis
to the organization or work unit, they conclude, near-perfect sex segregation prevails. The restaurant industry, for example, has become
more integrated with time, but the majority of individual restaurants
continue to employ only male waiters or only female waitresses to
serve customers. The results they describe conform closely to those
we would expect to find in an economy organized on the principle of
anti-matriarchy: women are found in positions of power and authority but, as they note, "women in positions of authority almost always
supervised other women, though it is also common for women to be
supervised by men."[22]

The Bielby-Baron conclusions are based on a sample of 290 economic establishments in California. Are they generalizable to the rest
of the economy? Unfortunately, only the Canadian survey allows us
to address this question directly. In the Canadian survey, all employees were asked to identify the sex of their immediate superior, the
person responsible for supervising their work or to whom they were
required to report. The question structure allowed for the possibility
that a respondent might be supervised by or report to more than one
person. Hence there is a small residual category ("mixed") of respondents who report to or are supervised by both a man and a woman.[23]
These data have been analysed elsewhere by Monica Boyd, Mary
Anne Mulvihill, and John Myles.[24] Here we present the highlights of
that analysis.

The answers of our respondents are unequivocal (Table 6.4).
While women are almost equally likely to report to either a male or a
female superior, men are almost never directly subordinate to a
woman. Indeed, to find such extreme distributions is rather rare in
the social sciences. In the entire Canadian economy, only 7 per cent

Table 6.5
Per Cent Female by Industry Sector, Employed Labour Force, Full-time and Part-
time Employees

Sectors	United States	Canada	Norway	Sweden	Finland
GOODS & DISTRIBUTION	31	24	24	24	35
Goods	32	21	24	23	36
Distributive services	28	31	23	25	33
POSTINDUSTRIAL SERVICES	61	61	57	67	68
Business, personal,					
& retail services	60	61	52	60	63
Social services &					
public administration	62	60	60	70	71

of all employed men are subject to the direct authority of a woman.
As a descriptive statement, the designation of gender relations in Canadian workplaces as neo-patriarchal is clearly warranted: men rule
over women and junior males; women rule over women but rarely, if
ever, over men.[25] Men are not, or will not, be ruled by women.

Clearly Engel's assumption that, once women enter the labour
market, relations of ruling based on sex will be replaced by relations
of ruling based on property, that capitalist powers would replace patriarchal powers, needs modification. Women do acquire capitalist
powers when they enter the public sphere – powers to allocate capital
and to rule labour – but only when it is unlikely that men will be subject to these powers. Paradoxically then, it is precisely through the
economic segregation of women into female job ghettos that they are
most likely to acquire effective powers over "the forces of production." As Rosabeth Kanter observes, "numbers" are a key element
shaping the corporate environment.[26] Stereotyping, tokenism, and
isolation characterize environments where women are a minority,
producing performance pressure and differential patterns of evaluation. Accordingly, Kanter concludes that as the ratio of women to
men in organizations begins to shift, we should expect patterns of
social relations between men and women to shift as well. By implication, then, there is every reason to expect postindustrialism to be a
force favouring women's access to positions of economic power.

DO NUMBERS MATTER?
POSTINDUSTRIALISM AND THE CLASS
PROSPECTS FOR WOMEN

Numerically, the labour force of traditional industrial labour markets was and is predominantly male (Table 6.5). In contrast, the la-

bour force of the postindustrial sectors is dominated by women. Men are in the majority in both goods production (manufacturing, construction) and distribution (transport, utilities, communication, and wholesale trade), the sectors associated with both the first and the second "industrial revolutions." Here we would expect few women to achieve significant positions within capitalist relations of ruling. In contrast, women dominate in the more "modern" business, consumer, and public services. Female-dominated work sites are more numerous (schools, health-care agencies), and there is less likelihood that women in authority will be required to exercise their authority over male subordinates.

There are reasons other than numbers to expect that gender differences in the distribution of positions of power and authority might abate in postindustrial labour markets. The first is the very "modernity" of the service industries. The growth of personal, business, and social services is a contemporary phenomenon, and, as Stinchcombe has shown, the organization of labour within firms, industries, and occupations tends to bear the imprint of the historical period of their foundation and growth.[27] Baron and Newman, for example, show that wage differentials between men and women are greater in "old" than in "new" job categories.[28] Second, state employment is more prevalent in the service sector, and studies of earnings differentials between men and women have shown that the gender gap narrows in the public sector, a result of both public policy and stronger labour unions.[29] Finally, postindustrial labour markets – and especially social and business services – tend to be not only "knowledge-intensive" but also "credential-intensive." Job-relevant skills in services tend to be acquired through the educational system rather than through on-going training and apprenticeship programs. This should benefit women, who are typically excluded from on-the-job training programs but who tend to have high levels of formal education.[30]

There is little question that postindustrialism has brought women into the exercise of economic power to a degree unprecedented in history (Table 6.6). In the United States, for example, women in postindustrial services fill almost half of all positions with power and authority, compared to less than 20 per cent of such positions in goods and distribution. And as the pattern of consistently positive signs in Table 6.6 indicates, women in all countries have greater access to positions of power and authority in postindustrial services than in the traditional industrial core. But the question remains as to whether postindustrialism also means that the rules of the game have changed. Have postindustrial work sites been "degendered"? Does women's *representation* in positions of power and authority more

Table 6.6
Women's Share of Decision-Making and Authority Positions by Industry, Full-Time
Employees Only (percentages)

Positions & Sectors	United States	Canada	Norway	Sweden	Finland
MIDDLE AND UPPER MANAGEMENT					
Goods & distribution	18	19	5	5	15
Postindustrial services	46	44	20	35	52
Difference	+28	+25	+15	+20	+37
DECISION-MAKERS					
Goods & distribution	9	13	7	8	27
Postindustrial services	45	39	22	38	57
Difference	+36	+26	+15	+30	+30
SANCTIONING AUTHORITY					
Goods & distribution	19	24	5	4	16
Postindustrial services	47	43	19	36	50
Difference	+28	+19	+14	+32	+24
TASK AUTHORITY					
Goods & distribution	19	15	8	6	16
Postindustrial services	46	47	24	37	53
Difference	+27	+32	+16	+31	+37

closely reflect their numbers? Has the law of anti-matriarchy been eroded?

The answer to the first of these questions is a clear no. In general, our results for all five countries do not support our postindustrial expectations. Women have not closed the gender gap in the more "modern" sectors of the economy. Of the twenty possible contrasts in Table 6.7, only three indicate that women are better represented in postindustrial services, four indicate no difference between sectors, and thirteen indicate that women's under-representation is greater in the postindustrial, than in the industrial, sector of the economy. In Sweden and the United States, postindustrial services provide somewhat more scope for women to participate in decision making, but these gains are not reflected in greater access to the formal managerial hierarchy. Rather than eroding the traditional sexual division of power, postindustrial labour markets appear to be the site of its consolidation (in the United States and Finland) and even growth (in Canada, Sweden, and Norway).

Some of the reasons for these results can be interpolated from closer inspection of differences among service industries. In those sectors of the service economy characterized by an unusual number of "good jobs," men have tended to appropriate an even larger share of power and authority, so that gender differences are augmented rather than diminished. Women's gains in postindustrial services are

Table 6.7
Women's Representation in Decision-Making and Authority Positions by Industry,
Full-Time Employees Only[a]

Positions & Sectors	United States	Canada	Norway	Sweden	Finland
MIDDLE AND UPPER MANAGEMENT					
Goods & distribution	−12	−4	−16	−17	−27
Postindustrial services	−16	−20	−24	−27	−27
DECISION-MAKERS					
Goods & distribution	−17	−7	−10	−11	−10
Postindustrial services	−9	−15	−14	−6	−17
SANCTIONING AUTHORITY					
Goods & distribution	−10	−7	−11	−13	−21
Postindustrial services	−10	−13	−19	−17	−22
TASK AUTHORITY					
Goods & distribution	−11	−7	−8	−11	−22
Postindustrial services	−11	−9	−14	−16	−19

[a] See note, Table 6.1.

largely confined to the low-wage and unskilled sectors of the service
economy.

To demonstrate the point, we divide the postindustrial sector into
high-end (business and public) services, where wages and job skills
are above average, and low-end (personal and retail) services,
characterized by low wages and limited job skills (see chapter 2). As
the results in Table 6.8 show (Finland is excluded because of small
sample size), women do comparatively well in the low end of the
service economy but very poorly in high-end business and public
services.

Here, however, our conclusions run into technical limitations imposed by the relatively small size of our national samples. Although
our data *suggest* that gender differences are larger in postindustrial
services than in goods and distribution, the number of cases involved
is not sufficient to provide statistically robust evidence for this conclusion.[31] Quite simply, it may be that our conclusions are a result of
sampling error. To test this assumption, Boyd, Mulvihill, and Myles
examined Canadian census data to determine if similar results could
be reproduced using census occupations.[32] The results were remarkably similar. For example, the "gender gap" – the percentage difference between men and women – in upper-management occupations
in 1981 (the time of our survey) was largest in business services
(−6.6), followed by social services (−5.0), public services (−3.3), distributive services (−2.9), retail services (−1.8), manufacturing
(−1.5), and personal services (−0.6).

Table 6.8
Women's Representation in Decision-Making and Authority Positions by
Postindustrial Service Sector, Full-Time Employees Only

Positions & Sectors	United States	Canada	Norway	Sweden
MIDDLE AND UPPER MANAGEMENT				
Personal & retail services	−6	−2	(−7)	(−13)
Business & public services	−11	−16	−22	−20
DECISION-MAKERS				
Personal and retail services	−4	−11	(−2)	(+8)
Business & public services	−11	−16	−18	−9
SANCTIONING AUTHORITY				
Personal & retail sevices	−6	−7	(−12)	(−5)
Business & public services	−11	−16	−22	(−22)
TASK AUTHORITY				
Personal & retail services	−5	−5	(−7)	(+1)
Business & public services	−13	−11	−17	−21

( ) indicates estimates based on an underlying industry sample of less than 50. For Sweden, cell
counts in personal & retail services are based on less than 20 cases. All other ( ) cells are based
on 38 or more cases.

None of this implies that women have not been gaining ground in
the class hierarchy, but there have been two offsetting trends in the
labour market: women have been improving their position relative to
men in lower-level management and supervisory jobs but losing
ground relative to men in upper-level management. As Boyd,
Mulvihill, and Myles show, the gender gap has fallen among middle
managers and supervisors in all industries except retail trade since
1971. In contrast, the gender gap in senior-management occupations has risen in all industries except social services.

Bringing these results together suggests the following. As women
have entered the labour force in ever larger numbers, a rising share
of supervisory and middle- management positions have also opened
to them. Women have acquired real economic powers in the public
sphere to a degree unprecedented in Western history. Our Canadian
results indicate that women encounter the "glass ceiling" to further
advancement near the top of the class pyramid, where they begin to
compete for positions that involve the exercise of significant authority over men, particularly over senior men. The result, as Mann suggests, is a form of neo-patriarchy, an economy ruled by senior males
in which women may rule women but not men. Postindustrialism
matters for women because the concentration of women in postindustrial services provides many more opportunities for the exercise
of power over other women but not because the glass ceiling has
been broken. Indeed, despite their small numbers in services, men

have, if anything, been more effective at appropriating class powers in postindustrial, than in traditional industrial, work sites.

CONCLUSION: GENDERING CLASS THEORY

Feminist critics of "male-stream" sociology have long argued, as Joan Acker has, that "theories that are silent about gender are fundamentally flawed." [33] We have argued that to have any meaning, such a claim must imply more than the fact that class processes have differential outcomes for men and women. Rather, what is required is to demonstrate that the processes themselves are "gendered" in some meaningful way. The feminist claim is that things are as they are not only because of class struggle and capitalist calculation but because of struggles over gender relations and patriarchal calculation. If such claims are correct, then class theories and even class descriptions that remain silent about gender are indeed "fundamentally flawed."

The results we have presented here indicate that a gender-neutral account of relations of ruling in modern capitalist economies is at least *descriptively* inadequate. More bluntly, what we have been calling class relations are not just class relations and what we have been calling a class structure is more than a class structure. Relations of power and authority in the modern workplace exist not only to regulate relations between capital and labour but also to reproduce a particular way of organizing relations between men and women. The class structures of the developed capitalist economies are also neo-patriarchal structures, a system of rule by senior males that by and large excludes women from exercising power over men. As women have moved from the domestic into the public sphere, the relations of ruling of the patriarchal household have moved with them.

While we have established that a class *description* without reference to gender is "fundamentally flawed," our research design and data do not allow us to go the extra step to show that a class *explanation* for this fact would be similarly flawed. It is conceivable (though we think unlikely) that the process generating a neo-patriarchal pattern of production relations is exclusively a class, not a gender, process. To determine which is the case exceeds the grasp of a study that from the outset was conceived to answer questions in class, not gender, analysis. Other studies of "male resistance" to rule by women persuade us, however, that neo-patriarchy forms part not only of the *explanandum* but also of the explanation. [34]

Our results confirm Paula England's observation that resistance to sex equality is greatest when it concerns face-to-face contact involving power in the workplace.[35] While the modern, postindustrial sectors of the economy provide women with access to public power and authority, their under-representation in these positions, as well as the gendered structure of these relations, means that postindustrialism has provided only marginal challenge to patriarchal relations of ruling. Our data do not allow us to explain this apparent resistance by men to women's exercise of power over them. Nor can we adjudicate among the debates in the growing body of feminist literature on this question. We do, however, conclude that this fact must be the starting point for further efforts to account for the position of women in the economic structure of modern capitalism.

7 Household Relations: Power Divisions and Domestic Labour

Patriarchal structures, like classes, are also "relations of ruling." As Dorothy Smith has forcefully argued, both the structures and practices of sexist political economy located in the state and the capitalist relations of production should be revealed. This means moving beyond the traditional "institutions of ruling" identified by a particularly masculine account of classes. She contends that "assertions of women's presence in class, of the significance of domestic labour in economic relations, let alone of the need for representation within political economy of the neglected areas of sexuality and motherhood, have not yet succeeded in shifting the central determination of the focus of political economy from the 'main business' of dominating the relations of ruling."[1]

As we have seen in chapter 6, the theoretical status of "patriarchy" is highly contested. Joan Acker notes, for "radical feminists" it has been "seen as a universal, trans-historical and trans-cultural phenomenon; women were everywhere oppressed by men in more of less the same ways." "Marxist feminists," she contends, have "explained patriarchal processes as functional for the mode of production" or as "located outside the mode of production in a separate system."[2] Since the fundamental content of patriarchy is unequal gender relations, we have chosen to focus specifically on how gender penetrates production and reproduction as part of a combined process. This has led us to an analysis of the household as the appropriate unit of study and the relationship between household and classes located in the paid labour force as the site of investigation.

This chapter and the next switch our attention from the "public" domain explored in chapter 6 to the "domestic" sphere where "private patriarchy" prevails. First, we will examine how forms of labour-force participation, class locations, and relative income each impact on household powers such as decision making, division of domestic labour, and attitudes towards gender issues. In chapter 8 we turn our attention to how the household acts to constrain the labour-market participation of women, particularly their careers. Combining the two perspectives, we explore the class of households and their effects on the attitudes of both partners. We are especially interested in understanding women's empowerment as they become class actors on their own. Finally, in chapter 9 we see how the culture of gender is shaped by social cleavages associated with race, ethnicity, and region. All of this continues to be located within the project of understanding relations of ruling based upon class, but our main business now becomes patriarchal practices based on sex.

Our initial focus is on relations within the household and the issue of power. One source of power we can measure is the income an individual brings from paid labour into the household. This apparently simple measure is, in fact, the outcome of a complex process. One's ability to earn income through participation in the labour market depends upon training, experience, and the availability for work on the one hand and conditions of work and pay on the other. Our main point is that these are not distinct practices. We argue they are necessarily connected relationships, especially with the commodification of life, where money mediates labour more often than ever before.

Heidi Hartmann's analysis of "the family" is particularly revealing. She identifies the "family as a locus of struggle ... a location where production and distribution take place," going on to observe that "members of families frequently have different interests [and] use family forms in various ways."[3] We would add that family members often have different powers. The nature of family relations is highly complex, as captured by Hartmann's comment that "family members have distinct interests arising out of their relations to production and distribution, those same relations also ensure their mutual dependence." The essence of patriarchy as expressed through households is men's command over women. According to Hartmann, "control over women's labour power is the lever that allows men to benefit from women's provision of personal and household services, including relief from child rearing and many unpleasant tasks both within and beyond households." In her words, "patriarchy's material base is men's control of women's labor; both in the household and in the labor market, the division of labor tends to benefit men."[4] Households are a locus of men's patriarchal command over women.

We find in what follows that families benefit men more than women in terms of the conditions governing their participation in paid labour. In other words, men and women sell their labour power under very different conditions. The domestic conditions from which women sell their labour power are a hindrance.

Domestic relations are highly gendered and have strong impacts upon paid labour. By gender we mean a set of complex social relations and structures that divide people around the process of reproduction. Reproductive work includes nurturance of families and raising children in the context of a patriarchal system based on sex. Throughout the following discussion, we examine gender using an analysis of domestic labour and its relationship with forms of paid labour, including attitudes challenging or supporting these social relations.

THEORIZING DOMESTIC LABOUR AND ITS EFFECTS

As mentioned in chapter 6, the "labour-supply thesis" derived from the "domestic-labour debate" places women's household subordination at the explanatory centre of their disadvantage compared to men's privileged labour-market position. A competing explanation, identified by Wally Seccombe, is the "employer-demand thesis," which contends that employer's drive for profit requires them to exploit women's labour-market weakness to keep wages low and to enhance authority structures within firms because "discrimination is profitable."[5]

A domestic *consequence* of the employer-demand argument, which devalues women's paid work, means that in the home men's careers have priority over women's since men's earning power is greater. It follows that women subordinate their less-valued working lives to the demands of other household members both in day-to-day matters and in longer-term planning for careers and training, including where to live, hours available for work, and domestic responsibilities. Each thesis acknowledges domestic labour, but in the labour-supply approach the domestic power relations determine inequality, while in the employer-demand approach domestic inequality follows from gendered divisions in the paid workplace as a consequence of the profit drive.

Christina Jonung's labour-supply-side account[6] begins in the household but relates to women's investment in education and training. Because of their likely domestic responsibilities, women are more likely to select a shorter range of training and occupations, which can be combined with domestic work. Her labour-market perspective reflects the reluctance of employers to invest training in women because of discrimination based on assumptions about women's careers. These reasons combine to create a vicious circle.

Two key matters follow for our analysis. The first implication is a critical class issue resulting from the feminization of the labour force and concerning the conditions under which women supply their labour and how these differ from men. Women's ability to supply their labour is affected by the fact that "working women" have "two jobs" (the other being primary responsibility for domestic work) and women's work-life cycle is subordinated to men's. The second implication is that employers exploit these weaknesses, particularly in wage relations, as they seek to minimize their costs. Women's struggles to overcome wage differentials in the labour force have the potential to transform domestic relations. Nordic women's wage conditions have been altered. The results of our data, however, demonstrate some Nordic differences in decision making within households over matters of empowerment and domestic labour with regard to the ability to negotiate the allocation of tasks. Later we will show a considerable gap between attitudes toward the sharing of domestic responsibilities and actual practices, especially for Sweden.

The gendered relationship between domestic and wage labour has been disputed.[7] But all feminist approaches agree, first, that domestic labour is a site of struggle interacting with the paid labour market and, second, that patriarchal power relations, whether in the domestic or labour-force realms, structure the experiences of both men and women. Sylvia Walby argues with reference to housework that there are three "dimensions" to domestic patriarchy: "firstly, that the domestic division of labour is a major form of differentiation of men and women; secondly, that this has significant effects on other aspects of social relations; thirdly, that this in itself is a form of significant inequality."[8]

The domestic sphere is a terrain of struggle where traditional male dominance and female subordination are contested. How this struggle unfolds affects how women encounter the class structure. In the words of Dorothy Smith, "The inner life and work of the family, and the personal reactions of power between husband and wife are understood as a product of how family relations are organized by and in the economic and political relations of capitalism."[9] Such relations, however, are not outside history, and fundamental changes do occur, impacting upon what Smith calls the "dependent family form," wherein the domestic tends to become separated from the rest of the economy. She focuses upon the material basis of such separations.

Earlier women's domestic labour was essential to subsistence. It had no substitutes. It has also been essential to advances in the family standard of living which would have been originally unobtainable without the interposition of women's work in the home. Women of both the middle class and working classes at different income levels could by their personal skills, their hard work and commitment, take the wage and salary, purchase materials and tools and combine these with labour and skill – their knowledge of cooking, cleaning, managing, laundering, shopping, etc. – to produce a subsistence level or better, essential for family health, comfort and under minimal income conditions for survival ...

Over time the labour women contributed to domestic production of subsistence was displaced by labour and skill embodied in the product of industry. Progressively capital has inserted a labour process embodied in the commodity into the home and has reorganized the work process there as it has reorganized so much in every part. At some point what women can contribute in the form of labour no longer balances off what she can earn and hence add to the purchasing power of the family.[10]

Smith articulates the intimacy of the relationship between reorganizations of relations within the household and the economy. They occur together in such a way that women are pushed from the household and drawn into the paid labour force. But there is more than commodification of domestic labour or the location of women's work at stake. Equally relevant are the power relationships that order and structure women's "place" in the household and labour market.

As women increasingly participate in paid labour, they acquire new economic resources through their class locations. At issue is how these new-found resources translate back into the household and influence such things as the domestic division of labour. Restructuring the domestic sphere is a contested terrain for patriarchal powers. At stake is not only the empowerment of women but a challenge to the privileges that have empowered men.

Meg Luxton has articulated some essential features of this power struggle through her investigations of gendered divisions of labour in a community's households, saying,

Because inequalities in the division of labour are based on male power, when women demand equalization of the work, they are challenging that power.

Some women were afraid that if they pushed for more male participation they would provoke their husband's anger and rage ...

While there is evidence to suggest that when women have paid employment they increase their own power in marriage, all of these women earned considerably less than their husbands. As a result, the men retained economic power (bread-winner power). Men can also use their greater earnings as a justification for not doing domestic labour.[11]

Women's paid labour-force participation under conditions where women earn less than men need not empower them at home. Moreover, there will be a struggle to translate increased obligations in paid labour back into more domestic leverage.

As with most aspects of life, besides the more obvious one of economic dependency, there is yet another dynamic organizing domestic responsibilities. As Luxton astutely observes: "When men do start doing domestic labour, women begin to lose control. Domestic labour has traditionally been the one sphere of female control and power. For most women, the kitchen is the closest they ever come to having a 'room of one's own.' It is difficult for many women to relinquish this, particularly if they are not compensated for that loss by gains made elsewhere – for example in their paid work."[12] At stake is not simply men's involvement in domestic labour but the very organization of that labour and its relationship with paid labour.

All these approaches agree, first, that domestic labour is a site of struggle interacting with the paid labour market and, second, that patriarchal power relations, whether in the domestic or labour-force realms, structure the experiences of both men and women. While the analysis of patriarchy as a system of power begins with domestic domination by men over women and children, it is also intimately associated with the organization of the paid labour force. Bonnie Fox concludes that patriarchy "is the production and reproduction of people that is both accomplished by gender relations and produces the gendered individual."[13]

Patriarchy is a cross-cutting set of power relations that interacts with other systems of production and reproduction; it does not stand on its own, hence it is not autonomous in its logic or operation. Consequently, patriarchy takes many forms and has a variety of expressions while still having some constants. Patriarchy, as a relationship between men and women individually and collectively, empowers men and diminishes women. Men are privileged by patriarchy; the power of women is attenuated.

The power relations inside the household are not isolated from what goes on in the paid labour force. There is a complex feedback between the two spheres. Men's powers in the labour market are enhanced by their domestic privileges. Women's labour-force participation is handicapped by excessive domestic obligations. On the other hand, the way rewards are gendered influences the relative strength each partner has in distributing domestic work. Traditional relationships, however, are now being challenged. We will focus on identifying the conditions that make a difference in domestic powers.

WHO DECIDES WITHIN THE HOUSEHOLD?

A basic starting-point for exploring power relations within households is to examine who decides key aspects of living arrangements. In four countries, respondents were asked a series of household decision-making questions, including, "Who has the most say about the overall *family budget*, that is, about how much of the family income goes for different general purposes, such as running the house, recreation, new clothes, and so forth?" and "Who has the most say in making *major financial decisions* in your household, such as a decision to take out a loan or buy a car?" These questions were asked only of those respondents currently living with a partner.

Questions concerning family financial decisions allow us to replicate within households issues similar to those examined within the paid workplace. The key distinction is between decisions concerning "major financial decisions" versus the "family budget," with the former corresponding to executive-like decisions governing strategic administration, while the latter are akin to the tactical administration of daily resource allocations within pre-set limits.

This type of analysis has been pioneered by Meredith Edwards in her report *Financial Arrangements within Families*. Edwards contends that "management of finance is akin to the implementation functions performed within any enterprise – carrying out of decisions which have already been made. The manager of family finances would handle family money and would make the actual payments. However, (s)he may not in fact have a major role in financial decision-making." This activity she calls "management," as distinct from "control," which involves "the decision-making aspects of family finances. It is akin to the policy-making functions of any enterprise."[14] Edwards found within Australian families that the one "who managed the finances in the family was not necessarily the person who controlled the finances. The results point to the need to distinguish between initiation of decisions and their execution."[15] This distinction also proves important in our comparative analysis.[16]

Table 7.1
Household Decision Making by Nation and Sex of Respondent[a] (per cent)

Who Decides	Reported by:							
	United States		Canada		Norway		Sweden	
	Women	Men	Women	Men	Women	Men	Women	Men
FAMILY BUDGET								
Woman	44*	33	29*	20	5	7	10	8
Man	21*	33	12	15	5	4	4	4
Equally	36	34	59*	65	90	89	87	88
	100	100	100	100	100	100	100	100
MAJOR FINANCES								
Woman	12*	5	8	6	3	3	2	3
Man	41*	50	27	31	15	16	15	15
Equally	47	45	65	63	83	81	84	82
	100	100	100	100	100	100	100	100
(N)	478	528	834	846	948	934	360	447

[a] Respondents who are currently living with a partner/spouse. The populations are the same for all nations with the exception of Swedish women, since no housewives were included in that sample. In all cases, men report on their wives, who may be housewives, and housewives were included in the other three samples of women.
* There are no significant differences between men and women in the Nordic countries. Differences in the distribution for men and women in the United States are significant at .05 level or better for both questions and in Canada only for family budgets.

We will show there are major national differences in household de-cision-making patterns. In North America both sexes report that men have more say in major financial decisions and women have more responsibility for "administering" the family budget. In the Nordic countries equality prevails for all types of household deci-sions. Men and women tend to agree in their reports on who decides. Table 7.1 shows general agreement, especially strong in the Nordic countries and least in the United States. This agreement between the sexes in reporting decision making has the methodological con-sequence of allowing us to merge who does the reporting, focusing the following tables on sex differences in who decides or does the work.

Major financial decisions tend to be taken by men and family bud-gets administered by women. Frequently men have executive powers over households resembling traditional patriarchies, but there are strong national differences. Canada is more egalitarian than the United States, with about two-thirds for each type of decision saying that they decide equally, while in the United States less than one-half report equality, the proportion dropping as low as a third. In the United States there is a consensus that men decide major financial matters (half the men and two-fifths of women say the men decide alone). This is a pattern consistent with traditional patriarchy. With the family budget the split is more even, with one, the other, or both deciding. Scandinavians claim the most equitable decision-making arrangements, with over four-fifths always reporting that partners decide equally. Few Nordic households could be described as traditionally patriarchal. In the United States, having an equal say falls to about one-half or less and in Canada it is around two-thirds. Women have more say in Canadian households than in U.S. households. Decision making in Canada's households is somewhat more likely to resemble Sweden and Norway. Most remarkable about the Nordic results is the overwhelming agreement by both sexes that these decisions are taken equally.

Edwards's distinction between taking financial decisions and their administration has meaning in North America, most especially in the United States, but not in the Nordic countries because of their uniformly egalitarian decision making. In Canada and the United States the distinction between major financial decisions and family budgets is an important indicator of traditional patriarchy. It is agreed by both sexes that men have more say in major financial decisions, akin to executive powers associated with traditional patriarchy, while women have more tendency to have a greater say in administering the family budget. Although a somewhat similar pattern prevails in the Nordic countries, it is much less pronounced, since equal decision making is the predominant pattern, with only a residual effect of men making the major financial decisions.

Do the propertied classes, which are the most male-dominated, carry decision-making authority from the workplace into the home? The answer is "somewhat." Even in the Nordic countries nearly a quarter of the households report that men make the major financial decisions. This compares to half that many in the employed classes. Canada's classes are quite torn on this issue: the old middle class follows the traditional U.S. pattern of male dominance, while the other classes are midway between the U.S. pattern and a common Nordic one.

Do household decisions vary by the class of respondent? Table 7.2 examines the four major classes in each of four countries with respect to reports on relationships concerning major financial decisions (reports by men and women are amalgamated). In each nation the capitalist-executive and old middle classes are least equitable in their decision-making and most male-dominated. For each class, the

151 Household Relations

Table 7.2
Major Financial Decisions by Class of Respondent (per cent)

	United States	Canada	Norway	Sweden
Who Makes Major Financial Decisions[a]		Capitalist-Executive Class		
Woman	3	8	1	2
Man	57	33	22	23
Equally	40	59	77	76
	100	100	100	100
(N)	(105)	(106)	(104)	(66)
		Old Middle Class		
Woman	4	4	1	8
Man	45	43	23	23
Equally	51	53	76	69
	100	100	100	100
(N)	(75)	(158)	(125)	(53)
		New Middle Class		
Woman	10	8	2	0
Man	45	24	14	9
Equally	46	68	85	91
	100	100	100	100
(N)	(239)	(333)	(366)	(163)
		Working Class		
Woman	9	7	3	3
Man	43	27	13	15
Equally	48	66	84	82
	100	100	100	100
(N)	(416)	(687)	(739)	(517)

[a] Answers collapse the sex of respondent, based upon the finding in Table 7.1.

United States is the most inequitable and the most male-dominated in decisions about major family financial matters. Canada again consistently stands equidistant between the United States and the Nordic countries for each class. In the United States there is little class variation in the decision making patterns, while in Canada the new-middle-class and working-class relationships tend to be the most equitable. Similarly, in Sweden and Norway it is the new middle class, followed by the working class, which occupies this most egalitarian position.

The propertied classes in all the countries are the least equitable and most male-dominated in their control over major financial decisions, but in the United States this pattern also extends to the non-propertied classes. Aside from the United States, where a type of propertied-class hegemony prevails, class differences are important in the relative decision-making power of men and women, with the split mainly between the propertied and employed classes. Nation, however, has the strongest effect, with the Nordic countries consistently more egalitarian in all classes and Canada caught between them and the United States.

THE CHANGING WORLD OF FAMILY INCOMES

The dynamics of the relationship between domestic and paid labour have varied as capitalism itself has changed, especially from subsistence production to the commodification of domestic work and the accompanying increased demand for women's paid labour. Since capitalism is not a homogeneous system, differences between nations should be expected.

A key feature of recent labour-force change in North America and Nordic countries has been the already-observed rise in women's participation. Finland has been outstanding for its high female labour-force participation, and Sweden "caught up" by the mid-1980s (see Table 2.5). In the youngest age group (15–24) women's labour-force participation in Sweden actually slightly surpasses men's.[17] Canada, Norway, and the United States lag behind by 4 or 5 percentage points. Finland and Sweden have near parity in labour-force participation rates by sex, but 45 per cent of Sweden's female labour-force participation is from part-time work. This often observed qualification of high "part-time" work for Swedish women will itself be further qualified in chapter 8, as it will be demonstrated that these workers are not like part-time workers elsewhere.

While official statistics in OECD countries tell the story of women's rising share of employment with persistent problems in their earnings relative to men, there is little research that looks inside the household *and* relates it to paid labour. We begin to address this "hidden" connection by first examining relations within the household, including both domestic responsibilities and decision making, then in the next chapter shifting the analysis to the relationship between the domestic sphere and paid labour. Along the way, attention will be paid to the way class interacts with gender to structure both the experiences and the ideas of men and women.

We ask whether women across classes confront similar experiences resulting from domestic responsibilities thus affecting their labour-market participation or whether their conditions differ in class-specific ways. Given the limitations of sample design and sample size, we ask these questions primarily for housewives, working-class, and new-middle-class women.

What impact does women's paid economic contribution make upon domestic divisions of labour and women's power within the household? To answer this question we will concentrate on two aspects of empowerment for women: decision making within the household and the allocation of domestic work.

A major effect of women's increased labour-force participation[18] has been the phenomenon of dual-earner families. Such families, as a share of all husband-wife families in Canada, increased from 34 to 62 per cent between 1967 and 1986, while traditional families, with only male breadwinners, shrank from 61 to only 26 per cent. Women are now in the paid labour force regardless of the family's child-care obligations. As of 1986, dual earner families (68 per cent) are only slightly behind traditional families (75 per cent) in the likelihood of having children at home.[19] Moreover, within these dual-earner situations, by 1987 the wife was the primary breadwinner for one in five families.

Wives still usually earn less than their husbands. Family responsibilities clearly effect women in these dual-earner families, often expressed through part-time work and career interruptions. Maureen Moore has conducted an interesting comparison of "primary-earner" wives versus "secondary earners." When wives earn more than their husbands, they tend to have greater post-secondary education and be in managerial or professional occupations. "But the most marked difference between the two groups of wives is work patterns. Three-quarters of wives who were primary earners worked full-time throughout 1987 compared to just under half the wives who were secondary earners."[20] Children matter. While 42 per cent of the "primary-earner" wives were without children at home, this compared to only 29 per cent of the "secondary-earners."

Research in the United States for the period 1940 to 1980 mapped changes in men's and women's income contributions to families. Sorenson and McLanahan found that "in 1940, the vast majority of married women were completely dependent on their spouses for economic support ... The situation is remarkably different in 1980 ... wives who are completely dependent constitute a distinct minority."[21] There persists, however, relative dependence by married women, which leads these authors to argue for the use of families as a unit of analysis for stratification; moreover, differences in relative

Table 7.3
Women's Income Dependency in Households in the United States, Canada,
Norway, and Sweden

	Dependency Level[a]	Dependency for Working Women[a]	% Totally Dependent
United States (1979)	58.8	36.6	35.5
Canada (1981)	59.0	36.3	35.9
Norway (1979)	55.7	41.5	25.0
Sweden (1981)	40.6	33.4	11.2

Source: Based on Barbara Hobson, "No Exit, No voice: Women's Economic Dependency and the Welfare State," Acta Sociologica 33,3 (1990): 240, Table 1.

[a] Dependency value of 0 would be an economically egalitarian union. A value of 40 means a gap of 40 percentage points; e.g., the man contributes 70 per cent and the woman 30 per cent of total income. A gap of 50 means the husband accounts for 75 per cent and the wife for 25 per cent.

dependence "may contribute to the development and persistence of gendered life chances."[22] We are interested in examining how the position of women within households affects their powers and the distribution of domestic responsibilities.

Barbara Hobson has conducted a comparative analysis of the distribution of financial resources within families, showing how "economic dependency of married women in the family is a crucial link in a chain of processes that perpetuates the weak bargaining position of women in the market."[23] She argues that a woman's earning contribution to family income "enables her to make claims about the division of household labor" thus influencing the "bargaining position" of family actors.[24] While she does not have systematic data to illustrate the effects on domestic power relations and the division of household labour, using the Luxembourg Income Data she does document levels of dependency within families.

Hobson measures dependency as the percentage-point gap between a man's and woman's household income contribution. She finds that in Canada and the United States there is a 59-percentage-point gap, compared to a 41-percentage-point gap in Sweden and 56 percentage points in Norway. National differences decrease, however, when only labour-force participants are examined. Still, there is a strong similarity within North America and difference with Sweden. While over a third of North American women are totally dependent upon a man's income and a quarter in Norway, in Sweden this proportion drops to 11 per cent.

Hobson finds a strong income difference between North America and Sweden. In Sweden 37 per cent of families have wives that are dependent on husbands for half or more of the total family income, but in the United States the corresponding figure rises to 63 per cent. For women working outside the home, 29 per cent in Sweden and 43 per cent in the United States are highly dependent (the woman contributes less than a quarter of the family income).[25] These figures demonstrate that there are national differences in women's income dependency, which presumably influence domestic power relations, including the division of domestic labour and decision making. Our data allow us to take Hobson's findings a step further and actually examine the effects of class and relative household incomes on domestic power relations.

SPOUSE'S RELATIVE INCOME

The relative contribution that spouses make to their household incomes can be used to illustrate that men and women have different experiences even within the same classes, particularly concerning their respective powers within the household. We are interested in how power differences created at the point of production interact with household relations. A spouse's relative income contribution will be used as indicative of "breadwinner" power within households, identifying conventional situations where men contribute the majority of income and unconventional relationships where women contribute an equal or majority share of the income. The unit of analysis now shifts from the individual to the household, since the individual men and women are reporting upon their place within the household income structure.

To what extent does the amount of money each partner brings into the household influence their domestic decision-making power? Table 7.4 examines both conventional and unconventional households. For men an unconventional situation occurs when their spouse contributes half or more of the household income. For women the unconventional situation occurs when the spouse makes half or less. These household types are explored in terms of how they affect who makes major financial decisions in each of the four nations.

When women make half or more of the income, their likelihood of making the major financial decisions consistently increases; in Canada, for instance, the increase for women is from 4 per cent in conventional households to 14 per cent when they make most of the household income. The differences, however, are not great and clearly do not overcome the national differences already observed. Declines for men and increases for women are most prominent in

Table 7.4
Spouse's Relative Income[a] and Major Financial Decisions by Nation (per cent)

Who Makes Major Financial Decisions	Conventional Household	Unconventional Household	Difference
		United States	
Woman	8	13	+5*
Man	47	43	−4
Equally	46	44	−2
	100	100	
(N)	(775)	(197)	
		Canada	
Woman	4	14	+10*
Man	32	21	−11*
Equally	63	65	+2
	100	100	
(N)	(1,280)	(380)	
		Norway	
Woman	2	5	+3*
Man	18	8	−10*
Equally	80	87	+7*
	100	100	
(N)	(1,434)	(410)	
		Sweden	
Woman	1	5	+4*
Man	17	13	−4
Equally	83	82	−1
	100	100	
(N)	(431)	(325)	

[a] In a conventional household the man earns over half of the income; in an unconventional household the woman earns half or more of the household income. No distinction is made by the sex of the reporter because of fundamental similarity. The only exceptions of note are U.S. men in unconventional households, who are more likely (+13 percentage points) than similarly placed women to claim that men make the major financial decisions, rather than equally as the women claim. Otherwise, there is virtual identity in reporting between the sexes.
* Indicates that the difference between conventional and unconventional households is significant at .05 level of confidence or better.

Canada. There is not much room for movement in the Nordic countries because they are so egalitarian, but in Norway there is still a substantial drop in men's powers. The pattern continues to persist whereby all the relationships in the United States are the most unequal and characterized by male dominance, while in Sweden and Norway there is overwhelming equality in decision making but some positive impact for women in unconventional situations. Canada again stands in the middle; when the spouses of Canadian men make less than half of the income, the men make the major financial decisions in 32 per cent of the cases, but in unconventional households this drops to 21 per cent.

For the allocation of family budgets (table not shown), the Nordic situation is once again uniformly egalitarian in decision making, ranging from 85 to 90 per cent of both men and women reporting an equal division of responsibility, regardless of the spouse's financial contribution. The United States remains strikingly different, dividing roughly into thirds. Unlike financial decisions, however, the household budget in the United States is much more likely to be under the control of women. Canada is more egalitarian than the United States but not nearly as egalitarian as Scandinavia. The main area where the relative income of the spouse matters is in the United States as reported by women. When U.S. husbands make half or less of the family income, 36 per cent report having family-budget responsibilities, but when their wives make at least half the income, the figure rises to 47 per cent. Women in the United States are more likely to have sole responsibility for family budgets when their husbands make most of the income. In Canada there is also a tendency for women to have more responsibility for family budgets. In the Nordic countries the overwhelming pattern is an equal sharing of this task, even more so than with major financial decisions. It seems that administering the family budget is more an obligation than a privilege.

There is a difference, mainly evident in the United States, between household decisions concerning broader "management" matters (analogous to executive powers) and those involving "administering" such decisions (analogous to new-middle-class powers). Women in the United States tend to be responsible for administering household budgets, especially when their spouses make most of the income. Most U.S. women are not responsible, or even equal, partners in major financial decisions. In the Nordic countries it is difficult to detect differences between the types of decisions made, mainly because both types of decisions tend to be taken by both partners equally. The Canadian household is definitely distinct from the U.S. situation in terms of decision making. This is especially evident where women make a greater income contribution. For instance, in U.S. unconventional households, 52 per cent of the men report that they alone make the major financial decisions but in Canada only 19 per cent do so. Once again, Canada's households resemble the Nordic pattern, with the United States the exception.

GENDER ATTITUDES AND RELATIVE INCOMES

Now we turn to some of the attitudinal effects of these household-income differences. How do men and women in different countries think about gender relations? The main focus will be on four questions asked about gender-relations in four countries. These questions, viewed separately and as part of a gender-attitude index, tap some important differences in the way each sex constructs its thinking about gender relations. There are a variety of dimensions to feminist consciousness, but our data limit us to two of these, based on four comparative questions. Two focus on issues of women and power in government and business (the public sphere), while the other two cover family structures in the sharing of household and child-care responsibilities (the domestic sphere). These are important dimensions covering key issues for feminists of all types, but we are necessarily silent here on other practices, such as women's careers, training, everyday work life, pay and promotion equality, domestic violence, sexist practices, and so on, which are equally significant. We can only claim to cover a limited range of feminist issues. As will be shown, there are some important differences between countries and classes in these gender attitudes.

The relative contributions of income by spouses again distinguishes between conventional households, where men earn most of the income, and unconventional ones, where women earn as much or more than their spouses. For illustrative purposes we have chosen to present two gender-attitude questions in Table 7.5, one representing "private patriarchy" on traditional families and the other representing "public patriarchy" on women in positions of power in government and business.

Are people's attitudes influenced by the income shares each partner brings to a relationship? A strong effect is evident for attitudes toward traditional family structures, especially in Canada. Canadian men have more progressive attitudes when their spouses earn as much or more than they do (60 per cent) compared to wives who earn less (26 per cent). For Canadian women, when their husbands earn the same or less than they do, there is a greater chance of having a progressive attitude toward families than when their spouses earn more. A similar effect is evident for both sexes in all four countries. Women are typically more progressive than men. The only ex-

Table 7.5
Spouse's Relative Income[a] and Gender Attitudes by Nation (percentage progressive)

	United States	Canada	Norway	Sweden
	Traditional Families[b]			
WOMEN				
Unconventional	47	55	66	64
Conventional	33	46	57	57
Difference	+ 14*	+ 9	+ 9*	+ 7
MEN				
Unconventional	32	60	57	62
Conventional	20	26	49	45
Difference	+ 12*	+ 34*	+ 8*	+ 17*
	Key Posts[c]			
WOMAN				
Unconventional	68	75	87	82
Conventional	52	76	80	82
Difference	+ 16*	− 1	+ 7*	0
MEN				
Unconventional	74	71	76	71
Conventional	47	56	63	66
Difference	+ 27*	+ 15*	+ 13*	+ 5

[a] For definitions of conventional and unconventional households, as well as relevant Ns, see Table 7.4.
[b] "It is better for the family if the husband is the principal breadwinner outside the home and the wife has primary responsibility for the home and children" (per cent disagree).
[c] "Ideally there should be *as many* women as men in important positions in government and business" (per cent agree).
* Differences between unconventional and conventional households significant at .05 level of confidence or better.

ception for traditional families is Canadian men in unconventional households. For the question on public patriarchy, men's relative income contribution to the household has a consistent effect, with greater support for women in positions of power as their wife's contribution increases. For women, however, there is more inconsistency, with virtually no effect for Canada or Sweden but a substantial one in the United States (where there was the most room to move).

U.S. unconventional men are interesting in how they split around the questions for private versus public patriarchy. They are as progressive as unconventional men in the other countries concerning women in key public positions but still very conservative with respect to traditional families.

Table 7.6
Spouse's Relative Income and Gender Attitude Index[a]

Households by Sex[b]	United States	Canada	Norway	Sweden
WOMEN				
Unconventional	.69	.84	1.24	1.29
Conventional	.49	.75	1.05	1.18
Difference	+.20*	+.09	+.19*	+.11
(N)	(434)	(820)	(892)	(336)
MEN				
Unconventional	.56	.84	1.01	1.01
Conventional	.28	.36	.76	.71
Difference	+.28*	+.48*	+.25*	+.30*
(N)	(481)	(828)	(897)	(421)

[a] Index ranges from −2 (anti-feminist) to +2 (pro-feminist), based on four items. See the text for the questions used.
[b] For household types, see Table 7.4.
* Differences between respondents in unconventional and conventional households significant at .05 level of confidence or better.

Overall, income share has more impact on men's views than on women's. In Canada, for example, the men whose spouses earn as much or more than they do are almost as progressive as women are on the issue of having women in key public positions. In the United States, men whose spouses earn as much or more than they do are even more progressive than women, the only time this occurs.

The empowerment that comes with women earning an equal or greater share of household income matters in all four countries in terms of promoting more progressive attitudes by their male partners. This suggests that when material conditions improve for women, then they have a greater positive impact on the thinking of their partners. Women also tend to adopt more progressive attitudes, especially towards traditional family roles.

Using four attitudinal questions associated with gender, Table 7.6 again distinguishes between conventional and unconventional households. Two of the questions in the index are the same as in Table 7.5, concerning traditional family roles and whether there should be as many women as men in important government and industry positions. As earlier, the two additional questions also represent private and public patriarchy. "If both husband and wife work, they should share equally the housework and children" and "There are not enough women in responsible positions in government and private business." These questions are added together from a 5-point scale between −2 and +2 to construct an index that reflects attitudes towards feminist issues. The most obvious result from Table 7.6 is that one's relative income contribution matters for how one thinks about feminist issues. The influences are greatest for men, many of whom become decidely feminist when their wives earn an equal or greater proportion of the household income. The effects for women are more modest. There are other conclusions that can be drawn from the same table.

Overall, the most progressive countries are Norway and Sweden, with Canada well behind but considerably ahead of the United States, which is by far the most conservative. Within Canada there is a relatively small difference between men and women in unconventional households. In conventional households, however, women are more progressive than men by a large margin. The pattern in the United States is similar except on a more conservative scale. In conventional Swedish households, men are much more conservative about feminism than the women. Norwegian men in conventional relationships are also much less feminist than women. These patterns suggest relatively harmonious gender attitudes within unconventional households in all the countries (with women tending to do some leading in the Nordic countries) but fairly sharp gender-attitude differences between the sexes in all countries for conventional relationships.

Attitudinal conflicts over gender-related matters are most profoundly felt within conventional households. Material conditions in unconventional households have produced an equalization of gender-related attitudes between men and women and more progressive attitudes as well. What differs between countries is the level of pro-feminist support. Sweden and Norway are the most progressive of the countries and the United States the least. Canada, as usual, is in between, with the most notable feature being the relatively progressive attitudes of Canadian men in unconventional relationships.

REPRODUCTIVE WORK: DOMESTIC
RESPONSIBILITIES

Given the outstanding social fact of women's increased labour-force participation, we explore the impact this has had on the organization of domestic labour. Aside from short periods devoted to the care of small children, women enter the labour force at rates resembling men's patterns. Women, of course, continue to experience the "double ghetto" (a phrase popularized by the Armstrongs in the late 1970s) of segregated work in the paid labour force and primary responsibility for domestic labour at home.

The domestic sphere is crucial for producing subsistence and obviously the intergenerational reproduction of workers. Our focus here will be on an understanding of how the domestic and reproductive spheres are associated with relations of subordination between spouses. How are the domestic and reproductive spheres divided between the sexes and what implications does this division have for women's labour-force experience? Reproductive activities associated with the biology of "motherwork" are a limited aspect of other gendered activities, which include child care and maintenance of households on a daily basis. These activities influence women's experiences within the paid labour market.

Harriet Rosenberg has produced an important statement on "motherwork" associated with child rearing, including the emotional stresses associated with post-partum and the responsibilities of child care. She has investigated "mothering as work," concluding that the social reproduction aspects of care giving are characterized by low control and high demands through isolation and continuous shift work.[26]

Duffy, Mandell, and Pupo, reporting on their own research and summarizing the reproductive and domestic labour literature, conclude:

When a married mother takes on full-time employment, she increases her weekly work-load by 50 per cent; no corresponding shift takes place in her husband's work-load. The wife works about 70 hours a week, although she reduces the number of hours she spends on domestic labour each week from 50 to 28. The time her husband spends on household work increases – to eight hours a week ... And when he increases his household involvement, he tends to become involved with pleasant childcare tasks, such as playing with or walking the baby, rather than undertaking the children's demanding physical care.[27]

Heidi Hartmann has argued that "time spent on housework ... can be fruitfully used as a measure of power relations in the home."[28] Following this argument, we explore some aspects of power relations in domestic relations by using, first, the relative share of time spent looking after children, then the gendered allocation of domestic tasks.

An important caveat about the following analysis of domestic labour is its focus on the distribution of tasks between men and women. We are restricted by the data to such information, but what has become evident in more recent literature is the equally important question of who organizes these tasks. In other words, who has ultimate responsibility to see that domestic tasks (including child care) are properly managed? Indications are that even when there is greater sharing in the execution of tasks, women still bear the managerial responsibilities, consequently the organization of domestic obligations will "be on their mind" all day (and all night) long, whereas men have the more straightforward jobs of simply performing appointed and often non-routine tasks associated with domestic work.[29]

CHILD CARE

Basic to reproductive responsibilities is care of children. In four countries, couples with children sixteen years of age or younger were asked about the division of child care. Responses have been divided into three categories: those who have *little* (zero to 40 per cent), *equal* (ranging from 41 to 59 per cent), or *most* of the responsibility (60 per cent to all). Men and women tend to agree that about a third of the men have an equal share of child care, with strong agreement between the sexes, except in Sweden, where the absence of housewives among women in the sample may influence the comparison (See Table 7.7). Swedish men and women disagree somewhat on the extent of equal child care, but they do agree on who does most. Swedish women claim in two-thirds of the cases to do most of the child care, virtually identical to women from the United States and Canada. Swedish men, however, give Swedish women even more credit, claiming in 71 per cent of the cases to do little themselves (this is because Swedish men include housewives as a referent in their responses, but Swedish housewives are not directly represented in the sample).

According to these broad national patterns, the most equitable nation in terms of sharing child care responsibilities is Norway. Sharing is far from equal, but Norwegian men, as reported by both sexes, are the most likely to participate in child care, well above the proportions reported in the other countries, where the agreed level is about a third reporting that men share equally.

There are some fairly major differences between women according to their labour-force status.[30] The more a woman works, the lower her share of child care (although always much greater than her partner's share, even when she works full time). In Sweden the part-timers have the greatest child-care responsibilities. In Norway there is a steady progression of increased women's responsibility for child care from full-time to part-time to housewives. Norway is on the leading edge of sharing child-care responsibilities. Among women

Table 7.7
Child Care for Partner with Children (16 years and under) by Nation and Sex*
(per cent)

Share of Child Care[a]	United States			Canada		
	Women	Men	Diff.	Women	Men	Diff.
Little	4	61	−57	3	60	−57
Equal	31	31	0	30	33	−3
Most	65	8	+57	67	7	+60
	100	100		100	100	
(N)	(239)	(302)		(474)	(456)	
	Norway			Sweden		
	Women	Men	Diff.	Women	Men	Diff.
Little	1	52	−51	3	71	−68
Equal	43	42	+1	32	21	+11
Most	56	6	+50	65	8	+57
	100	100		100	100	
(N)	(529)	(501)		(200)	(263)	

[a] Little (0–40%), equal (41–59%), or most (60–100%) of the time spent caring for children relative to one's partner.
* All differences between male and female percentage distribution profiles are significant at the .05 level of confidence or better.

employed full time, 59 per cent report an equal sharing. Canada is not far behind at 49 per cent equal. As earlier results lead us to expect, the United States is the least advanced, with only 38 per cent reporting equal sharing. But even in Sweden, women employed full time do most of the child care (44 per cent equal). This pattern is even more accentuated for Swedish women working part time, over two-thirds of whom do most of the child care. Swedish women employed part time are even higher than part-timers in the United States (65 per cent) in relative child-care responsibilities.

In Canada 62 per cent of part-timers do most of the child care, but in Norway this drops to 46 per cent. A woman's labour-force status obviously impacts on her child-care burden. It is highest for housewives, but also consistently higher for women with part-time paid work compared to those with full-time paid work.

Does class matter in terms of sharing child-care responsibilities? The data (not shown here) indicate that it does not. Men in all classes are equally unlikely to contribute to child care. Women in all classes confront a common problem concerning child care in terms of their partners. In no class is there generalized equal sharing of this responsibility, and in all classes most women do most of this aspect of

Table 7.8
Sex Differences* in Household Tasks by Nation (percentage-point difference,
women over men)[a]

	United States	Canada	Norway	Sweden
Meal preparation	+74	+74	+73	+63
Grocery shopping	+53	+44	+38	+44
Post-meal clean-up	+60	+63	+54	+58
House cleaning	+68	+72	+70	+58
Laundry	+76	+79	+80	+70
(N)	(1,010)	(1,678)	(1,918)	(802)

[a] Percentage-point difference between women and men when they do "most" of a task (60 per
cent or more). For example, in the first cell, U.S. men do most of the meal preparation in 9
per cent of the households, but women do most in 83 per cent, a difference of +74.
* All differences between men and women are significant at .05 level of confidence or better.

domestic work. Domestic responsibilities, of course, encompass more
than child-care responsibilities. Also important are the household
tasks, to which we now turn.

HOUSEHOLD TASKS

Rarely can such consistency across nations (and agreement in reporting between the sexes) be found as with these results on the divisions
of household tasks by sex. There appears to be almost a "universal
law of domestic practices," whereby women do meal preparations,
house cleaning, and laundry, with some sharing – under the general
responsibility of women – for post-meal clean-up and grocery shopping.

Respondents who live with a partner were asked to report how
much involvement they have with a series of household tasks, reporting the share of work done by themselves and their spouses. The results are summarized for the five main household tasks in Table 7.8.
Once again there is remarkable agreement between men and women
on their respective contributions to domestic tasks. On virtually every item for every country, men and women are mirror images of
one another. This gives us considerable confidence in the results as a
fairly accurate reflection of the actual division of domestic labour
and permits us to combine the reports by men and women. The
scores reported in Table 7.8 are the percentage-point differences between women and men when the do "most" of the work associated
with a domestic task. A score of +70, for example, would result
when 80 per cent of the women do most of a task and only 10 per
cent of the men do most. Equal sharing would result in a score of
zero.

Table 7.9
Number of Household Tasks for Which the Respondent* Does the Majority of Work
(share of five household tasks[a])

Task[a] Share	United States		Canada		Norway		Sweden	
	Women	Men	Women	Men	Women	Men	Women	Men
None	6	78	5	76	6	75	5	72
Some	13	17	14	19	16	20	18	24
Most	81	5	81	5	77	5	77	4
	100	100	100	100	100	100	100	100
(N)	(475)	(524)	(833)	(845)	(965)	(953)	(270)	(365)

[a] None = zero; some = one or two; most = three, four, or five. Number of tasks for which the respondent does the majority (60 per cent or more) of the work. Tasks identified in Table 7.8.
* All differences in the profiles of men and women are significant at .05 level of confidence or better.

There is remarkable similarity across countries on the relative contributions by men and women to each task. For cooking meals, only Sweden has a somewhat different profile, with slightly more sharing. This difference results from the Swedish sample, which is only for employed individuals. Even in that sample, nearly three-quarters of the women do most of the cooking and the same proportion of men do little, a pattern confirmed by examining only the active labour forces for other countries, which are then virtually identical to the Swedish results. Shopping for groceries is the most equitably shared household task, with nearly a third in all countries (except the United States at a quarter) reporting equal sharing of this task. The least equitable country is the United States. Elsewhere about half the men do little and half the women do most of the grocery shopping. Cleaning up after meals follows groceries for men's participation, with nearly a quarter sharing this task but over two-thirds reporting that men do little and women do most. Routine general house cleaning follows the meal preparation pattern, with only Sweden differing from the others with nearly a quarter reporting equal sharing and two-thirds reporting men do little and women most. Laundry is the strongest universal, with consistent agreement across the countries that women do most of this task and men make little contribution. Table 7.9 summarizes the number of tasks for which individuals do a majority (60 per cent or more) of the work. In about 5 per cent of the households everywhere either the man does most of the housework or the woman does very little. These are clearly exceptional. The typical case, covering three-quarters of all households, is where the man does the majority for none of the tasks and the woman does the majority for most of them.

Table 7.10
Gender Divisions* of Yard Work and Home Maintenance for Canada
(percentages)

Task Share[a]	Yard Work		Home Maintenance	
	Men	Women	Men	Women
Little	22	53	15	60
Equal	26	28	18	22
Most	52	19	68	19
	100	100	100	100
(N)	(845)	(833)	(845)	(833)

[a] See Table 7.7.
* All differences in the profiles of men and women are significant at .05 level of confidence or better.

In each country, men and women are mirror images, with incredible consistency both between the sexes and internationally. There is little to pick between the four countries, especially since Sweden has nearly the same record for women performing the majority for most of the tasks when only the currently employed populations are compared. Our findings support those of Phyllis Moen and others that "Swedish women, like their U.S. counterparts, continue to perform the bulk of the household chores."[31]

Only the Canadian survey asked about two other types of household labour, involving more traditional male tasks. For yard work or gardening, men are significantly involved (with figures nearly the inverse of grocery shopping), yet even here nearly half the women have some significant involvement. With home maintenance, about two-fifths of the women are involved even though the majority of the work is done by men. These two tasks illustrate the twin points that there are tasks where men perform the majority of household labour but that even these are not nearly as exclusively the domain of one sex or the other as the previous five tasks proved to be. There is also the obvious point that the five tasks where women concentrate are routine in the sense that they are virtually daily and on-going whereas yard work and home maintenance are more intermittent undertakings, thus imposing fewer restrictions on the practitioner.

Using the Canadian data for illustrative purposes, it is possible to demonstrate a strong association between the spouse's relative contribution to household income and the allocation of domestic tasks. Share of income accounts for some of the patterns, but sex is the greatest source of division. In terms of meal preparation, for example, women report they do most or all of that work in 88 per cent of the cases when they earn less than men, 74 per cent when they earn equally, and 63 per cent when they earn more than the men with whom they live. Men pretty much confirm the women's reports, saying they do little or none of the cooking 84 per cent of the time when women earn less than them and 65 per cent when women are equal earners; even when women earn more, 43 per cent do little or no meal preparation. Across each of the household tasks the pattern holds whereby women's economic power independently impacts upon the allocation of domestic labour but never overcomes the fundamentally gender-structured divisions. Patterns in the other countries are similar.

Class also influences the gender allocation of various household tasks in Canada. Capitalist-executive and old-middle-class men are less likely to contribute to cooking meals or grocery shopping than those from the new middle and working classes. New-middle-class women seem to be best able to resist exclusive responsibility for meal preparation, grocery shopping, post-meal clean-up, and housekeeping, with less impressive inroads into laundry. The most affected activity for new-middle-class women is post-meal clean-up, where husbands are at least equally responsible over a third of the time. Around housekeeping there is a notable split on both class and gender lines. The capitalist-executive and old middle classes have the most rigid gender division, while the working and new middle classes have the greatest male contribution. New-middle-class women report greater equality than do men. Again, laundry is a universal, with the only notable exception the even greater shirking of this responsibility by capitalist-executive men. Yard work is more evenly distributed, with old-middle-class men contributing less than male counterparts in other classes, while working-class men are especially active in yard work or gardening. Home maintenance is an area of considerable gender disagreement (cutting across all classes except the working class, where women agree with the men's assessment). Capitalist-executive, old-middle-, and new-middle-class men all claim considerably more contribution to home maintenance than they are credited with by women from these classes.

Overall, capitalist-executive and old-middle-class men are the least active in performing household tasks, with greater involvement by men from the new middle and working classes. Women in all classes have primary responsibilities for these tasks, with the main resistance coming from new-middle-class women, who have demanded greater equality in domestic chores. For working-class women the results are more mixed, with some success in getting more equality with grocery shopping but little gain around the traditional tasks of meal preparation, house cleaning, or laundry. Outside the house, working-class women do little, but women from other classes share in those tasks, which are somewhat recreational and more irregular.

Having summarized our findings about both relative income contributions to households and the division of domestic responsibilities, we can combine these two dimensions into household types.

HOUSEHOLD TYPES: ECONOMIC POWER AND THE DIVISION OF DOMESTIC LABOUR

Thus far, two dimensions of household power have been explored: the relative contribution each partner makes to the household's total income and the domestic division of labour. We can use these dimensions in combination to produce a typology of households which follows changes occuring in the relative powers of men and women. In constructing our typology we build upon the divisions already examined. For the income contribution to the household we follow the distinction between conventional and unconventional households. Recall that in a conventional household the man earns over half of the total family income; in an unconventional household the woman earns half or more of the household income. For the division of domestic labour, we have distinguished between those who do "most" and those who do "little." This leaves a substantial middle ground for "equal" covering a range of 40 to 59 per cent.

In *traditional* households the man earns most of the income and the woman does most of the domestic labour, with men contributing little to domestic labour and women providing less than half of the income. As women improve their economic power and are able to make demands for more equitable sharing of domestic responsibilities, these traditional households are subject to change. In *transitional* households the new economic power of women is not yet reflected in men's adjustment to doing more domestic work, resulting in a lack of correspondence between income contribution and the sharing of domestic duties. In other words, the woman earns half or more of the family income, but the husband does not contribute equally to domestic labour. In *modern* households, changes in the sharing of domestic labour have occured. The defining feature of a modern household is one where the man does at least 40 per cent of the domestic work (the majority for at least two of the five domestic tasks identified earlier).

Theoretically, it is possible to divide the "modern" type into situations where the man earns most of the income and others where

Table 7.11
Household Relationships by Nation and Sex

Household Types	United States	Canada	Norway	Sweden
	Women			
Traditional	63	63	65	55
Transitional	18	18	14	23
Modern	19	19	21	23
	100	100	100	100
(N)	(448)	(822)	(925)	(258)
	Men			
Traditional	83	79	76	56
Transitional	11	16	20	40
Modern	6	5	5	3
	100	100	100	100
(N)	(511)	(836)	(927)	(344)

women earn as much or more than the man. In practice, however, there are very few situations where the man reports earning less than half of the income and contributing equally to domestic labour (never over 2 per cent of our national samples). There are more instances where the man earns most of the income and does share equally in the domestic labour. We have chosen to group these two sub-types under the category "modern." Our typology better fits women in our sample, largely because they are more likely to claim equality in obtaining household incomes than men attribute to them. This accounts for the higher share of modern women in our typology than modern men.

Hence what we conceived as a fourfold typology turns out in practice to have three distinctions: traditional households, where men bring in the money and women do the housework; transitional households, where women bring in at least an equal share of the money but still do most of the housework; and modern households, where the housework barrier is finally broken and men contribute equally.

In all four countries, the majority of households are traditional for both men and women. This is to be expected. Transitional and modern relationships, as reported by women, are also fairly common, with some lead shown by Swedish women. Once again, we must qualify the results for Swedish women since housewives were not sampled there (although the men reported on families where there were housewives). There need not be any qualification for the results as reported by Swedish men, who are clearly more likely than other men to find themselves in transitional households. This is a result of the relatively high incomes for Swedish women because of labour's wage-solidarity practices, yet the slow response by Swedish men to an equitable distribution of household tasks. When only the currently employed are examined, the Swedish level for transitional men rises to 52 per cent (as do the other countries in proportion: the United States to 20 per cent, Norway to 32 per cent, and Canada to 27 per cent).

In the next chapter we will return to the household types established here, but first it is interesting to see the effect of class, focusing on a comparison between the working and new middle classes. Table 7.12 makes it evident there are quite different effects for men and women. For women in all four countries, those in the middle class are less likely to be traditional and more likely to be modern in their household relationships. The difference is very great in the Nordic countries, with middle-class women much more likely to be modern and working-class women traditional. The differences are more modest in North America, but still in the same direction. Class does matter for empowering women within the household. Obviously middle-class women bring a greater share of the family income into the home and are able to effect some changes in the distribution of domestic labour – at least, more so than working-class women. Middle-class Nordic women even drop to less than half in traditional household relations.

The situation for men is quite the opposite. Middle-class men are more likely to be in traditional relationships than working-class men, especially in Sweden, Canada, and Norway. In the United States there is less effect. This suggests that middle-class men not only bring a greater share of the income into their households than working-class men, but they do not make adjustments to their sharing of domestic duties even when their partners match or exceed their income. Middle-class men are much more reluctant than working-class men to share in domestic duties.

Does an individual's class matter in the distribution of economic power and domestic duties? Class does have some effects, but they are attenuated by the basic sex division that occurs within each nation and the differences between nations. Sweden emerges as the exceptional nation, mainly because women there tend to earn incomes within classes similar to men's incomes. When this income pattern combines with the failure to adjust the division of domestic labour, it produces a much higher level of transitional relationships for Swedish men than elsewhere. Generally, relationships in the United States

Table 7.12
Household Relationships by Class, Nation, and Sex

	Working	Middle	Diff.	Working	Middle	Diff.
			Women			
		United States			Canada	
Traditional	65	60	−5	64	59	−5
Transitional	18	18	0	15	18	+3
Modern	17	22	+5	21	23	+2
	100	100		100	100	
(N)	(272)	(116)		(474)	(156)	
		Norway			Sweden	
Traditional	61	44	−17*	57	44	−13
Transitional	17	17	0	24	20	−4
Modern	23	39	+16*	20	37	+17*
	100	100		100	100	
(N)	(373)	(107)		(202)	(45)	
			Men			
		United States			Canada	
Traditional	81	82	+1	74	85	+11*
Transitional	12	14	+2	20	11	−9*
Modern	7	4	−3	6	4	−2
	100	100		100	100	
(N)	(217)	(166)		(394)	(223)	
		Norway			Sweden	
Traditional	72	80	+8*	49	66	+17*
Transitional	23	16	−7*	47	32	−15*
Modern	5	4	−1	4	2	−2
	100	100		100	100	
(N)	(357)	(258)		(184)	(87)	

* Differences between classes significant at .05 level of significance or better.

tend to be the most traditional, but this pattern is fairly consistent with the one found in Canada and Norway. In all countries, men are more often traditional than are women. This means women are more often in transitional relationships or in ones where they contribute at least an equal or greater share of the household income. They account for a fifth of all women. Modern women who have husbands that share domestic duties account for a similar share. Together they represent a noteworthy trend in challenging traditional household relations.

This approach to an individual's class and household type shows that it is unsatisfactory to look only at the individual when trying to understand the household. Even when we can get the individual to report on a household relationship, there remains the problem of having only the individual's class as a point of reference. In the following chapter we will address this difficulty. Just how domestic responsibilities and the division of powers within the household impact in return upon the paid labour of women is the subject of the next chapter. Included will be a more detailed analysis of household relationships, which uses the class of household rather than only the individual's class.

CONCLUSION

As the complex relationship between class and gender in different nations begins to unfold, the salience of the link between domestic and paid labour becomes more evident. England and Kilbourne are among the few who have sought to "explain why men generally have more power than women, and why power flows from earnings more than from domestic work." They argue that since women have lower earnings and more domestic responsibilities than men, they have lower "marital power" because of "(1) cultural forces that devalue traditionally female work and encourage women to be altruistic, (2) the fact that the beneficiaries of much domestic work are children rather than men, (3) the fact that some domestic work involves making investments that are specific to a particular relationship rather than 'general,' and (4) the fact that even 'general' investments in domestic skills are less 'liquid' than earnings because they do not ensure survival until one finds another partner."[32] Their account is particularly intriguing because they attempt to include both cultural and structural restraints imposed by the role of housewife in their explanation of the weaker powers of women. A weakness from our perspective, however, is their acknowledged decision to take "the typical division of labor by sex as given,"[33] whereas we attempt to see what happens when the "typical" is challenged, either by women earning as much as men or men contributing equally to the housework.

In this chapter we have explored who decides in domestic politics and who does domestic labour in the context of who is empowered by bringing income into households. We have examined situations where women make equal or greater economic contributions to households and ones where men make equal or greater contributions to domestic labour especially to see if these arrangements affect how people think about gender relations and act toward the domestic division of labour. We can conclude that these "atypical" situations do indeed matter, especially affecting the attitudes of men. When women bring a greater share of income into the household, men become more progressive in their views of women and even modify somewhat their behaviour toward domestic work. In class terms, we can also conclude that the propertied classes are more patriarchal than the new middle or working classes. We have the added advantage of comparing at least four nations, with the pattern of United States traditionalism, Nordic progressiveness, and Canadian "in-betweenness" on decision making between the sexes. At the level of actual practices, however, Swedish men's contribution to domestic labour has not kept up with Swedish women's greater economic contribution to households, especially in the working class.

Our results indicate that there are major material conditions in terms of economic contributions to household incomes, the allocation of the domestic division of labour, the class of the participants, and even the nation where they live which all contribute to how both men and women think about important gender issues. At the heart of such issues is the relationship between domestic and paid labour, a relationship that continues to undermine the powers of women and enhance those of men.

8 Linking Domestic and Paid Labour: Career Disruptions and Household Obligations

Households make demands on their members and do so in ways that are highly gendered in their impacts. Most often women are the dependent labourers, whose motherwork and housework have a negative bearing upon their relationship to paid labour. Women's lives are contigent upon husbands, children, parents, and household obligations. Martin Meissner and his colleagues concluded from their research in the early 1970s, "Women and men have a different relationship to work organizations, to the class structure, and to the means of controlling the value of different kinds of labour."[1] Women are more likely to experience disruptions in their employment as a result of their domestic labours and the demands these make on paid employment. Disruptions resulting from the unequal sharing of domestic responsibilities cause women's careers, earnings, and positions within decision-making structures all to be adversely affected.

People experience class not only as individuals but through households, both *within* the household and *between* the household and the labour market. We say "people" but in fact the experience is specifically gendered. Men tend to be empowered by their households, while women have their powers diminished because of domestic responsibilities. A person's labour-market status (such as part-time paid worker, full-time paid worker, or housewife) is the result of a complex set of relationships. As the Armstrongs have pointed out, "it should not be forgotten that these [labour-market] choices are very much limited by women's domestic responsibilities and by the work that is available."[2] The conditions under which women make their labour-market decisions include such factors as the availability of day care, of some equal sharing of domestic labour, of attractive, well-paid work, and of accessible or appropriate training. None of these factors exist in isolation.

The work women perform in the paid labour force, the nature of their careers, and their availability for work are all contingent upon their relationships to others. While more women engage in paid labour for longer periods of time with fewer stoppages than ever before, they nevertheless experience the labour force differently from men. Duffy, Mandell, and Pupo have captured an essential aspect of this difference when they find, "Frequently, any plans they [women] may have are short-term and contingent on the activities or inclinations of others ('when my children go to school'; 'because my husband got a new job') ... The major features of most women's lives are the products of external forces, not the women's personal predilections."[3] Let us begin with one key indicator of these gendered differences: labour-force disruptions.

LABOUR-FORCE DISRUPTIONS

The Canadian survey posed a series of questions to people who have lived or are currently living with partners, asking whether their household or family responsibilities ever prevented them from engaging in a series of labour-force activities. These answers are summarized in Figure 8.1. Only 18 per cent of the men had experienced any of these disruptions because of household or family responsibilities, but 54 per cent of women had such interferences. For men, the major impediment concerned accepting a transfer, with some limitations on changing jobs, but both these pale beside the figures for women, over a third of whom have been prevented from accepting a full-time job and looking for a job, with well over a quarter unable to accept a transfer and a part-time job. While 38 per cent of the women in the sample (1,054) experienced two or more of these disruptions, the same can be said for only 7 per cent of the men (973). Clearly domestic responsibilities bear much more heavily upon women's careers than they do on men's.

Women of all ages have experienced disruptions to their careers. While younger women are somewhat less likely to have experienced the various disruptions, for the obvious reasons that they are less likely to have had children and have had less labour-force opportunity to experience disruptions involving transfer or promotion, still, over half have had at least one disruption, nearly the same level as older women. Interestingly, more young men than older ones have had disruptions, amounting to nearly a quarter of the youngest group. This may reflect

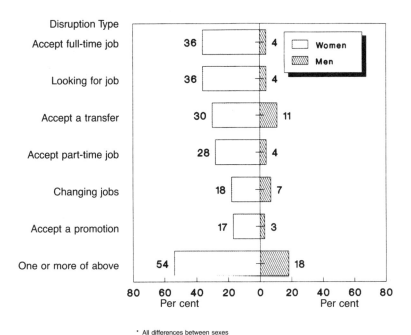

Figure 8.1
Labour-Force Participation Disruptions by Sex of Respondent

changes in two-job households and some changes in domestic politics arising from the career demands of women.

Table 8.1 refers to the current status of Canadian women living with partners. Women currently employed full time, not surprisingly, have experienced the least disruption to their work life. For each of the other statuses, accepting a full-time job because of household or family responsibilities is their greatest career barrier. Similarly, looking for a job is high on the list. Women working part time (less than 20 hours a week) have particular difficulty with accepting promotions. For housewives it is getting into the paid labour force that has been most difficult, whether looking for a job or accepting full- or part-time employment. The unemployed have been fairly hard hit across the board in looking for or accepting full-time work, but their greatest relative difficulty is accepting a transfer because of household or family responsibilities. As argued above, it is women who sacrifice for "others" in their careers. They are considered the secondary member of the household when it comes to paid work. Employment status has virtually no impact on men's experience of disruptions.[4]

Table 8.1
Women's Labour-Force Disruptions by Current Employment Status, Canada
(percentages)

		Employment Status			
Disruption Type	Full-Time	Part-Time (20–34)	Part-Time (1–19)	Unemployed	Housewife
Accepting full-time job	20	46	49	38	42
Looking for a job	22	37	42	35	45
Accepting a transfer	28	35	29	33	25
Accepting part-time job	18	31	36	28	32
Changing jobs	19	18	20	18	14
Accepting promotion	13	21	28	21	15
One or more of above	45	62	59	52	59
(N)	(336)	(125)	(66)	(140)	(330)
Men: One or more	18	13	32	17	—
(N)	(735)	(46)	(13)	(154)	—

Having children impacts strongly upon women's career disruptions (as Table 8.2 illustrates) *but is far from the whole explanation.* Even 43 per cent of women with no children have had at least one disruption because of household or family responsibilities, compared to only 17 per cent of men, regardless of how many children they have. Having children has no effect whatsoever on men in terms of these disruptions, yet there is a clear cumulative effect for women, with the greatest increase from none to one, especially in the activities of accepting full-time work and looking for a job or even accepting part-time work. More than two children mostly effects accepting promotions or changing jobs.

The Armstrongs are particularly important within Canadian scholarship for introducing the notion of *The Double Ghetto*, as the title of their book so neatly captured. They combined an analysis of the segregated nature of women's paid work with an examination of work in the home. As they express the relationship, "While women's work in the home places restrictions on their ability to work outside the home, many of these factors are also a function of the kind of work women perform in the industrial unit. The dual demands of work in both the home and the labour force have a direct effect on women's labour force participation."[5]

The essential insight of the Armstrongs' work has been to focus on the two jobs that most women have and how domestic responsibilities affect their paid labour-force involvement. The situation evolves

Table 8.2
Women's Labour-Force Disruptions by Number of Children, Canada (percentages)

	Number of Children			
Disruption Type	None	One	Two	Over Two
Accepting full-time job	23	36	49	49
Looking for a job	23	36	46	52
Accepting a transfer	30	31	28	29
Accepting part-time job	21	29	31	37
Changing jobs	17	18	14	24
Accepting promotion	15	57	63	66
One or more of above	43	57	63	66
(N)	(428)	(211)	(227)	(185)
Men: One or more	17	16	18	18
(N)	(399)	(199)	(206)	(169)

whereby "men's jobs are primary, women must do the adjusting. Therefore, women take jobs that allow them to fulfill their household responsibilities."[6] The Armstrongs were eager to point out that women worked because they were required to do so by economic necessity in most instances *and* that they were essentially handicapped in the paid labour force by primary responsibility for the household. Sex segregation developed within the paid labour force is reinforced by the strongly gendered division of domestic responsibilities.

In reviewing analytical and empirical developments concerning women's work in the household and paid labour market, Wally Seccombe notes, concerning women's double day of labour based on time-budget studies, that

the overall distribution of labour in marriage has become *more unequal* in the post-war period. Whether we calculate this distribution on a daily or weekly basis (where the shift is modest), or more adequately on a lifetime basis (where the determination is apparently severe), the evidence is unambiguous. Despite the rise of feminism and positive changes in mass consciousness concerning women's rights, women's position has nevertheless regressed in this *fundamental* aspect of gender relations.[7]

The extent of a woman's domestic responsibilities is reflected in her experience of disruptions, especially in looking for a job and accepting full-or part-time employment. On the other dimensions there is less difference. Men who share the domestic tasks equally or do most of them also have more disruptions caused by household responsibilities than men in traditional relationships where their wives do most of the domestic work. Table 8.3 illustrates that progressive

Table 8.3
Women's Labour-Force Disruptions by Household Tasks, Canada (percentages)

Disruption Type	Traditional Households	Progressive Households[a]	Difference[b]
Accepting full-time job	40	25	−15*
Looking for a job	41	26	−15*
Accepting a transfer	29	23	−6
Accepting a part-time job	30	17	−13*
Changing jobs	16	10	−6*
Accepting a promotion	17	12	−5
One or more of the above	58	45	−13*
(N)	(566)	(268)	
Men: One or more	16	27	+11
(N)	(801)	(44)	

[a] Progressive households have a somewhat "equal" sharing of household tasks. This means that men do most of the work for three or more of the five tasks outlined in Table 7.8. For women it means they do less than the majority of the work for three or fewer of the five tasks. Men required a more "generous" definition than women in order to raise the number of cases from 25 to 44. In traditional households, women do 60 per cent or more of the work for four or five of the five tasks.

[b] A − sign indicates a decrease in disruptions; a + sign indicates an increase.

* Differences between household types significant at .05 level of confidence or better.

households where men make major contributions to household tasks increase men's experience with disruptions (+11 percentage points) to the same degree as they decrease women's disruptions (−13 percentage points). There is a substantial relationship between the sharing of household tasks and labour-market behaviour, a relationship relevant to both the freedom of men and the restraints for women. Even the most "progressive" men do not reach the level of penalty experienced by the least domestically responsible women.

Does class influence the disruptions women experience with domestic responsibilities? To some extent but not much. Capitalist-executive women have had more difficulties with promotions than women from other classes. Working-class women have difficulty accepting full-time work or looking for a job, while old-middle-class women have trouble accepting part-time or full-time work because of their household responsibilities. Overall, working-class women more frequently encounter domestic barriers. Among men, those in the new middle class have the greatest experience of barriers, while capitalists-executives have the least. New-middle-class women have had the greatest difficulty with transfers. Working-class women find being prevented from taking full-time work or looking for a job the most common household barriers preventing them from entering the labour force at some point.

Do women have similar problems with career disruptions across classes? Some problems are common, such as having to change jobs because of family responsibilities or even looking for a job. Within the labour market, however, other barriers are more class-specific. New-middle-class women, for instance, have the greatest problem with accepting transfers, capitalist-executive women are more likely to be impeded in accepting promotions and old-middle-class women have the most difficulty in accepting work. Compared to men, however, there appears to be much more that binds women together across classes with respect to their career disruptions. Men and women in all four classes *appear* to live in totally different worlds when it comes to the effects of domestic responsibilities on labour-force disruptions, regardless of class. The appearance, however, is deceiving. They live in the same world but share it unequally.

LABOUR-FORCE STATUS

By 1986 women's share of the labour force reached half in Sweden and Finland (48 per cent) and nearly half in Norway, the United States, and Canada (43 to 44 per cent). Reporting on the Canadian situation, Duffy, Mandell, and Pupo say, "In 1931, only 3.5 per cent of all married women engaged in paid labour. Even at mid-century, only 10 per cent of married women were paid workers ... Today 66 percent of women with employed husbands and children under age sixteen work for pay."[8] Women's labour-force participation has changed rapidly in Canada and elsewhere, especially for women traditionally considered unavailable for paid work. Still labour-force status fundamentally distinguishes men from women.

There are few national differences for men's labour-force participation rates and little change between 1973 and 1987 except, if anything, a slight drop.[9] In the prime age group (age 25–54) there is virtually no variation for men between the five countries (ranging from 93 to 95 per cent). Women, on the other hand, have consistently increased their labour-force participation rates. Canada has the greatest increase (21 percentage points), in part because it started well below the others. Finnish women moved the least (6 percentage points), in part because they began with the highest rates. Sweden has the highest rate for women, including those in the prime age group, where the rate rivals the already high level for Swedish men. Norwegian women began the period with North American–like rates but ended in line with the Nordic countries. Women in all the Nordic countries have considerably higher rates (80 to 90 per cent in the prime age group) than in North America, where there is now little national variation (71 per cent in Canada, 72 per cent in the United States). Even though women are approaching the same labour-force participation rates as men, they still have radically different labour-force statuses.

Part-time work is one distinctive feature of women's labour-force status. There are two outstanding features in discussions of part-time status. One is the substantive fact that it is a highly gendered practice. The other is a matter of definition: just how many hours constitute part-time? Some nations report a cut-off of 30 hours (as in Canada and Norway) and others 35 hours (as in the United States and Sweden), thus complicating official international comparisons. It has also become a common finding in comparative research to point to the fact that much of the extraordinarily high labour-force participation by Swedish women is actually part-time, thus somehow diminishing its significance. The classic point made by observers is that the Swedish rate is so high for women because of their high proportion of part-time work. In the 25 to 54 age group for women, 21 per cent in both Canada and the United States are part-time, but in Sweden the share of part-time rises to 45 per cent, with 42 per cent in Norway. Table 8.4 will confirm this observation.

The comparisons in Table 8.4 are less than perfect since there are two definitions of part-time used (also, neither the proportion of involuntary part-time for Norway nor the part-time figures for Finland are available). Still, there is a clear difference within nations by sex, with the greatest gaps in the Nordic countries. Men show little variation. Both Sweden and Norway have very high part-time rates for women, nearly twice those for North American women. A much higher share of Nordic part-timers are women. Again, the Nordic–North American pattern persists.

There is a noteworthy difference in part-time work between the countries, however, focusing upon the share who are involuntary part-time workers (that is, wanted to work more hours). Sweden has the lowest rate of involuntary part-time workers, especially among women, indicating that their part-time status is a chosen one. Over a quarter of the part-time labourers of both sexes in Canada are involuntary. In Canada, for part-time male workers between ages 25 and 54 years, 59 per cent are involuntary, compared to 29 per cent for women; it should be kept in mind that only 2 per cent of Canadian males in that age group are part-time, compared to 21 per cent of women. Part-time work and women are virtually synonymous in

Table 8.4
Proportion of the Labour Force Working Part-Time

		% Involuntary*	Female Share of Part-Time
UNITED STATES (1987)	*Under 35 Hours*		
Men	10	24	
Women	26	17	68
CANADA (1987)	*Under 30 Hours*		
Men	8	28	
Women	25	26	72
NORWAY (1986)	*Under 30 Hours*		
Men	8	NA	
Women	43	NA	82
SWEDEN (1987)	*Under 35 Hours*		
Men	7	15	
Women	45	12	86

Source: OECD, *Employment Outlook* (Paris, September 1988), 21–2, 149, Tables 1.4, 1.5, and 5.5.

* In Canada and the United States "involuntary" means they could not find full-time employment; in Sweden it means they wanted to work more hours.

Sweden and Norway. In Canada and the United States a greater share of part-time work is done by men, even though women still form the clear majority.

By shifting from the OECD data to the Comparative Class Structure Project data, the different definitions of part-time work can be removed and an alternative division point within part-time work used. After a closer examination of the Swedish situation, we have adapted a twofold definition of part-time work that can be applied across the four nations under study. We distinguish part-time workers who have fewer than 20 hours per week from those with 20 to 34 hours. Full-time is defined as 35 hours or more, a reasonable designation given the struggles currently under way in Europe to reduce the weekly standard hours to 35 hours from its current 37½- to 42-hour range. As will become evident, the distinction between the two types of part-time workers captures a key difference, especially for Sweden, in the character of part-time work.

More Norwegian women work part time than Swedish women, but a greater share of them work under 20 hours a week, compared to Sweden, where more part-timers work from 20 to 34 hours. The North American rates are higher for full-time work than in the Nordic countries, but a much smaller segment works 20 to 34 hours per week. This helps to explain why much lower proportions of

Table 8.5
Employment Status of the Employed Population by Nation and Sex (per cent)

	Women			
Weekly Hours	United States	Canada	Norway	Sweden
Full-time (35 or more)	76	70*	46*	49*
Part-time (20–34)	17	20	33*	35*
Part-time (1–19)	7	10*	21*	16*
	100	100	100	100
(N)	(679)	(733)	(642)	(482)

	Men			
Weekly Hours	United States	Canada	Norway	Sweden
Full-time (35 or more)	92	90	92	85*
Part-time (20–34)	6	7	6	5
Part-time (1–19)	2	3	3	9*
	100	100	100	100
(N)	(800)	(1,017)	(1,015)	(611)

* Difference with the United States significant at .05 level or better.

women in the previous table report that their part-time work is involuntary in Sweden compared to North America. A high proportion of Swedish women choose to work reduced hours but not necessarily the irregular work of under 20 hours per week. As a result, less than half the Nordic women work full time. In North America the pattern is one whereby nearly three-quarters of employed women work full time, with similar patterns in both countries. Men vary only a little between the countries, nearly all are employed full time.

Table 8.6 compares women who work full time (35 or more hours per week) with those who work part time for 20 to 34 hours per week, focusing on the class effects of employment status.[10] In all the countries, part-timers are more likely to be working class and less likely to be new middle class. Swedish part-time women workers in the 20- to 34-hour category are the most likely to be in the working class (85 per cent). One of the prices they pay for working part time is confinement to the working class. These findings confirm those of Elisabet Nasman for Sweden. She contends, "Part-time work is most common among working-class women even though they do not re-

Table 8.6
Women's Employment Status[a] by Class and Nation

	United States			Canada		
Class[b]	Full-Time	Part-Time	Diff.	Full-Time	Part-Time	Diff.
Property	12	11	−1	7	12	+5
Middle	28	19	−9*	27	20	−7
Working	61	70	+10*	66	69	+3
	100	100		100	100	
(N)	(515)	(116)		(515)	(146)	

	Norway			Sweden		
Class[b]	Full-Time	Part-Time	Diff.	Full-Time	Part-Time	Diff.
Property	7	6	−1	7	1	−6*
Middle	22	18	−4	19	14	−5
Working	71	76	+5	74	85	+11*
	100	100		100	100	
(N)	(296)	(209)		(236)	(169)	

[a] Full-time is defined as 35 or more hours per week; part-time includes only 20–34 hours per week.
[b] Property class combines capitalist-executives and old middle class.
* Differences between full-time/part-time categories significant at .05 level of confidence or better.

ceive economic compensation for their reduced working hours. The possibility to work part-time is used to a very small extent by men."[11]

Swedish part-time work has been subjected to detailed investigation by Marianne Sundström. She examines labour-market legislation associated with part-time work. According to Sundström, since 1979 parents employed full time are guaranteed the right, until the child is eight years old, to reduce their hours to 75 per cent of full-time.[12] Nasman's research indicates that few men have taken advantage of this provision.

Sundström's study finds that from 1970 to 1980, three-quarters of the growth in women's employment was in part-time work (defined as less than 35 hours per week). There has been a steady increase in the hours worked by part-timers. In 1970 60 per cent of the part-time women workers were employed 20 to 34 hours per week, but by 1985 this proportion had grown to 83 per cent.[13] Whereas the growth in North American part-time work has been concentrated in the commercial service sector, in Sweden this area has not been the leading edge of part-time women's work. Instead, employment in the public sector has been particularly important, especially for health-care workers.

A combination of factors account for the rise in Swedish part-time work, but specific to Sweden has been the rise in wages for women compared to men as a result of the labour movement's wage-solidarity practices. Women were assured of wages and benefits equitable to those of men. Along with spouses' separate taxation since 1971, increased public child care and a greater gap between employed women and housewives for social benefits (especially "paternal insurance"), these changes narrowed the gap for entitlement to such benefits between full- and part-time workers. Anyone working over 17 hours a week in Sweden is entitled to "the same social and labor-law rights as the full-time worker."[14] Little wonder Swedish women concentrate in the longer hours of part-time work. But, as we will soon see, since Swedish women have organized their lives to look after household responsibilities, this tends to undercut pressure on Swedish men to change their old habits of avoiding domestic work.[15] It has been the Swedish employers, rather than Swedish husbands, that share child-care responsibilities with Swedish women.

The character of Swedish women's rapid entry into the paid labour force requires some further explanation. Direct political measures designed to encourage and facilitate women's labour-force participation include, as mentioned, the separate taxation system for spouses so that there is an incentive for income to be spread between family members; public day-care places were expanded; parental insurance was based on labour-market entitlements. Because of Sweden's virtually universal unionization, plus its solidaristic wage policy, there has developed a narrower wage gap between men and women. Moreover, the famous active labour-market policies have meant easier re-entry for training. All these measures, as Inga Persson has argued, were directed at the "supply side" but without similar attention to "the demand side of the labour market (i.e. eliminating discrimination against women and their exclusion from certain occupations and positions) and the opportunities for Swedish women to achieve leadership positions. For example, the Swedish law on equal status between men and women seems to be more toothless and less effective than the American one."[16]

Sundström contends that the increase in the number of part-time women workers is the reason for legislative changes, so that "the supply-side of the labour market" and "the demand for labour" have "(mainly) gradually adjusted to the changed composition of female labor supply," which in turn is "also largely influenced by public policies."[17] In North America it may be structural (demand-side) factors, such as occupational and industrial segmentation, while in Sweden the individual (supply-side) conditions promote part-time work.

Because of Swedish women's part-time work and paid absences (87 per cent of child-care absences are taken by women, although short-term sick care is more evenly distributed), there are major differences by sex in the time spent on market work (35.9 hours per week for men in 1984, 20.4 hours per week for women) and non-market work (16.0 hours for men, 29.4 hours for women).[18] Swedish women spent an average of 18 hours more per week on household tasks and active child care, while men spent an average of 4 hours more on maintenance. Aside from the fact that Swedish men have substantially more free time than women, this difference means that some of women's labour-market-based entitlements (including pensions and sick and unemployment payments) are reduced by the unequal allocation of non-market work.[19] Adversely affected are the labour-market *careers* of women, especially their opportunities for advancement to supervisory and managerial posts.

Part-time work in North America has come to be associated with young people and women as cheap, flexible employees to populate the growing commercial service sector. Strong labour organizations in Sweden have weakened the drive for cheap labour and ensured that part-time working women receive proportionate wages and benefits. Part-time work in Sweden allows women to reduce their paid labour time to fulfil household and child-care responsibilities without the same penalties as North American women. Still, in Sweden this means that part-time women workers are heavily concentrated in the working class and have less prospect for new-middle-class work or even jobs in the capitalist-executive class, which continue to accrue to men. In the United States this appears to be less the case. Labour-force status has less impact on class throughout North America since part-time participants have a similar class profile to full-time workers.

LABOUR-FORCE STATUS AND GENDER ATTITUDE

Beside part-time paid work, the other distinctive status for women is "housewife." "Housewife" is a complex social category. To be a "housewife" is a *status* like that of a full-time or part-time worker. Obviously full-time and part-time workers also do housework (at least the women do), but a housewife does not currently have a paid location in the labour-force, nor is she unemployed, that is, currently seeking a job. Many housewives, however, do have an independent class experience based upon their past labour-force participation. A "housewife" is defined as a woman not currently in the paid labour-force, not retired, and not seeking employment, but living with a partner. In the class scheme used here, most housewives are assigned to a location based upon their labour-force experience, and a residual of individuals without that experience remain as "unclassified housewives."

As might be expected, housewives are very diverse. Ann Duffy's study of thirty housewives in southern Ontario provides an in-depth understanding of contemporary conditions creating this status.

Many considerations intersect to push or pull women into or out of paid employment – including whether the family can get by without a second income; how heavily the domestic responsibilities are; whether there are attractive child care alternatives; how women conceptualize their maternal responsibilities; whether husbands support their wives' paid employment; and whether manageable, attractive paid work is available. Which factors predominate depends on the individual woman's life circumstances (such as the presence of a new-born infant, a disabled child, or a helpful mother-in-law), the community or region in which she lives (which determines her employment opportunities and the availability of daycare) and such social and economic pressures as rates of inflation and unemployment.[20]

The conditions that produce housewives have been steadily changing since the end of the Second World War. There has been a consistent erosion of the subsistence aspects of domestic production and its substitution by commodities and commodified services. The decline of self-sufficiency has changed the role of housewives, increasing the need for wage labour as a way to pay for commodities.[21]

Pat Connelly, in her classic study *Last Hired, First Fired*, documents the changes experienced by married Canadian women in their labour-force involvement since the Second World War. She identifies a set of women she calls "an institutionalized inactive reserve army," who are housewives, different from the unemployed, to be called upon only in extraordinary times such as the labour shortages during the world wars.

The bulk of the institutionalized inactive reserve ... is made up of married women who are living with their husbands ... If the husband's wage is insufficient to buy the commodities necessary to meet a reasonable standard of living in Canada, then the housewife has two alternatives to prevent the family's standard of living from declining. First, she can intensify her labour in the home; that is, she can cook more and use fewer of the costly prepared foods, mend rather than buying new things; shop more carefully, and generally try to stretch her husband's wage. Second, she can seek employment outside the home if jobs are available.[22]

The forces at work within the contemporary economy, however, press in the direction of the second strategy since "productivity in the industrial sector has risen significantly relative to the productivity in the domestic sphere. As capitalism develops, the housewife has to work more hours in the home to make up for one hour spent in producing wage goods."[23]

Pressures like those identified by Connelly move women from the status of housewives in the "institutionalized inactive reserve army" into some segment of the active labour-force. These segments include full-time employment, part-time employment, or unemployment (seeking work), thus decreasing the share of married women with the status of housewife. Pat and Hugh Armstrong have brought an interesting perspective to these developments. Beginning with the observation that married women have always worked but mainly in the household where they could

produce food, sew clothes, do laundry, take on boarders or do other domestic chores, without selling their ability to work for a wage ... women were supporting their own reproduction in a way that allowed them to combine this work with the labour they had little chance of escaping – childbearing and caring responsibilities ... Instead of seeing women's domestic work as substituting for the wage, we should be seeing the wage as what becomes necessary when, like men, they have no alternative means of providing for their own needs.[24]

Such transformations in the conditions of women's domestic work, the Armstrongs anticipate, will vary by class.

What effect does one's labour-force status have on the way an individual thinks about gender? Table 8.7 gives the scores on the four gender issues discussed earlier for the various statuses available from each of the national surveys. As previously noted, not all the countries included a full range of statuses. To begin with Canada, the most feminist are women employed full time and the least, men who work part time (20–34 hours worked). Canadian men cluster very closely together, whether working full time or variations of part time and unemployed (only ranging between .47 and .66). Women are much more dispersed, with housewives the least progressive (very close to men), followed by shorter-hour part-timers, longer-hour part-timers, then the unemployed, and, of course, full-timers (with the women's range from .62 to 1.10). Men are more homogeneous in their gender attitudes than are women, who tend to have a wider range of views differing quite substantially from housewives to full-time employees.

Earlier research on a sample of American women by Eric Plutzer

Table 8.7
Gender-Attitude Scale[a] by Status, Sex, and Nation

Status	United States		Canada		Norway		Sweden	
	Women	Men	Women	Men	Women	Men	Women	Men
Full-time	.68	.38	1.10	.52	1.33	.78	1.30	.85
	(455)	(650)	(509)	(899)	(281)	(892)	(220)	(489)
Part-time	.58	.42	.84*	.47	1.13*	1.11*	1.17	.98
(20–34)	(103)	(47)	(146)	(68)	(204)	(57)	(158)	(29)
Part-time	.41*	.34	.67*	.66	.98*	.81	1.23	.79
(1–19)	(42)	(15)	(72)	(29)	(132)	(25)	(66)	(52)
Unemployed	1.02*	.38	.96*	.54	1.04*	.69	na	na
	(41)	(15)	(208)	(273)	(171)	(170)		
Housewives	.41*	na	.62*	na	.98*	na	na	na
	(138)		(328)		(310)			

[a] See Table 7.6.
* Difference from mean scores of full-time employees significant at .05 level of confidence or better.

found a fairly small, but consistent, effect of working life (measured by present participation in the labour-force, whether the respondent ever worked, number of hours worked, and their share of the family income) on support for feminism, especially concerning attitudes towards traditional gender roles at the workplace and responsibilities in the family.[25] Our results support these findings but also make contrasts with American men and the much greater variations by work-life statuses in the other three countries.

In the United States there is low overall variation, with the exception of unemployed women. The most progressive men are long-time part-timers. There is a gap between housewives and women working full time in the United States, but it is not nearly as great as in Canada or Norway, where housewives have also been surveyed. In all the countries there is a large gap between men and women working full time, ranging between .30 in the United States and .58 in Canada. Sweden tends to have the most feminist women, closely followed by Norway. In Norway there is more variation, in part because more statuses were surveyed. Still, women working full time lead the way and short-hour part-timers are the least progressive, tied with housewives. In Norway there is a gap among the women working part time, with those working under 20 hours per week considerably less progressive than those working 20 hours or more.

Our results support the general proposition that the greater women's labour-force attachment, the more feminist their attitudes. This is especially true for housewives, who have the least feminist attitudes, and women who work full time in the paid labour force, who have the most. Unemployed women (that is, those seeking work) also have strongly feminist attitudes, typically even more so than women who work part time. Several explanations consistent with our findings have been offered by Ethel Klein in her book *Gender Politics*. She argues that women's labour-force experience shows women that they are capable of doing traditional men's jobs, thus undercutting stereotypes; that financial independence arising from earning incomes demonstrates to women the prospect of breaking traditional roles; and that the work world's discriminatory practices confront working women more directly than housewives.[26]

Each of these experiences makes feminist propositions more meaningful for women, whereas men have a much more uniform set of attitudes, less directly influenced by their material circumstances in the labour force (as opposed to those mediated through their wives, as we will see).

The attitudes of both men and women towards gender issues are influenced by their economic clout, as measured by the share of income they contribute to their household and their status in the labour-force. The more women contribute economically to the household, the more likely they will have progressive ideas about women *and* the greater the likelihood their spouses will also have progressive attitudes. The greater a woman's attachment to the labour-force, the more progressive her attitudes toward feminist issues. For men, the opposite is the case. Men whose labour-force attachment is full-time have the least progressive attitudes towards feminist issues. The notion is supported that some men feel threatened by women working full time and that women working full time in the labour-force feel the need to struggle.

CLASS OF HOUSEHOLD

Our purpose here is to determine the implications various types of households have for women's labour-force participation and household responsibilities. We argue that our typologies allow us to examine the household as a unit of analysis rather than rely only on individuals isolated from families. Concerning the particularly thorny issue of women's class, the British Class Structure Project poses the following questions on the fundamental matter of the appropriate unit for class analysis: "Are social class locations most appropriately attributed to families, according to the labour market position of the 'head of household'; to individuals, as individuals, each according to his or her own position in the market; or by some composite measure that takes account of the possibly different market and work situations of the man and woman who make up a particular family grouping?"[27]

Following a detailed investigation utilizing the British data and a thorough assessment of the theoretical and methodological issues, they conclude:

Social classes comprise neither families nor individuals but individuals in families. It is for this reason, therefore, that the study of class is properly conducted at different levels of analysis. In this way the collective effects of women's limited access to economic and political power on the reproduction of positions within the structure can be explained, as well as the complex determination of life-chances accruing to individuals in conjugal units. That there is no all embracing scheme which captures the complexity of both processes perhaps need not worry us unduly.[28]

Most survey-based class studies – indeed, empirical class analysis in general – use only individuals as the unit of analysis. Class analysis based only on labour-force participation is also a limited perspective since, as argued, much of the actual experience of class occurs through the unit of the household or family. This is especially true for the key social category "housewife." As discussed earlier, to be a "housewife" is a status rather than a class. Housewives may experience the class structure directly through prior labour-force participation or indirectly through their spouses.

The appropriate unit of analysis for studies of class in households has been hotly contested. Is it the individual or family? If the family, then is it to be regarded as a homogeneous unit and are men and women given equal weight in determining a household's class, or should the "head of household" be determinant? What significance is to be attached to "cross-class" households?[29] We take the approach of examining households in terms of class but also note the sex of the class bearers. This means, for example, that instead of examining a household only as a mixed working – new-middle-class unit, we also distinguish the sex of each partner.

We offer a new way to describe households.[30] We focus on the class *composition* of the household, distinguishing by sex and concentrating on the effects for women in terms of their empowerment. We are interested, for instance, in whether the class of a woman's husband mediates her own class characteristics. Is a woman's life experience altered by the person with whom she is living? And does she alter his understanding of the world?

Since our interest is the relationship between men and women within households rather than the problematic of "cross-class" families, which is concerned with the classification of households by class in so-called direct and mediated class locations,[31] we need not be vexed by that classificatory debate. We are interested here in the relationship between two people in terms of their respective household contributions. The one aspect of the debate important for us is whether a person's current status (namely, "housewife") should be seen as "neutral," such that the class of the husband determines the class of household, or should we look into the labour-force career of the woman to determine her class? Generally, we use the woman's career as determinant of class location, contending that women's labour-market experience has a bearing on their empowerment. In some instances, the current status of housewife must be invoked. It is used, however, not in an "invisible" way by dissolving into the husband's class, but as a specific status to be interpreted.

Table 8.8 provides the national breakdowns for four of the main household-class combinations. It distinguishes between men and women within these households in terms of their relative contribution to the income of the households. Unconventional situations are used because they best reveal households where women have the greatest economic equality. Recall that unconventional households are those in which the woman earns half or more of the family income.

The patterns, as shown in Table 8.8, are very consistent across the four countries for both sexes. There are fewer unconventional households if the man is new middle class, and an increase if he is working class. For women there are more unconventional households when she is new middle class and a decrease when she is working class. The situations contrasted here focus first on households that have a new-middle-class man with a working-class woman, comparing them to households where both are working class. The second comparison is between households consisting of a new-middle-class woman with a working-class man, compared to households where both are middle class. By altering the sex of the various class combinations rather different results occur.

Generally, the household arrangements producing the least conventional patterns for spouse's relative income occur when the man is working class and the woman is new middle class. In these households women are empowered. The country with the most unconven-

Table 8.8

Household Class by Spouse's Relative Income by Nation (per cent of the active labour force with unconventional households ˜)

As Reported by:	Both Working (1)	Man Middle/ Woman Working (2)	Diff.* (1–2)	Both Middle (3)	Woman Middle/ Man Working (4)	Diff. (3–4)
WOMEN						
United States	36	17	+19*	33	42	−9
Canada	32	23	+9	7	55	−48*
Norway	26	11	+15*	20	30	−10
Sweden	41	28	+13*	32	55	−23
MEN						
United States	14	11	+3	46	56	−10
Canada	32	20	+12	39	56	−17
Norway	38	22	+16*	44	71	−27*
Sweden	63	45	+18*	44	89	−45*

˜ Unconventional households occur when the woman earns half or more of the family income. Differences are percentage-point differences from one column to the next.

A − sign indicates a decline in the percentage-point difference for unconventional households, and a + sign an increase.

* Differences between columns are significant at .05 level of confidence or better.

tional households is Sweden, mainly because women tend to have incomes more equal to those of men. The country with the lowest level of unconventional households, for men is the United States. This occurs especially when both partners are working class or the woman is working class and the man new middle class. When the woman is new middle class, there are fairly high rates of unconventional households, either if her partner is new middle class or especially if he is working class.

The differences between class combinations is generally greater than between countries, with the notable exception of Sweden. When the woman is new middle class, it tends to produce the most unconventional household. Even when both are working class, however, there is still a fairly strong tendency for unconventional households. Obviously, where the woman is a housewife, the situation is a conventional household (and only in Canada, Norway, and to a lesser extent the United States do the samples allow for systematic analysis involving housewives). As women increasingly enter the labour-force and demand greater equality of payment, there is a greater tendency for more unconventional households.

Does a woman's class of household impact upon her experience of labour-force disruptions? The answer is yes, especially when both partners are new middle class or when a working-class woman is attached to a new-middle-class man. The strongest impediments are in

Table 8.9
Women's Labour-Force Disruptions[a] by Household Class, Canada (per cent one or more career disruptions)

	Both Working	Man New Middle/ Women Working	Difference
	54	68	+14*
(N)	(245)	(126)	
	Both New Middle	Man Working/ Women Middle	
	66	51	−15
(N)	(49)	(76)	
Difference	+12	−17*	

[a] See Chart 8.A for a listing of disruptions. A + sign indicates an increase in the percentage of women with career disruptions; a negative sign indicates a decrease.
* Differences significant at .05 level of confidence or better.

looking for a job, accepting full-time work, and accepting transfers. If we compare the disruptions for women when both are working class to those for working-class women with new-middle-class men (+14 percentage points), the greatest differences are in looking for a job and accepting part-time work. When the sexes are reversed by class, it becomes much less confining for the woman (−17), especially in accepting full-time employment and looking for work. These same dimensions improve for women in the middle class if they are with a working-class man (−15). Finally, when both are new middle class, there is an increase (+12) for the woman over when both are working class. This time the woman's largest disruption difference is over changing jobs, a finding that indicates a man's new-middle-class job takes precedence over a woman's of the same class. Among those currently in the labour-force, new-middle-class women attached to working-class men have the least disruption (but still over half), with the main difficulty being accepting a transfer.

Clearly, a woman's individual class position matters, but so too does the household class. The attitudes and experiences of women are influenced by their class situation, as is the strength of decision making they have been able to achieve within relationships.

GENDER ATTITUDES BY HOUSEHOLD CLASS

Typically, the literature on households and attitudes (which deals with class orientations) contends that a woman's class attitudes are

Table 8.10
Household Class and Gender Attitudes by Nation*

As Reported by:	Both Working (1)	Man Working/ Woman Middle (2)	Diff. (1–2)	Both Middle (3)	Woman Working/ Man Middle (4)	Diff. (3–4)
WOMEN						
United States	.57	.60	+.03	.97	.45	−.52*
Canada	.86	.83	−.03	.96	.95	−.01
Norway	1.12	1.56	+.44*	1.40	1.05	−.35*
Sweden	1.30	1.42	+.12	1.20	1.11	−.09
MEN						
United States	.38	.71	+.33	.54	.38	−.16
Canada	.57	.79	+.22	.84	.78	−.06
Norway	.90	1.04	+.14	1.01	.77	−.24
Sweden	.92	.83	−.09	.98	.90	−.08

A + sign indicates an increase in the gender index score (that is, more feminist attitudes); a − sign indicates a decrease.
* Differences are significant at .05 level of confidence or better.

shaped by her husband's class, at least in the United States and the United Kingdom. In Sweden there is some indication that a woman's own class has an independent effect. We alter two of the factors typical of the traditional literature. We examine gender attitudes instead of class attitudes and ask whether a wife's class affects her husband's attitudes. Table 8.10 compares the attitudes of various household-class combinations for four countries.

Women's class has a fairly consistent, but not universal, impact on men's gender attitudes. Everywhere but Sweden, when a middle-class woman is with a working-class man, compared to where both are working class, the man's inclination toward feminism rises. It falls everywhere when a working-class woman is combined with a new-middle-class man, compared to both being new middle class. Similar results occur for women, except in Canada, where there is almost no effect. Other results in the table indicate there is a general rise in support for feminism by both sexes, comparing homogeneous middle-class to working-class households. Whenever the man has greater class power, there tends to be a decline for feminism by *both* partners.

DOMESTIC TASKS AND HOUSEHOLD CLASS

Meg Luxton has shown some insights into the relationship between entering the paid labour force and the allocation of domestic labour between the sexes. Her study of households in Flin Flon, Manitoba, found that "when their paid work time and their domestic labour time are added together, the women doing both jobs put in about 12 hours more than full time housewives each week."[32] There were also key class differences in responses by men when their spouses entered the paid labour-force. According to Luxton, "the working class men did not increase the amount of time they spent on domestic labour on work days but on weekends they did half an hour more, spread over two days. In contrast, with one notable exception, the middle class men actually reduced the amount of time they spent on domestic labour when their wives took on paid work."[33] Class location, both of individuals and households, and its impact upon domestic arrangements have received relatively little systematic empirical attention.

Is there a difference in the sharing of household tasks based on the household class? When both partners work outside the home, working-class husbands appear to be somewhat more willing to share than are new-middle-class ones, especially when the woman is new middle class and the man working class. This suggests that new-middle-class women are better able to pressure their spouses into some greater household responsibilities than are working-class women.

The greatest sharing of tasks is among couples where both are working class or when the man is working class and the woman is new middle class. The least sharing occurs when the woman is a housewife, both in combination with a new-middle-class male and, to a lesser extent, a working-class man. When both partners are new middle class, there is some pressure towards sharing, as there is when the male is new middle class and the woman working class.

Table 8.11 shows that only in the situation where the woman is new middle class and her spouse working class (column 2) is there any significant sharing of tasks, especially so in Norway and Sweden. When the situation is reversed in the Nordic countries (that is, the woman is working class and the man new middle class, column 4), the woman's share of domestic tasks goes up.

Once again the results indicate that a woman's class power does influence the division of domestic responsibilities. Also evident from these results, however, is that combinations where both partners are of the same class continue to favour the man. Only when the woman has *more* class power is she able to translate that into relatively less domestic work (columns 1–2 and 3–2). When the man has more class power (column 4), women tend to have greater domestic burdens (in 10 out of 12 combinations).

Only the surveys for Norway and Canada permit combinations

Table 8.11
Household Class by Women's Share of Domestic Tasks[a]

	Both Working (1)	Man Working/ Woman Middle (2)	Diff.[b] (1–2)	Both Middle (3)	Woman Working/ Man Middle (4)	Diff. (3–4)
United States	83	74	−9	87	87	0
Canada	75	70	−5	88	86	−2
Norway	71	56	−15*	68	86	+18*
Sweden	81	54	−27*	78	85	+7
Other Differences	(1–3)	(2–4)		(3–2)	(1–4)	
United States	+4	+13		−13	+4	
Canada	+11*	+16*		−16*	+11*	
Norway	+3	+30*		−12	+15*	
Sweden	+4	+31*		−24	+4	

[a] Per cent of relationships where the woman does most of the majority of the household tasks. Most means 60 per cent or more; majority means at least three of five tasks.
[b] Differences are percentage-point differences from one column to the next. The differences are signed so that a − indicates a woman does less domestic work and a + means a greater share.
* Differences between household classes significant at .05 level of confidence or better.

involving housewives, but in both instances the share of women's responsibilities is overwhelming. Where the woman is working class and her spouse new middle class (column 4), there is also virtually universal agreement on the high degree of women's domestic responsibilities. When both partners are new middle class (column 3), there is some effect in the Nordic countries but little in North America.

Women in all classes and in all combinations of class households perform most of the domestic work. Class, however, does influence women's share of the domestic tasks, since they are able to utilize their economic power to effect some changes. There are some national effects, with Sweden and Norway more equitable than the United States. Canada occupies its usual median position. It is the *combined* effect of class and gender that best reveals the relative power of domestic partners.

The classes in Table 8.12 take into account the class composition of the household, using Canada as an illustration. Household types were discussed at the end of chapter 7. They are a combination of spouse's contribution to household income and the domestic division of labour. The most traditional types occur when a new-middle-class man lives with a working-class woman or both are middle class. The most likely situation for a transitional or modern relationship is in

Table 8.12
Household Types by Household Class, Canadian Women

	Both Working (1)	Man Working/ Woman Middle (2)	Diff.ᵃ (1–2)	Both Middle (3)	Woman Working/ Man Middle (4)	Diff. (3–4)
Traditional	64	50	−14*	78	78	0
Transitional	11	21	+10	9	9	0
Modern	25	30	+5	13	13	0
	100	100		100	100	
(N)	(243)	(72)		(48)	(124)	

Other Differences	(1–3)	(2–4)		(3–2)	(1–4)	
Traditional	+14	+28*		−28*	+14*	
Transitional	−2	−12*		+12	−2	
Modern	−12	−17*		+17*	−12*	

ᵃ Differences are percentage-point differences from one column to the next; a + sign is more and a − sign less.
* Differences between columns significant at .05 level of confidence or better.

households where the man is working class and the woman new middle class or both are working class. The greatest increase in traditional relations (+28 percentage points) occurs in mixed-class households when the sexes are reversed (column 2–4) and the greatest decline when the man is working class and the woman new middle class, compared to both middle class (column 3–2). As with household tasks, an increase in a woman's class power leads to a more modern household.

Table 8.12 reports only for Canadian women. Canadian men parallel their results except that men concentrate in the "transitional" type to the exclusion of "modern," and, unlike the women, where there is no difference, when both are middle class, the men are less traditional (+11 percentage points) than the combination of new-middle-class man and working-class woman. In other words, for middle-class Canadian men, having a working-class wife makes the relationship more traditional than having a new-middle-class wife.

Contrasting new-middle-class men's situation when they live with a working-class, compared to a new-middle-class, woman produces the expected results. The men are much less likely to be in traditional relationships and more likely to be transitional when their partners are new middle class than when they are working class. Exactly the same pattern emerges for working-class men when their partners are working class: they are then more traditional, but when their partners are new middle class, they tend to be transitional. Comparing men in relationships where both partners are working class, the United States is most traditional (84 per cent), with Norway (61 per cent) and Canada (59 per cent) between it and Sweden (36 per cent), which is the lowest. In Sweden 60 per cent of men in relationships where both are working class can be classified as transitional. Similarly, when the man is new middle class and the woman working class, 42 per cent of Swedish men are transitional. These results support our findings about more equitable incomes by sex in Sweden but the lack of a corresponding movement around domestic labour (which would make them modern).

We can comparatively identify the most progressive household-class types for women. These again occur when the man is working class and the woman new middle class. In Canada 30 per cent of women in this situation are modern, in the United States 26 per cent, and Norway 42 per cent. Unfortunately, there are too few cases in Sweden to analyse.[34] The least favourable configuration occurs when working-class women and new-middle-class men are together. These are primarily traditional households: 78 per cent in Canada, 80 per cent in the United States, 77 per cent in Norway, and 65 per cent in Sweden. Each is the highest share of traditional households for each category in all combinations. Clearly the class one brings into a household relationship strongly influences the combined distribution of economic power and allocation of domestic tasks.

GENDER ATTITUDES AND HOUSEHOLD TYPES

Do household relationships affect gender attitudes? Transitional men and women in all four countries are generally more progressive than men and women in traditional households on the gender index. "Modern" women, in turn, are considerably more progressive than those in transitional households. While there are not sufficient cases of "modern" men to analyse, it is clear that household type has a stronger influence on the gender-index scores of men (ranging from +.25 to +.55 for men) than of women, who are more marginally affected by the traditional to transitional shift. How people think about gender issues in general is influenced by their household arrangements.

We can also break the index down into one of its key components. When households are organized traditionally in terms of who brings the most income and does most of the domestic work, this is reflected in more conservative attitudes about what is the preferred family structure (more strongly so for men than women). As would

Table 8.13
Household Types by Gender-Attitude Index for Nation and Sex

Household Type[a]	United States	Canada	Norway	Sweden
		Women		
Traditional (1)	.45	.74	1.01	1.19
Transitional (2)	.61	.73	1.11	1.27
Modern (3)	.83	.96	1.36	1.28
Difference (1–2)[b]	+.16	−.01	+.10	+.08
Difference (2–3)	+.22*	+.23*	+.35*	+.01
		Men		
Traditional (1)	.26	.35	.77	.66
Transitional (2)	.56	.80	1.02	1.03
Difference (1–2)	+.30*	+.55*	+.25*	+.43*

[a] There are less than 50 cases of "modern" men in every country.
[b] The differences are in the gender index, with a + sign indicating an increase in feminist orientation and a − sign indicating a decrease.
* Differences significant at .05 level of confidence or better.

be expected, traditional households tend to support families where the husband is the principal breadwinner and the wife in charge of the house and children. In the United States (81 per cent of men and 71 per cent of women) and less so in Canada (74 per cent of men and 65 per cent of women), there is a close correspondence between the material conditions and attitudes. In the Nordic countries, however, about half of the men and women in these household arrangements do not assert that they are the "best" type of arrangements. Even within traditional families in Sweden and Norway, there is more of an openness to non-traditional households. Such openness, however, is even more pronounced in non-traditional households.

In discussing the future of family politics in the United States, Kathleen Gerson predicts, "A 'family gap' between people living in traditional versus non-traditional households may well become as important or more important than the much-heralded gender gap." By this she means that women with poor employment opportunities will seek to preserve traditional households where men provide the economic support, while women without such support will press for equality at home and work, thus creating two groups of women with opposed stakes in family politics.[35] Our evidence is that household types do indeed effect gender attitudes. This is in addition to the persistent sex (and national) differences already discussed. Households do have major effects for the individuals living within them.

EDUCATION AND GENDER ATTITUDES

One of the issues of special importance for postindustrial societies is
the role of education in preparing people for change. We have demonstrated that major changes are underway in gender relations
within the four nations under study. Of interest is whether education
has a liberating influence on attitudes towards gender issues. Davis
and Robinson conclude that "well-educated people tend to be less
favorable toward efforts to reduce gender inequality than less well-
educated people," thus supporting their "reproduction thesis" over
the "enlightenment thesis" whereby more education produces
greater awareness of equality for all. The "reproduction" argument
is that education leads to awareness but also acceptance of the inequality, so the better educated are "*less* favorable to intervention to
reduce inequality." Their results indicate a greater awareness or per-
ception of inequality with more education, but higher "acceptance"
of gender inequality. They speculate this "may be due to education's
emphasis on credentials rather than government intervention as the solution to group disadvantage," therefore the better educated are less
supportive of state-directed measures to reduce gender inequalities.[36]

We prefer a version of the reproduction thesis that specifically
takes the respondent's sex into account and sees women as potential
contenders for educated men's privileges. It appears that men with
post-secondary training in the United States, Sweden, and Canada
may well feel threatened by competition from more women in key
positions in a way that men without such training are not threatened.
We ask, Is there a relationship between level of educational attainment and the attitudes men and women have toward gender issues?
Table 8.14 indicates a strong correspondence.

Generally the higher the education level, the greater the feminist
sensitivity in each nation. The only exception is in the United States
for men between pre-secondary and secondary levels, where there is
a slight decline, although men with post-secondary training are more
progressive towards feminism than their less-educated counterparts.
These are relative statements, however, and U.S. post-secondary –
trained men are much less progressive than men elsewhere. Indeed,
all those from the United States are less progressive in their attitudes
in every category, with the exception of Canadian men who have not
graduated from secondary school.

Those most progressive towards gender issues are Norwegian
post-secondary women, followed by Swedish and Canadian post-
secondary women, with U.S. post-secondary women well back (even below the post-secondary Nordic men and Swedish secondary men).

Table 8.14
Gender-Attitude Index by Education, Nation, and Sex

	Pre-Secondary	Secondary	Post-Secondary
UNITED STATES			
Men	.36	.31	.46*
Women	.36	.60*	.78*
CANADA			
Men	.24	.50*	.60*
Women	.62	.93*	1.14*
NORWAY			
Men	.64	.77	.95*
Women	.87	1.16*	1.43*
SWEDEN			
Men	.75	.90	.93
Women	1.14	1.25	1.35

For sample sizes, see Table 8.15.

In all cases (except for men in the United States), the differences in mean scores between respondents with pre-secondary and post-secondary education are significant at .05 level of confidence or better.

* Indicate differences in mean scores of respondents across pre-secondary–secondary categories or secondary–post-secondary categories are significant at .05 level of confidence.

There is little variation by education on the "private patriarchy" issue of whether couples should share equally in housework and child care if both spouses work outside the home. There is, however, a more complex relationship between gender and education level on "public patriarchy" issues.

We now break the gender index into two of its key components. On the matter of the traditional family, whether it is better for the family if the husband is the principal breadwinner and the wife has primary responsibility for the home and children, there is a consistent increase in the degree of progressiveness with the level of educational attainment for both sexes in every country. Educational level has a positive influence on issues of private patriarchy.

There is a more complicated relationship between educational attainment and attitudes towards women in public power, at least for men. People were asked to respond to the statement that ideally there should be as many women as men in important positions in government and business. In the United States, Sweden, and Canada the most-educated men are the *least* progressive on this issue (in Norway there is little difference for men by level of education). Among American men, there is a steady *decline* in agreement on the issue of

Table 8.15
Progressive Attitudes toward Gender Issues by Education (percentage progressive)

	Pre-Secondary	Secondary	Post-Secondary	(N)
		Traditional Family[a]		
UNITED STATES				
Men	10	22*	35*	(749)
Women	19	36*	49*	(619)
CANADA				
Men	16	35*	47*	(1,228)
Women	27	45*	63*	(875)
NORWAY				
Men	36	49*	74*	(1,010)
Women	45	57*	82*	(660)
SWEDEN				
Men	39	57*	74*	(618)
Women	49	62*	82*	(475)
		As Many Women[a]		
UNITED STATES				
Men	63	53*	49	(743)
Women	56	63	62	(619)
CANADA				
Men	61	65	57*	(1,229)
Women	73	80	78	(874)
NORWAY				
Men	65	66	64	(1,007)
Women	76	82	85	(657)
SWEDEN				
Men	74	72	58*	(610)
Women	85	82	79	(473)

[a] See Table 7.5 for questions.
In all cases the differences in mean scores between respondents with pre-secondary and post-secondary education are significant at .05 level of confidence or better.
* Indicates differences across pre-secondary–secondary categories or secondary–post-secondary categories are significant at .05 level of confidence or better.

having as many women as men in power. Ironically, in the least-educated category, more men than women agree with the notion of expanding women's public power, but for the post-secondary category many more women than men support the idea. A similar phenomenon occurs for Swedish men, with support decreasing signifi-

Table 8.16
Education by Gender Index for Sex, Class, and Nation

	Women		Men	
	Working	New Middle	Working	New Middle
UNITED STATES				
Secondary	.61	.82	.28	.37
Post-secondary	.66	.95	.54	.48
Difference[a]	+.05	+.13	+.26*	+.11
CANADA				
Secondary	.95	.92	.51	.62
Post-secondary	1.16	1.11	.60	.82
Difference[a]	+.21*	+.19	+.09	+.20*
NORWAY				
Secondary	1.12	1.35	.79	.73
Post-secondary	1.42	1.52	.90	1.16
Difference[a]	+.30*	+.17	+.11	+.57*
SWEDEN				
Secondary	1.21	1.60	.92	.95
Post-secondary	1.42	1.26	1.04	.74
Difference[a]	+.21*	−.34	+.12	−.21

[a] Differences in the gender index with a + sign indicate an increase in feminist orientation, while a − sign indicates a decrease.
* Differences significant at .05 level of confidence or better.

cantly among the post-secondary group. There is also a slight decrease for Swedish women. In Canada, women change very little by education level, while men peak in agreement among the secondary level and drop below the support from pre-secondary – training level for the post-secondary category. In Norway there is little variation for men and a slight increase in support for the proposition from the more-educated women. Better-educated men seem threatened by attacks on public patriarchy.

As noted, there is a general tendency for more progressive gender attitudes as the level of education increases within each class. This certainly holds for Canada and Norway. In the United States this tendency generally holds (the exception being a decline of .11 from pre-secondary to secondary for working-class men). In Sweden the pattern holds for the working class but not the new middle class. For both sexes the new middle class with post-secondary training is less progressive in Sweden than those with less schooling by a fairly substantial margin. (These figures are based upon 40 cases of Swedish new-middle-class women with post-secondary training and 55 cases of men.) For both sexes in Sweden, the working class with post-secondary training is more progressive than the new middle class. (There are 91 cases of Swedish working-class men and 97 cases of women with post-secondary training.) Education, at least at the post-secondary level, does not have a progressive influence for the Swedish new middle class, although it does for the working class. For Sweden, at least, educated new-middle-class men *and* women seem to reject the notion of intervention to improve the power positions of women, while in all the other countries these same types of people are the most likely to call for such interventions.

For women in the United States, class has a greater impact on their gender attitudes at the secondary and post-secondary levels than does the increase from secondary to post-secondary training. For men from the United States, however, the shift in the level of formal training has more impact than class. For Canadian men, both class and education have similar, more progressive impacts, while for women, class has little effect, but level of education does make a difference.[37] In Norway there is a strong class impact for new-middle-class men, especially at the post-secondary level. For Norwegian women, both class and education have impacts of similar magnitudes. As discussed, the Swedish impact for post-secondary training in the new middle class is regressive (a decline of .30 for men and .16 for women, compared to the working class). Otherwise there is little class impact for men but a major progressive impact (+.39) for women at the secondary level of training.

Gender attitudes are altered by education in all countries, but not in a simple way. In Norway, and to a lesser extent in Canada and the United States, more education for middle-class men means they will be more progressive. In Sweden the pattern is reversed. Indeed, for both Sweden and the United States, working-class men with post-secondary schooling are more progressive than their new-middle-class counterparts. For women the positive effects of education and class are fairly consistent, with the notable exception again of Swedish new-middle-class women with post-secondary training. It should be kept in mind, however, that these Swedish women still score much higher than any category in the United States and Canada or even any category of men in Norway and Sweden.

There is no universal law that more education leads to more progressive gender attitudes. Sweden is a case in point. The educated middle class in Sweden, both men and women, backtrack on support for gender issues. This backtracking, however, is for issues of public patriarchy involving actions to increase women's powers in business and government. For issues of private patriarchy, no such reversal occurs. A closer examination of the question concerning having as many women as men in positions of power shows that post-secondary education has a negative impact for men in all four countries. We think this indicates a perceived threat by well-educated men who are competing for power positions in postindustrial societies. They are not likely to bow out of public power without a struggle, even if they are willing to concede some changes to traditional family structures.

CONCLUSION

The division of domestic responsibilities is intimately associated with people's relationship to the labour-force. For women, this has meant that these responsibilities have inhibited their paid working lives, while men have benefited both within the household by being re-lieved of an equitable responsibility for domestic work *and* within the paid labour force, where they have been advantaged over women burdened by their household duties. Employers have used women's weaker labour-market positions to keep wages down, thus further weakening women's economic power within the household. This en-tire system is reinforced by patriarchal ideologies and practices that privilege men over women.

Still, there are important gender differences within this broad pat-tern based upon nation, class, and status. The more economic clout a woman has within the household, as determined by her relative in-come contribution, the more say she has in making key financial and budgetary decisions. This economic clout is closely associated with her class position, especially for a few capitalist-executive women but more notably for a substantial number of new-middle-class women. There are some key national differences that transcend class and gender. Overall, the Nordic countries are much more equitable in their household decision making than is the United States, with Can-ada suspended in the middle. This pattern holds across classes and between sexes, whether in conventional or unconventional house-holds, as indicated by spouse's income contribution.

In terms of actual practices, Swedish men stand out as the least progressive in sharing child-care responsibilities, while U.S. men re-semble Canadian men. Norwegian men are the most equitable. For household tasks, however, Swedish men become more involved and U.S. men are the least likely to share responsibilities. Nevertheless, women in all these countries overwhelmingly carry the greatest load of domestic responsibilities.

Men in the propertied classes have made the least contribution to domestic work, while new-middle-class women were able to com-mand greater sharing than those from other classes. Using the household class, it was demonstrated that most sharing occurs when both partners are working class or a new-middle-class woman is living with a working-class man. The least occurs when women are housewives. These general patterns were upheld for all four countries, but again the overwhelming share of domestic work falls to women in every case.

Household responsibilities were shown to disrupt women's labour-force participation in Canada, especially for those currently other than full-time workers. A majority of women in all age groups had some disruption. Number of children affected the experience of disruptions, but even women without children were much more likely to be disrupted in their careers than all types of men by a margin of 43 per cent to 17 per cent. These disruptions affected women from all classes, although working-class women were most severely impacted. Progressive households where there is a more equal sharing of household tasks have the twin effects of decreasing women's labour-force disruptions rather substantially (by −13 percentage points) and increasing men's disruptions by a like amount (+11 percentage points).

Canadian men in unconventional households have attitudes toward traditional families very similar to the progressive attitudes of Nordic men and women; indeed, men in these unconventional income positions (where their wives earn as much or more than they do) are more progressive in some ways than Canadian women. Canadian women, while more progressive than U.S. women, are not as progressive as Nordic women on a variety of gender-related issues. Canadian men in unconventional income situations are therefore a key bridgehead for progressive gender issues.

The employment status of men matters little to their gender attitudes, but status matters a great deal for women, especially since many women are housewives (the least progressive women's status), while women employed full time are the most progressive. Full-time working Canadian women more closely resemble Nordic women working full time in terms of their gender attitudes than do their U.S. counterparts. The greater a woman's attachment to the labour force, the more her attraction to feminism.

Women are empowered *inside* the home when their class power exceeds men's (as in households with working-class men and new-middle-class women). When partners are of the same class, there are different effects: both working class is more liberating for women than both new middle class. When both have new-middle-class careers, it is the man's that takes priority.

Women with relative class power have a positive influence on their partner's attitudes towards gender issues, and, inversely, men with relative class power have a reverse effect on women's attitudes. More powerful men tend to dampen women's feminist expectations.

Household-class combinations strongly influenced the attitudes of men toward traditional families, while men living with women working outside the home are much more progressive than those living with housewives. Housewives everywhere tend to be the least progressive women on gender issues. Again, men are more homogeneous in their views and women more diverse with respect to gender attitudes. The lack of unity on the part of women follows from their much more diverse statuses since some women obviously are housewives and others much more likely to be part-time workers, while men are concentrated in full-time status. At the foundation of the differences between men and women, however, is their radically distinct attachment to household responsibilities both on a day-to-day domestic level and at the broader level of careers. The basic gender difference in the intersection between domestic and paid work is fundamental to an understanding of work performed by both sexes.

So, how are families changing? We summarized the changes in income and domestic labour contributions into household types. For women we were able to examine three types: "traditional," where the woman does most of the domestic work and the man brings in most of the money; "transitional," where the woman contributes equally to the household income but there is no reciprocity in men's contribution to domestic labour; and "modern," where there is basic equality in both income and domestic work. It was more difficult to identify "modern" men because they are more reluctant than women to state that their wives contributed as much financially as they do. Still, it was possible to highlight some directions of change. The most modern relationships occur when a working-class man is with a new-middle-class woman, followed by homogeneous working-class families.

Men's gender attitudes are especially influenced by household types, with a major increase in support for feminist issues in all four countries in transitional situations. Women tend to be more strongly influenced by modern arrangements when they are most feminist.

Households are complex sites, where class and gender relations meet to mediate a variety of demands on an individual's behaviour and attitudes. These demands greatly influence the way Nordic and North American women experience the world since households tend to weaken their powers while enhancing men's. We have shown that the more women are attached to the labour force, the more progressive they are on feminist issues and the more influence they exert on their husbands' ideas and – however gradually – their practices in sharing domestic responsibilities. Age and, to some extent, education appear to work toward a more favourable approach to feminist issues, but the way remains contested by traditional men, who have the most power to lose. Before equality can be achieved in the paid labour-force, much more attention to equality in the domestic sphere will be required. The point will not only be to change the attitudes of men but their domestic practices. The ongoing sites of struggle include the workplace and the household. In every case, it is the combination of class and gender factors that mediates the practice of inequality.

9 Social Cleavages and the Political Cultures of Gender

Feminism is about more than class relations or even domestic powers; it is about multiple forms of relations of ruling. As argued earlier, patriarchy is about senior males ruling within families and privileging male powers in public life. Here we explore how people's attitudes about gender relations interact with social cleavages based on race and ethnicity and territorial divisions based on region and nation. Gender is an essential element in how people think about themselves and define what they believe to be "right, just, and proper." No resistance ever takes place in a social vacuum. As often as not, identities, loyalties, and interests are based on race, sex, region, and nation. Gender struggles, we will argue, are conditioned by the particular cultures associated with the other major cleavages that have shaped the development of North America, especially the French-English division in Canada and race and region in the United States.

In the previous two chapters we have sought explanations for variations in gender attitudes within the household, in women's labour-force attachments, and in cross-class households. But there are other sets of influences beyond individuals and households that include historical and organizational forms which are also salient for influencing people's cultures and experiences. As Patricia Armstrong and Patricia Connelly have reminded us, "Feminists have become more aware of the contradictory nature of their struggles and of the different consequences for women in different classes, in different racial and ethnic groups and in different regions of the country and of

Table 9.1
Gender Attitudes of the Employed Labour Force by Country, Age, and Sex[a]

Panel A	United States	Canada	Norway	Sweden
Total	.50	.72	.95	1.02
Men	.38	.51	.80	.85
Women	.64	1.01	1.19	1.24
Difference	+.26*	+.50*	+.39*	+.39*
(N)	(1,327)	(2,086)	(1,639)	(1,092)

Panel B	United States		Canada		Norway		Sweden	
Age & Sex	Men	Women	Men	Women	Men	Women	Men	Women
14–29	.62	.91	.75	1.15	.89	1.31	.97	1.49
30–49	.31	.63	.45	1.00	.85	1.22	.90	1.21
50+	.12	.38	.27	.73	.63	.94	.65	.97

[a] The gender-attitude index is defined in chapter 7 by a combination of four questions. Its maximum value is 2.0.
* Differences in mean scores are significant at .05 level of confidence or better.

the world."[1] We are already aware of the strong country differences in gender attitudes (see Table 9.1). There is a distinct spectrum of views, consistent for both men and women across each age group in all four countries included here. The United States is the least progressive in its gender scores; Sweden is the most progressive. In all four countries the differences between the sexes are pronounced.

Just as there is a "universal" sex difference in these countries, so too is there a consistent pattern by age. Younger people are much more progressive on gender issues than older cohorts.[2] In the Nordic countries the main division is between the old and middle-aged, while in the United States the split is between the young and middle-aged, suggesting a sex gap in when feminist attitudes were accepted by different generations. In Canada the split is between middle-aged and older women but for men between the youngest and middle-aged. The age breakdowns indicate that the influence of feminist ideologies came earlier in the Nordic countries than in North America. Whereas in North America the middle-aged are still quite traditional, in the Nordic countries only the oldest group is distinctively less progressive, but still slightly more so than the youngest Americans.

Having established such clear national differences, our purpose here is to examine intranational patterns along the lines identified by Armstrong and Connelly. We should expect to find fairly strong interactions since, as they tell us, the feminist literature reports "com-

Table 9.2
Gender Attitudes of the Employed Labour Force by Sex, Country, Class, and Union

	Women				Men			
	United States	Canada	Norway	Sweden	United States	Canada	Norway	Sweden
CLASS								
Working	.59	1.02	1.14	1.25	.39	.50	.79	.90
Middle	.88	1.03	1.40	1.33	.46	.69	.84	.80
Difference	+.29*	+.01	+.26*	+.08	+.07	+.19*	+.05	−.10
UNION[a]								
Never union	.62	.92	1.09	1.16	.46	.52	.70	.55
Union	.70	1.11	1.24	1.25	.30	.50	.85	.90
Difference	+.08	+.19*	+.15*	+.09	−.16*	−.02	+.15	+.35*
CLASS & UNION								
Working/Never	.57	.92	1.10	1.20	.52	.58	.58	.66[b]
Working/Union	.63	1.11	1.15	1.26	.29	.46	.84	.92
Difference	+.06	+.19*	+.05	+.06	−.23*	−.12	+.26*	+.26

[a] "Union" includes people who are currently or have ever been union members.
[b] Only 27 cases; all others over 50 cases.
* Differences are significant at .05 level of confidence or better.

plex and often contradictory processes that provide the basis for action, raising clues for a more systematic understanding of how gender, class, race/ethnicity, region/nation and ideology intersect."[3]

We will build upon the questions posed earlier about how sex and class divide the feminist project and add new questions concerning race/ethnicity and region/nation. We have come to expect new-middle-class women to be the leading feminists. Women in all four countries from the new middle class identified in Table 9.2 are indeed more progressive than those from the working class. When we find the paradoxical situation where subordinate groups such as working-class women, Québécois women, immigrant women, or women of colour are especially progressive in their gender attitudes, we must wonder about the complexity of gender resistance. Of particular interest is how the union movement influences the women's movement.

Traditionally, unions have represented the industrial, male working class. Often their interests were tied to exclusionary practices based on the maintenance of "the family wage" and a wife "at home." The postindustrial service economy has seen a rapid unionization of women, including an extension of union organization to the new middle class. The "old" union movement and "new" union movement have promoted different ideologies about gender relations.

Unions can either retard or promote women's interests, so we should not expect universal answers to the question of how unions influence gender attitudes. Instead, we should seek to find the conditions under which there are either progressive or regressive influences and address them with a better- informed understanding.

Are class and gender issues at odds? The labour movement has had different effects on the women's movement. For women, most especially from the new middle class, union experience enhances feminist attitudes. Those with union experience are more progressive than those without, a finding consistent for women in both the working and new middle classes. Women's greater support for feminist issues as a result of being in the union movement may follow from frustrations with patriarchal attitudes in the unions or stem from empowerment gained through experiences facilitated by the unions. We can only demonstrate the association, not the cause.

Nordic women are more feminist in our terms, but the leading edge is clearly found among the unionized new middle class, also the leading category in the United States. In Canada this is less clearly the case since there is a strong similarity with the unionized working class, a puzzle to which we return shortly.

For men a very complex set of relations are evident. In the Nordic countries, unionized men in both the working and new middle classes are fairly progressive. Men outside the union movement, however, are less progressive. In North America, unions have a regressive effect on men's gender attitudes, particularly in the United States.

Men, especially in North America, contradict at least one of each of the patterns followed by women. Within the North American labour movement, there is a large sex difference in both the working class and the new middle class. This sex split is equally great in both Canada and the United States. It is difficult to examine the union effect in a Nordic context since there are so few cases of non-union members, reflecting the hegemony of the labour movement in those countries. There are simply not enough cases of the new middle class in the Nordic countries without union experience to analyse (only 58 men *and* women combined in Norway and a total of 18 in Sweden). In North America, however, there is good reason to examine the union effect. There is a departure in North America of the pattern found for women whereby union experience has a progressive influence. Men with union experience are less progressive than those outside the labour movement. This phenomenon should be explored and explained.

The heterogeneity of North America, moreover, extends beyond the role of organized labour to issues of territory and ancestry. The most basic cleavages shaping their respective histories are the French-English divide in Canada and the racial division in the United States. The French-English difference has a territorial base founded in the provincial status of Quebec that has been accentuated over time, whereas the territorial quality of the U.S. racial difference (North-South) has been diminished by massive migrations of blacks to the North.

Internal heterogeneity has long been a factor invoked to account for the peculiar class politics of North America. Immigration, mixed ancestries, and regional settlement patterns over vast territories have distinguished the "new world" North America from the "old world" of Europe, including the Nordic region. Persistent as an issue in the United States is the division by race (especially blacks, Hispanics, and Asians) and in Canada the special place of Quebec as a distinct social formation and the on-going practice of immigration from diverse sources. Ironically, as we enter the 1990s, an important issue for Europe has become the international movements of people, especially a mixing of people with different ancestries, and the reassertion of various nationalisms. Europeans may benefit by understanding the North American diversity.

Specifically for North America, we will be asking whether ethnicity, immigration, race, and region divide the working class and the new middle class on gender issues. Are these key social cleavages important for the gender orientations of the two main classes and the sexes in North America? We are especially interested in knowing whether distinctive cleavages exist among women by class, ancestry, region, and union membership. Are there different feminisms that follow the lines of social cleavages in North America or is there a common feminism?

ETHNICITY IN CANADA

Class, gender, and ethnicity provide three principal pillars of social differentiation in Canada. Analytically, it is the relationship among these divisions that proves most challenging. Danielle Juteau-Lee and Barbara Roberts claim, "One of the most crucial questions in ethnic and women's studies is the relation between class, sex and 'ethnicity.' In Canada these have been among the crucial determinants of people's experiences ... But there is very little extant on the three factors taken together."[4] Traditionally, analysts have focused upon the way gender and ethnicity divide classes in the sense of fragmenting opposition to the dominant powers in a society. More recent formulations, however, indicate a more complex reality. As Floya Anthias and Nira Yuval-Davis tell us, "As well as ethnic and gender divisions being used for class goals, class divisions can provide the material conditions for ethnic and gender groups, for these will give unequal access to economic resources ... [which] structure their relationship to each other and give differential political power to different groups."[5]

The way that class and ethnicity interact has long been the marquee issue in Canadian social sciences, especially as highlighted by John Porter's famous study *The Vertical Mosaic*, in which he argued that these two aspects of Canadian social life had special importance in their combination.[6] Much less attention has been paid, however, to the combination of class, ethnicity, and sex.[7] We ask an even more neglected question. Do men and women of different ancestries have the same gender attitudes?

To begin with the basics, do ancestry characteristics still affect Canadian work-life experiences? Yes.[8] One indicator of ancestry is language, the battleground for much of Canadian politics.[9] When the language of the interview is used as an indicator, there is a major difference in the respective class profiles. Of those interviewed in English, 26 per cent are in the new middle class and 12 per cent in the old middle class, compared to 20 and 6 per cent respectively for the French group. In the working class, we find 68 per cent of the French-speaking, compared to 56 per cent of the English-speaking. Such results suggest a persistent class difference between the two official language groups in Canada, supporting in a general way the conclusions reached by Porter for the 1950s. What Porter (and most other analysts of ancestry) failed to ask, however, is whether sex structures the relationship between class and ancestry. We argue that sex does have an important effect on how backgrounds relate to people's thinking about the politics of gender.

The effects of ethnic ancestry for the working class are the most telling. Both men and women with French ethnic origins are over-represented in the working class. Men of French ancestry are much more likely to be in the working class (60 per cent) than those of British (47 per cent) or other European (45 per cent) origins. European (25 per cent) and British (30 per cent) women are over-represented in the new middle class, compared to French women (17 per cent).

In a direct contrast between the British and French, Canada's two "founding" groups, women have the most obvious differences, concentrating British women in the new middle class and a higher share of French women in the working class (78 per cent) compared to the British (64 per cent). A similar gap separates working-class French and English men, but the difference is spread over each of the other classes, with the greatest share falling to the old middle class. The fact that so few French men are in the old middle class reflects the rapid decline of agriculture in Quebec and the demise of the traditionally independent professions. The French of both sexes are now the most proletarianized of the major ancestry groups, the least likely to be working on their own account, and among the least likely to be directing the work of others. The British men and women, on the other hand, are most likely to be directing others. Is Canada still characterized as a "vertical mosaic" whereby class and ethnicity intersect in ways that reproduce stratification? The answer would have to be yes, especially for French Canadians.

Peter Li concludes his recent study *Ethnic Inequality in a Class Society* by calling for research on the way "ethnicity and race serve as a basis of fractionalizing the class structure."[10] Nearly all of the work on ethnic stratification in Canada has focused on issues of access to occupations, income, or education. There is little account of sex or gender. In Li's case, for example, sex/gender enters his analysis only as something "to be controlled for" rather than as a category of analysis. We seek to move beyond the traditional problematic by including sex as an analytical category, examining gender attitudes, and looking at the classes and unions as actors in the process of producing these attitudes.

Most of the feminist literature on class, ethnicity, and gender has focused upon participation in the labour market or on divisions of domestic responsibilities. Our concern here is with gender attitudes by sex and ethnicity within the context of work. Still, we can see how the findings that emerge from the participation literature are reflected in gender attitudes. Anthias and Yuval-Davis say, "We would suggest that within Western societies, gender divisions are more important for women than ethnic divisions in terms of labour market subordination. In employment terms, migrant or ethnic women are usually closer to the female population as a whole than to ethnic men in the type of wage-labour performed."[11] Our gender attitude results for Canada provide some support for such a position. Women of European origin are more similar to those of British origin than to European men (Table 9.3).

Our special interest is in the "chemistry" of the combined effects of class, sex, and ethnicity for the way people think about gender issues. By using the gender index we can chart the combined effects for the two major classes by sex. The largest cleavage is between those of French ancestry and all others, including those of British and European origins. The findings about the French reinforce

Table 9.3
Gender Attitudes in Canada for Ethnicity by Sex, Class, and Union

Panel A	French	British	European	Diff. from French British	European
Total	.81	.71	.60	−.10*	−.21*
Men	.62	.53	.44	−.09	−.18*
Women	1.03	.87	.74	−.16*	−.29*
(N)	(689)	(1,040)	(642)		

	Women			Men		
Panel B	French	British	European	French	British	European
CLASS						
Working	1.14	.85	.84	.57	.52	.42
New Middle	.91ᵃ	1.03	.86	.84	.66	.68
Difference	−.23	+.18*	+.02	+.27*	+.14	+.26*
UNION						
Never	.88	.82	.79	.58	.49	.51
Union	1.32	1.00	.86	.66	.52	.39
Difference	+.44*	+.18*	+.07	+.08	+.03	−.12
CLASS & UNION						
Working/Never	.92	.78	.83	.48	.59	.59
Working/Union	1.33	.93	.86	.61	.50	.31
Difference	+.41*	+.15	+.03	+.13	−.09	−.28

ᵃ Only 44 cases; all others over 50 cases.

* Differences are significant at .05 level of confidence or better.

those concerning the strength of the working class and unions for women. The interesting comparison in terms of "unpacking" the "Rest of Canada" is the contrast between the British and Europeans.

For women, there is little class effect for the Europeans, but members of the British new middle class clearly are more feminist than their working-class counterparts. The same pattern holds for the effects of unionization alone and together with the working class. The effects of each factor are small for the European women but substantial for the British. It is with the men that we gain greater insight into who are the bearers of patriarchy. For British men unionization has little influence, but there is a strong negative impact for European men. Outside the unions there is virtually no difference between the two types of men. Inside the unions, however, the differences are substantial for the working class (.19). For both there is some negative union and working-class effect, very much different from the

French, but the influences of class and union are much smaller for British than European men. Again reinforcing an earlier finding, French working-class men outside the union movement are less progressive than either the British or Europeans.

These results help us address the issue of the class base for feminism in Canada. The evidence suggest that no class differences appear for European women, but a fairly striking contrast appears for the two charter groups. British middle-class women, and French working-class women are not only the most progressive but each is also relatively large in size.

The results suggest that we can expect the greatest pressure for gender reforms from French working-class women and from British-origin new-middle-class women, and the greatest resistance from working-class men of all three backgrounds. The large gap between men and women in the working class for the French and in both classes for the British suggests potential sites for gender conflict but could also be interpreted for the French as providing a larger pool of progressive middle-class men from which to draw allies. Major differences of opinion over feminist issues exist between the sexes across ethnicities.

Traditional ethnic analysis in Canada leaves a puzzle in seeking to account for the social practices that produce such differences in attitudes toward feminist issues. To help explain them, we must shift our unit of analysis from ethnicity to nation, whereby the Québécois are understood as a distinct social formation.

THE CANADIAN-QUÉBÉCOIS EXPERIENCE

At least until the 1980s, the Canadian labour movement was not especially noted for its progressive stance on women's issues. As Grace Hartman, long-time president of the Canadian Union of Public Employees, said in the late 1970s, "It is an indisputable fact that unions have not done as much for working women as they could have. With some exceptions they have not led the fight for improved day care, maternity leaves with pay, abortion on demand, and equal pay for equal value. These are regarded as low priority items by unions which tend to reflect male values."[12] Like so much else in Canada, however, there are two realities. While Hartman's characterization rings true for the English-language trade union movement, in Quebec something very different was occurring. The Quebec trade union movement since the early 1970s was at the centre of a complex set of forces and changes. It had only recently broken from the conservatism of confessional unionism and was caught in the swirl of an emerging nationalism, all of which give a very different context to the development of feminism within Quebec.

Their own language, culture, institutions, and political state, in which English-speakers are a small minority, make the Québécois a distinct society within Canada. As a result, feminism in Quebec has tended to evolve separately from English Canada, especially since the women's movement was associated with nationalism in the 1970s and influenced by developments in France during the 1980s.[13] The Quebec trade union movement also has a distinctive history and traditions, forming a special relationship with the women's movement.

More than in English Canada, the development of the Quebec labour movement has succeeded in placing feminist issues on the social agenda. Most notable has been the Confederation des syndicats nationaux (CSN), established in 1960 to replace the Catholic Confederation of Labour (1921–60). Alongside the CSN, teachers' and nurses' unions have led the way for women in the Quebec labour movement. Quebec had the highest rate of women's unionization in the country by 1980 (31 per cent compared to the national average of 24 per cent), while men were virtually identical to the national average (39 per cent). As a result, 34 per cent of Quebec's union members were women.[14] According to Hélène David, women's issues became important in the Quebec union movement in the mid-1970s, and committees supporting women's rights were included in the trade unions since 1976.[15] Most notable was the Federation des affaires sociales (FAS) with 450 unions and 80,000 members, 72 per cent of them women. FAS launched its influential women's committee in 1980.[16] Heather Jon Maroney notes that "the Quebec federations" concern with the global aspects of 'la condition féminine' is exceptional."[17] Similarly, William Coleman contends that "the trade unions in Quebec played a pivotal role in bringing sex issues out from under the cover of nationalist struggles."[18]

The Québécois women's movement has been led from the working class rather than the new middle class. This is evident in our data and may in part be explained by the relatively small number of French new-middle-class women as well as the extraordinary concentration of French women in the working class. Moreover, the Quebec women's movement has been organized linguistically by the Federation des femmes du Québéc rather than from the federal level.

A direct comparison of the Québécois and the rest of Canada on gender attitudes demonstrates that a clear cleavage exists, especially between the women (a difference of .21). Our data allow us to take

Table 9.4
Gender Attitudes in Canada for Québécois by Sex, Class, and Union

Panel A	Québécois[a]	Rest of Canada	Difference
Total	.81	.67	+.14*
Men	.60	.50	+.10
Women	1.05	.84	+.21*
(N)	(517)	(1,937)	

	Women		Men	
Panel B	Québécois	Rest of Canada	Québécois	Rest of Canada
CLASS				
Working	1.19	.88	.58	.49
New middle	1.07[b]	.92	.69	.68
Difference	−.12	+.04	+.11	+.19*
UNION				
Never union	.90	.81	.45	.53
Union	1.40	.98	.69	.45
Difference	+.50*	+.17*	+.24*	−.08
CLASS & UNION				
Working/Never	.96	.81	.39[c]	.66
Working/Union	1.36	.97	.66	.40
Difference	+.40*	+.16*	+.27	−.26*

[a] Québécois are defined as of French ethnic origin living in Quebec.
[b] Only 30 cases; all other over 50 cases unless noted.
[c] Only 40 cases.
* Differences are significant at .05 level of confidence or better.

advantage of the fact that the labour movement and women's movements have had a distinctive combination in Quebec, different from that found in the rest of North America.

Several features should be pointed out. The first is a class issue. Typically the new middle class is more progressive on gender issues than the working class. For the Québécois, however, working-class women are more progressive than women from the new middle class. Moreover, Québécois working-class women are much more progressive (.31) than those in the rest of Canada. What about the effect of unionization? Among the non-unionized, there is little difference between Québécois women and those from the rest of Canada (.09). But the union effect for Québécois women is much larger (+.50) than the effect in the rest of Canada (+.17). As a result, there is a tremendous difference between Québécois union women and union women in the rest of Canada (.42 difference). A similar difference exists for women in the working class with union experience

(.39). Feminism has had a clear impact on working-class Québécois women and the union movement. Second-wave feminism has much deeper roots in the working class and labour movement in Quebec than outside it.

A telling interview with Madeleine Parent, a long-time union organizer in the Quebec textile industry and leading francophone feminist, gives some context to new-middle-class English feminism and working-class French feminism. She recounts her experience with the National Action Committee (NAC) on the Status of Women in Ottawa, the main federal forum where French- and English-speaking women come together.

I went to the NAC's founding meeting in 1972. I knew that some professional women, and others who were well-off but socially aware feminists, were planning to organize in order to put forward changes in our sexist laws ... I felt that it was terribly important that a much broader spectrum of women be involved in this undertaking. I felt that working class women, blue collar women working in factories should also be there, as well as women from various minorities, so that our particular needs would be considered in the battle. It was important that working class women be a voice in that movement.

When asked how this has worked out in practice, she replied: "Well, it is not without its tensions and difficulties. Certain women who are well-educated and who are favoured by their economic conditions, tend to assume a leadership role more easily ... it is not easy to bring blue collar working women into NAC."[19]

The francophone trade union movement, with strong feminist leaders like Madeleine Parent, gave the working-class women of Quebec a special encouragement that brought them up to or beyond the level of support for feminism more typical of new-middle-class women elsewhere. The Quebec feminist movement "took off" during the same time as the rise of democratic unions. The breadth of the women's movement in Quebec has included the working class since its beginnings and now has a strategic leadership role in representing other "popular groups," including minorities and native women.

What of the labour movement's influence on men's attitudes on gender issues? Men outside the labour movement are more progressive in the rest of Canada than in Quebec. In the rest of Canada, union men are less progressive than men outside the unions (−.08). But in Quebec the pattern is again reversed (+.24). Progressive gender effects are strongly indicated by the large effect for the unionized working class, which is even greater (.26) for the Québécois.

Outside the labour movement the working-class men in the rest of Canada are much more progressive (.27 difference). In the rest of Canada the labour movement is clearly conservative in its effects for men. This is not the case for women; they too are empowered, albeit not at the levels experienced by Québécois women.[20]

Quebec feminism has had a complex relationship with the national question; it has been both spurred and shunned by nationalism. Since the late 1960s a growing number of Québécois women became feminist and through the mid-1970s many of these worked in alliance with the nationalist Parti Québécois, helping them form a government in 1976. This was the heyday of Quebec feminism, when Lise Payette was minister for "la condition féminine." But the experience was a disappointment and Quebec feminists soured on the Parti Québécois, so much so that Payette refused to run for re-election in 1981. The PQ's second term in office (until 1985) was disillusioning for the women's movement, just as it was for the Quebec labour movement when the PQ in February 1983 entered into one of the most bitter confrontations in labour history with Quebec state employees, many of whom were women (nurses, teachers, and clerks).[21]

Isabella Bakker has argued that "the Quebec women's movement (as opposed to its English-speaking counterpart) was more conscious early on of the need to define its goals as explicitly political" because it had to resist subordinating itself to the national struggle.[22] The women's movement has had to direct its political actions at the subcentral level of government because in Canada so many of the issues effecting women are provincial in their jurisdiction, such as pay equity, education, health, and many labour-market policies.

We have evaluated the effects of unions on gender attitudes in Canada at the same time as posing a distinction specifically in terms of the "national question" that combines ethnicity and region. The Québécois – rest of Canada division is not only a regional split but represents two social formations with different organizations of class and gender because of distinctive labour and women's movements, each with its own internal relations. As our earlier findings would lead us to expect, Québécois working-class women are more progressive than their new-middle-class counterparts. But that is not the main story in terms of the labour movement, which has had a progressive effect for men and women of both main classes.

To summarize our findings, the Québécois tend to be more progressive on gender attitudes, but this is not universally the case (see Table 9.4). Québécois men with no attachment to organized labour are less progressive than their counterparts from the rest of Canada.

While organized labour has a progressive effect on gender attitudes in Quebec, this is not so for men from the rest of Canada. Women and Québécois men with union experience are all much more progressive. Union experience has been particularly strong in its impact on Québécois women. We can conclude that unionization has had an especially liberating effect for Québécois women but has also had a progressive impact for Québécois men. In "English Canada," unions have had a much more ambiguous influence, strengthening women's feminism but failing to bring their male members to a more progressive position on gender issues.

IMMIGRATION AND REGION IN CANADA

Having established a basic cleavage between the Québécois and the rest of Canada over the way class and unionization influence gender attitudes, we now seek to "unpack" the "rest of Canada," which itself is far from homogeneous. The primary social cleavages we examine are immigration and region.

Strongly associated with the issue of ethnicity in Canada has been the practice of immigration. Winnie Ng claims, "Immigrant women remain the 'muted shadows,' the silent partners of our society and the women's movement."[23] Others have argued they "suffer a triple oppression" as women, workers, and immigrants.[24]

Canada has been, and continues to be, a society built on immigration. Aside from the native peoples, all Canadians trace their roots outside. The French are the longest residents among those tracing their ancestry abroad. The British are next. There was steady immigrant recruitment through the immediate post–Second World War period (mid-1950s). It was in the postwar era that European immigration increased rapidly, building upon a base created in the first decade of this century. Since the seventies, larger immigrant flows have been from Asia and the Caribbean. As Frances Abele and Daiva Stasiulis have observed, "Feminist scholarship is beginning to expose the web of social relations that constitute both the class location and the practices of immigrant and minority women."[25]

Monica Boyd's analysis has been one of the few to treat sex as an analytical category with respect to immigrant status. She says her research, especially for immigrant women, "tempers the imagery of immigrant success and social equality" that promotes Canada as an "open society." Rather she "emphasizes the importance of birthplace and sex as factors underlying the Canadian mosaic."[26]

Since we are trying to "unpack" the rest of Canada, Table 9.5 reports

Table 9.5
Gender Attitudes in the Rest of Canada by Immigrant Status by Class,
Sex, and Union

Panel A	Native-Born[a]	Foreign-Born	Difference
Total	.69	.60	+.09
Men	.54	.32	+.22*
Women	.84	.88	−.04
(N)	(1,513)	(402)	

	Women		Men	
Panel B	Native-Born	Foreign-Born	Native-Born	Foreign-Born
CLASS				
Working	.85	1.04	.55	.23
New middle	.93	.89	.75	.43
Difference	+.08	−.15	+.20*	+.20
UNION				
Never union	.80	.88	.54	.45
Union	.96	1.09	.52	.23
Difference	+.16*	+.21	−.02	−.22
CLASS & UNION				
Working/Never	.78	1.00	.65	.64[c]
Working/Union	.95	1.08[b]	.49	.06
Difference	+.17*	+.08	−.16	−.58*

[a] Native-born includes only the non-Québécois; that is, the "rest of Canada"
born in Canada.
[b] Only 48 cases; all others over 50 unless noted.
[c] Only 26 cases.
* Differences are significant at .05 level of confidence or better.

only on immigrant status exclusive of the Québécois. At first glance
there is little overall difference between the native- and foreign-born,
but when sex is taken into account it becomes clear that there is little
difference among women (.04) but a large one among men (.22).[27]

The most notable feature for the women is that the foreign-born
resemble Québécois women in that the working class is more progressive than the new middle class. Moreover, foreign-born women
are even more positively influenced by unionization than are native-
born women, and these differences combine around the working
class and unionization.

While foreign-born women are slightly more progressive than
their native-born counterparts, the foreign-born men are decidedly
less progressive. There is an important qualification, however, since
this difference among men is large only inside the union movement

(.29); it is extremely large within the unionized working class, where the gap reaches enormous proportions (.43), producing the differences of −.58.

As we have come to expect, sex has a strong impact for all categories. Immigrant status itself has a strong impact, but it is radically different by sex since immigrant men are very traditional but immigrant women strongly progressive. This would indicate a difference of opinion within the immigrant communities on gender issues, even greater than the already considerable sex difference within native-born Canadians. Immigrant men in Canada may well have the most to lose in terms of reformed gender relations since their traditional patriarchal reliance upon the domination of women's labour, especially domestic work, is challenged within Canada by feminist views. Immigrant women, however, have the most to gain through feminism and its struggle against patriarchy. All this adds up to evidence of strained domestic relations among immigrants.

The final feature we use to examine the heterogeneity of the rest of Canada is region, based on provincial clusters. These include the four western provinces, Ontario, and the four eastern provinces. Ontario (9.1 million) and Quebec (6.5 million) have similar sized populations, while the East is fairly small (2.3 million) and the West somewhat larger (7.4 million).

Regionalism exists in virtually all countries, but regions are especially prominent in Canada, a vast nation, thinly populated with strong sub-central levels of the state and radically different regional economies.[28] For men it is the West that is so distinctive, with a huge old middle class and a small working class. The East tends to have a large new middle class for both sexes (and a small capitalist-executive class). Barrett and Hamilton show a particular sensitivity to the regional diversity of Canadian feminism, saying for example, "Much feminist political work has been provincially based, and its fortunes have risen and fallen with different governments in the provinces." [29]

When we examine region in Canada using traditional provincial clusterings, the basic cleavage between Quebec and the rest of Canada persists. There is some hint of more progressive views about gender issues in the East than in the West or Ontario, but the fundamental division is one that separates Quebec.

Quebec is quite distinctive for women, with notably more working-class and few new-middle-class positions; for men from Quebec there is a similarity with other areas for the new middle class but somewhat higher than others for the working class. Quebec has long been recognized for the role of its new middle class in social change,[30] but now we can see that this has been a particularly masculine develop-

ment; Quebec women have found themselves largely excluded from the new middle class.

Our primary interest is in how political regions interact with the cultures of class and gender. Quebec and the East stand out as the most progressive areas for gender attitudes, with the most traditional in the West, followed by Ontario.

There are some regional features of interest that help us differentiate the rest of Canada based on regional divisions. On the matter of class divisions, the greater progressiveness of the new middle over the working class holds across the country for men but is only supported for women in Ontario. Ontario new-middle-class women (1.04) are more progressive than their working-class counterparts (.88), but elsewhere this pattern breaks down. For the effect of unionization, however, there is a positive effect across the country for women, with the greatest difference in Quebec (+.40), as expected, but also for Ontario (+.22), the West (+.16), and the East (+.12). These results hold for unionized members of both the working and new middle classes. For men, however, both the West and Ontario have a negative union effect (−.09 each), compared to somewhat positive effects in Quebec (+.08) and the East (+.06). Tracing this further, we find that Ontario working-class union men are much more traditional than their non-union counterparts (−.36), a result not repeated in Quebec (+.16) and only marginally sustained in the West (−.07). Among unionized men there is a basic split between Ontario (.34) and Quebec (.59) on their support for gender issues.

During the early 1980s the Ontario labour movement was experiencing a major feminist challenge. According to Rosemary Warskett, it "gathered steam and depth throughout the eighties" beginning with "Organized Working Women (oww), an informal group devoted to bringing together union feminists across union lines, who took up this role. As a non-constitutional body within the ofl (Ontario Federation of Labour), oww represented union feminists' determination to build their strength within the movement ... its influence was felt in the form of resolutions to ofl and union conventions. Thus its very presence raised questions about who has power to assert demands and make decisions."[31] This helps us make sense out of our findings for Ontario. Working-class and new-middle-class women unionists were certainly empowered in Ontario by these events, as indicated by their high gender-attitude scores (1.01 and 1.34 respectively), but the male unionists were threatened. As Warskett reports, "By the end of the seventies union feminists were actively working to change the policies of the ofl and their own unions."[32]

The feminist challenge within the Ontario labour movement met with male resistance. Our data support such a conclusion. The non-union working-class men in Ontario had fairly high scores (.70) in supporting feminist issues, especially when contrasted to those with union experience (.34), thus highlighting a large backlash effect (−.36). Unlike male unionists in Quebec, who were at least somewhat persuaded to support women's causes, in Ontario many male unionists were threatened by feminism.

This analysis reinforces our findings about the distinctiveness of the Québécois and their combination of union and women's movements. It also tells us, however, that the new-middle-class character of the women's movement is a particularly Ontario feature for women. The union movement everywhere has had a positive influence for women but not at the levels evident in Quebec. The backlash by unionized men has been confined to Ontario westward and as a working-class response, is really Ontario-centred.

U.S. POLITICAL SPACE AND RACE

Both Canada and the United States are geographically vast countries but populated in radically different ways. The 250 million residents of the United States are "squeezed" into a territory smaller than the area that houses a tenth as many Canadians. Regional conflicts in Canada have been expressed in many ways but not so violently as the North-South struggle of the Civil War in the United States. That country has been characterized by shifts in power from the Northeast to the West Coast and relocation of production to the low-wage South. A main feature of postwar America was the mass migration of southern blacks to northern industrial cities.

A major characteristic distinguishing the United States from Canada and the Nordic countries is the historic significance of racial divisions.[33] An obvious limitation of our data, however, is the small U.S. sample size available to evaluate subtle racial differences, forcing us to use a fairly crude white – people-of-colour distinction in asking the question, Does race matter?

As would be expected, race does matter in the United States. In terms of the structures of class, people of colour are the most concentrated in the working class. Our main question, however, concerns gender cultures. For both sexes, people of colour are more progressive on gender issues, especially so for women. Race tends to increase the heterogeneity of gender orientations in the United States.

Of the differences in the class profiles by race in the United States, the primary divide is around ownership or control of property rights. White men have higher representations in the propertied classes (22 per cent to 11 per cent). There are identical proportions in the new middle class (32 per cent). The largest difference for men of colour is the higher share in the working class (57 per cent compared to 46 per cent). For women of colour, there is a greater presence in the working class (69 per cent) compared to white women (62 per cent). The basic class structure differences evident here, however, are no greater than those between British and French origins in Canada. Our primary interest is with gender attitudes as influenced by race.

Black feminists in the United States have criticized white feminists for their "double standard" in writing about race. bell hooks says, "In much of the literature written by white women on the 'woman question' from the nineteenth century to the present day, authors refer to 'white men' but use the word 'woman' when they really mean 'white woman.' Concurrently, the term 'blacks' is often made synonymous with black men."[34] There is a complex relationship between the civil rights movement and the feminist movement in the United States. Leslie Cagan, for example, argues that the empowerment black women gained from the civil rights movement spilled over as they sought freedom as women.[35] On the other hand, Bonnie Thorton Dill contends that black women in the United States "have felt called upon to choose between their commitments to feminism and to the struggle against racial injustice."[36]

Foremost it is important to understand that experiences for women of colour are different from those for men of colour. Our results (Table 9.6) illustrate that both race and sex cleavages are present at about equal levels of difference. Women are more progressive in both categories, but women of colour are more progressive (.24 difference) than white women, just as men of colour are more progressive (.21 difference) than white men. Overall, people of colour are more progressive on gender issues than whites, a finding supportive of Catherine Ross's results for black Americans and specifically for middle-class blacks.[37] (Among people of colour, the "others" are more progressive than blacks.[38]) In all instances the new middle class is more progressive than the working class and women are more progressive than men, sustaining the general pattern found earlier for Canada.

To find that middle-class women are more progressive on the gender-attitude scale does not mean that the two groups are necessarily part of the same social movement. Sheva Medjuck reports, "Black groups are often very suspicious of the feminist movement and dismiss it as a white, middle-class bourgeois movement."[39] Still, both

Table 9.6
Gender Attitudes in the United States for Race by Sex, Class, and
Union

Panel A	People of Colour	Whites	Difference
Total	.68	.47	+.21*
Men	.55	.34	+.21*
Women	.82	.58	+.24*
(N)	(244)	(1,302)	

	Women		Men	
Panel B	People of Colour	Whites	People of Colour	Whites
CLASS				
Working	.75	.52	.51	.34
New middle[a]	.99	.79	.55	.45
Difference	+.24	+.27*	+.04	+.11
UNION				
Never union	.75	.56	.67	.43
Union	.92	.65	.43	.25
Difference	+.17	+.09	−.24	−.18*
CLASS & UNION				
Working/Never	.66	.50	.69[b]	.49
Working/Union	.91[c]	.57	.31[b]	.24
Difference	+.25	+.07	−.38*	−.25*

[a] People of colour in the new middle class based on 38 men and 32 women; all
others over 50 unless noted.
[b] Men of colour in the working class based on 37 never union and 33 union.
[c] Only 30 cases.
* Differences are significant at .05 level of confidence or better.

types of women are positively influenced by the new-middle-class
effect.

The union effect is strong for women of colour and positive for
white women but negative for both types of men. These patterns
persist and are deepened for the combination of working class and
unionization. Working-class women of colour with union experience
are very progressive, much more so than their white counterparts
(.34 difference). There is little difference for unionized working-
class men by race. Both groups are negatively impacted in terms of
their gender attitudes. There are not sufficient cases available to talk
about the effects of unionization for middle-class people of colour,
but for whites the same patterns persist as for the working class, with
unionization having a positive influence for women (+.18) and a
negative one for men (−.13).

The race cleavage in the United States is subject to the effects of sex, class, and unionization. Comparing two countries, U.S. whites are distinctively less progressive than all Canadian ethnic groups, but U.S. people of colour could easily be matched to the British in Canada and are even more progressive than European migrants to Canada. Québécois remain the most progressive in a North American comparison, while American whites are the most traditional in the same context. Race matters for gender orientations in the United States, just as ethnicity does in Canada, but once again the divisions by class and sex are equally significant. None of these factors should be neglected in explaining the way people think about their lives and how they organize their actions.

As with the national comparisons, when we introduce race into the gender and union relationship in the United States, the women with union experience are more progressive. Women of colour with union experience are especially feminist, reaching levels that would not be out of place in Canada outside of Quebec. For men, however, the backlash cuts across racial lines. Both are less progressive if they have union experience. Men of colour with union experience are as likely as whites without union experience to be more traditional. The civil rights movement has generally had a progressive influence on the women's movement but has not overcome the fundamental gendered division within the U.S. trade union movement. Within North America only the Québécois have broken through the gender barrier, in the sense that unionized men are more progressive than the non-unionized. Lest someone conclude there is an end of gender conflict *within* the union movement, it should be kept in mind that the gaps between unionized men and women remain as great when the union movement has a progressive effect (.71 for Québécois, .39 in Norway, and .35 in Sweden) as it does elsewhere (.43 in the United States and .53 in the rest of Canada; see Table 9.2). Even when unions shift men to more progressive positions, they do not make them nearly as feminist as women. Whereas in Canada there has been relative autonomy for the Québécois labour and women's movements, in the United States the same movements have not had an independence through language and territory in which to develop distinctively. The influence of Quebec being a distinct "nation" with its own political space and institutions has mattered greatly for the development of Québécois social movements. U.S. blacks have been embedded in the dominant labour movement and to some extent the women's movement, lacking access to the same kind of territorially dominated political institutions as the Québécois have used to influence gender attitudes.

Ancestry, combined with sex and class, affects the way people think about gender issues. Gender becomes *part of* the way groups construct their cultures and formulate their political struggles. All three factors impact upon gender attitudes. Sex-blind class analysis fails to capture the subtlety of ancestry combined with class.

Given the nature of our data, we can also evaluate the effects of U.S. regionalism on the formation of classes and its consequences for gender attitudes. It will become evident that at least the cultural side of regionalism, as expressed through gender orientations, has stronger effects, as mediated by class and sex, in the United States than in Canada.[40] This illustrates the importance of looking beyond the structural side of regionalism to its cultural expressions.

Regional divisions in the United States have deep historical roots. The American Civil War of the 1860s is not so long ago in cultural memories as to wipe out a basic North-South division (the Mason-Dixon line). An East-West split has long been built upon the basis of old money versus new. Today the cleavages are constructed around different divisions but are nonetheless real. The Northeast represents the old industries and financial centres with a traditional working class. The Midwest is more agrarian, small-town America. The South is the pocket with cheap labour, anti-unionism, and traditional conservativism. The West Coast is the mecca for the high-technology industries, where new ideas flourish. In terms of class profiles, the United States is fairly complicated, with the West Coast having the most distinctive profile for men, including a large new middle class, but for women the profiles of the Northeast and West Coast are very similar, as are those of the Midwest and South (although the Midwest is more new middle class and the South more working class).

Within the United States, the Midwest and the South appear similar, as do the Northeast and the West Coast, especially for women. The Northeast has a higher proportion in the capitalist-executive class, and the West Coast is higher in the new middle class and low for working-class men. It should be kept in mind that the U.S. West Coast is numerically dominated by California, thus accounting for the high new-middle-class content.

The main question, however, is whether there are distinctive regional "cultures" of gender attitudes. Here again, in the United States there is a tendency to pair the Midwest with the South and the Northeast with the West Coast. The latter pairing is the most progressive.[41] The main cleavage in the United States is between the Midwest and South on the one hand and the Northeast and West Coast on the other. Both coasts are relatively progressive in the

Table 9.7
Gender Attitudes in the United States for Region by Sex, Class, and
Union

Panel A	Coastal America[a]	Middle America[a]	Difference
Total	.63	.41	+.22*
Men	.48	.30	+.18*
Women	.78	.52	+.26*
(N)	(567)	(914)	

	Women		Men	
Panel B	Coastal America	Middle America	Coastal America	Middle America
CLASS				
Working	.69	.48	.51	.28
New middle	1.01	.64	.48	.44
Difference	+.32*	+.16	−.03	+.16
UNION				
Never union	.75	.49	.57	.41
Union	.82	.61	.41	.17
Difference	+.07	+.12	−.16	−.24*
CLASS & UNION				
Working/Never	.67	.45	.67[b]	.47
Working/Union	.73	.57	.43	.09
Difference	+.06	+.12	−.24	−.38*

[a] Coastal America includes the Northeast and the West Coast; Middle America
includes the Midwest and the South.
[b] Only 49 cases; all others over 50.
* Differences are significant at .05 level of confidence or better.

United States, but they sandwich a conservative core running
throughout the centre and South.

Given the clear patterns found in our more detailed analysis, we
have chosen to collapse U.S. regions into their most basic cleavage,
which means a division between the middle of the country (including
the Midwest and South) and the coastal areas (including the Northeast and the West Coast). Table 9.7 shows the effects of this basic
cleavage in terms of gender attitudes. The cleavage effects both men
(.18 difference) and women (.26 difference).

As we have come to expect, class, unionization, and their combination all have positive influences for women in both regions of the
United States. The effect of the cleavage, however, is considerable for
women. Working-class women in coastal America are more progressive than in middle America (.21 difference), as are new-middle-class

women (.37). These differences are similar for the effects of union-ization and are compounded by the effects of class and union. Women in the two regions are subject to the same social forces, but there is a clear axis of difference whereby women in coastal America are consistently more progressive than those in middle America.

The situation for men is much more complicated. The working-class and union men, especially working-class union men, are much more progressive on the coasts than in middle America. In all in-stances, unionization has a reverse effect for men in the United States. The key difference based on region, however, is in the levels. Working-class men in coastal America are much more progressive on gender issues than those in middle America (.34 difference).

Given these findings, it would be difficult to argue there is a truly national pattern of gender attitudes in the United States. A major at-titudinal cleavage runs through the middle of the country. This cleavage is most pronounced within the trade union movement but primarily impacts upon working-class men in middle America. The American labour movement has not been progressive for men throughout the country, but there is a particular pocket of traditional views centred in middle America directed against the freedom of women. It needs to be stressed, however, that women throughout the country are more empowered by the union movement in their gen-der views.

When we look at North America as a whole, there are really three social spaces for gender attitudes. The Québécois, whether desig-nated as residents of Quebec or French Canadians, have the most progressive social space. The labour movement there has had a pro-gressive influence for both men and women, and it has the highest level of support for feminist issues. The middle ground is occupied by the rest of Canada and coastal America, which have strikingly sim-ilar profiles (compare tables 9.3 and 9.7), not differing by more than .06 on gender attitudes overall for men and women. In this social space, being new middle class has a progressive influence and being a union member a mildly progressive impact for women and a some-what regressive one for men. The final space is occupied by middle America. It is appreciably more traditional in its views on women's freedoms. The labour movement still has a positive effect for women but "middle American" men in the labour movement are extremely traditional, especially in the working class. Whereas union experi-ence for working-class Québécois men has a +.27 effect, in middle America the same effect is −.38. Union experience is clearly a con-tingent fact for North American men, although it is a consistently positive factor for North American women and Nordic people of both sexes. Unions matter for the experiencing of gender attitudes, but how they matter requires much more specific investigation.

CONCLUSION

Social cleavages based upon ethnicity, race, and region within North America are meaningful for the way gender attitudes are influenced by sex and class. Each division has experiential and organizational forms that develop historically and influence the ways relations of ruling evolve. All are aspects of the relations of domination and subordination, and each matters in terms of the politics of gender. Divisions such as those we have identified prioritize different social relations and have different effects in terms of the actors they mobilize. Knowledge of how they interact can help in understanding alliances and cleavages across divisions. We should be aware that at the concrete level, the terrain is likely to be very complex; still, certain contingent patterns do appear.

We can place findings about internal differences in the relationship between the union movement and gender attitudes within an international context. For women, union experience consistently means increased progressiveness on gender attitudes. This is most dramatically apparent for Québécois women, who rise to extraordinary levels of support for feminism when they have union experience, but it holds for all four of the nations examined. Women's support for gender issues seems to be energized by the union movement. Union experience for men, however, differs greatly by nation. In Sweden and Norway and for the Québécois, there is a correspondence between union experience and support for gender issues. In the rest of Canada and the United States, however, there is a collision between the labour movement and the women's movement. The data suggest a mild backlash by unionized men against women's issues in the rest of Canada and an unmistakable backlash in the United States. Men in English-speaking Canada and in the United States who have been part of the labour movement appear to be threatened by the claims of the women's movement. The underlying reasons for such different responses by men and women to the union movement can only be speculated on here, given the limitations of our data. They may well be men's reactions against affirmative-action programs or women's responses in favour of the union's advocacy roles.

In Sweden, Norway, and Quebec, the union movement during the decade from the mid-1970s to the mid-1980s was a powerful and progressive force influenced by the women's movement. Unionized women in each of these locations were stimulated toward feminist positions and demands, while at the same time unionized men were drawn along in their stances towards gender issues. In the rest of Canada and the United States, however, the labour movement has had a much more contentious relationship to the women's movement. Women with feminist attitudes have been attracted to the labour movement and have promoted their positions through it, but there has been a backlash on the part of men, who are even more conservative inside the unions than outside. It may well be that the already vulnerable position of established unionists in the United States has been even further threatened by women's demands for reform.

Especially in Sweden but also in Norway, men outside the labour movement are more traditional, a pattern repeated for Québécois men. This makes especially important the opposite effect in the United States (see Table 9.2), an effect that persists by class, race, and region. Ironically, feminists in the United States are much more likely to find receptive male allies outside the labour movement than inside, even though women unionists are more receptive than those lacking union experience.

By introducing ancestry and region into the account of how gender orientations are formed, we have discovered that the heterogeneity of views in North America compared to the Nordic countries is, at least in part, the result of these social cleavages. Moreover, we have discovered that regional differences in the United States have particularly strong influences on how gender issues are thought about. Indeed, regional differences turned out to be even greater in the United States than in Canada for forming these attitudes. In both cases, however, the *combined effects* of class, sex, and either ancestry or region made the greatest difference in discovering patterns in gender orientations.

We have tried to remove the "social vacuum" that often surrounds thinking about gender by introducing the social cleavages of ancestry and region into the analysis of North America. In so doing, we have begun to understand the relatively more heterogeneous patterns in North America, compared to the more homogeneous findings in the Nordic countries. Struggles over gender issues in the Nordic countries are less encumbered by the social cleavages of diverse ancestry, strong regional splits, and unevenly developed trade unions characteristic of North America. Both classes and sexes find the social cleavages of ancestry and region to complicate their respective cultures in North America, with the United States no more exempt from these complexities than is Canada. The *combined* impact of class, sex, and political regions accounts for the variations. While it may be argued that region or sex or class fragments gender orientations, it can equally be argued that together they produce significant pockets of culture which may sustain these perspectives.

Are there different feminisms in North America based upon social cleavages? North America does have different feminisms. Class, sex, *and* unionization are not universal in how they interact with race/ethnicity and region/nation to form gender cultures. If we begin to move beyond individuals and structures and into organizational forms, such as trade unions, that mediate structures and agency, then it becomes apparent that there are many potentially different futures for feminism. The labour movement can organize a backlash to feminist issues, or it can help to lead the feminist struggle. Feminism can just as well be the banner of subordinate women as the hallmark of the middle class. There are as many influences on gender attitudes as there are social cleavages; the deeper the social cleavage, the greater the variations in feminism and the more relevant human agency.

10 After Industrialism

From its origins in nineteenth-century social thought, sociological theory has been preoccupied with separating the present from the past and identifying trajectories toward the future. For everyone, the cataclysmic changes brought about by the end of feudalism, the spread of markets, and the technological revolutions associated with industrialism were matters for astonishment and wonder. How had this happened? What would the future be like?

To postwar observers of the 1950s and 1960s, the answers to these questions seemed reasonably clear. Modernity was to be understood in terms of the revolution in the forces of production that drove the transition from an agrarian past to the industrial present. Industrialism required cities, an educated labour force, and new kinds of social relations based on *individual* capacities, preferences, and rights rather than *group* identities based on ethnicity, religion, and other kinlike affiliations.

Industrialism also meant a new class structure, as farm sons and daughters left field and village to become factory workers and housewives in Detroit, Oshawa, and Kalmar. The old urban middle class of independent shopkeepers was displaced by supermarkets and merchandising chains. The social contours of *industrial* society seemed clear, if only for a moment. Men went to "work" on the shop floor or in the office; women, after a brief interval as an office or sales clerk, went home to raise families.

But no sooner was this imagery of an industrial society in place, than its material base began to erode. Manufacturing employment peaked in North America in the fifties and sixties and then declined, first in relative and then in absolute terms. Women left the home for paid employment, usually to do "feminine" work assisting men, caring for them, or tending children. New technologies in goods production increased demand for producer services (engineering, legal, financial) and reduced demand for factory operatives and other "direct producers." Rising affluence and the "working mother" increased demand for a variety of personal and social services once provided in the home or with the "volunteer" labour of women. "Big government" became a major source of employment alongside "big business," as schools, health care, and social services expanded. Something called postindustrialism had arrived and with it came a new intellectual debate to define its contours: What had changed? Where is it going?

POSTINDUSTRIAL CONVERGENCE?

In one important respect, postindustrial economies closely resemble their industrial predecessors and one another. At their peaks stands a small, predominantly male "ruling class" of corporate owners and senior executives. By our count, the capitalist-executive class represents no more than 5 to 6 per cent of the work force in both the North American and Nordic countries. Like industrial capitalism, postindustrial capitalism remains a form of rule of the many by the few. But despite continuity with the past, we have observed five major ways in which postindustrialism appears to break with the past.

1 *The Decentralization of Capital*   Since the seventies the "old middle class" and small employers have reversed their historical decline and become an "ascendant class" in some countries (chapter 2). In North America and elsewhere, postindustrialism has brought an end to the long-term tendency of capital to centralize in fewer and larger units of production. The "rule of the few" *appears* to be weakening, giving way to more and smaller workplaces and more self-rule (self-employment). Observers have been quick to point out that much of this change may be illusory: many small firms and the self-employed have traded one form of dependency on big capital for another. The exact mix of dependency and market freedom embedded in these changes remains to be determined. The implications for workers, however, are less ambiguous. As Marx observed, the centralization of capital in fewer and fewer hands also tends to concentrate workers in fewer and larger work units, increasing the possibility they will join together in their struggles against capital. But the inverse is also

true: corporate downsizing and fragmentation weakens labour unions and leads to declining wages and job stability. The expansion of non-working-class places for some (small capitalists and the self-employed) simultaneously intensifies the proletarian character of other places in the class structure.

2 *The Decentralization of Decision Making* Postindustrialism has brought about a "new managerial revolution," not only in quantitative terms but qualitatively as well. Postindustrial managers are different (chapter 4): more likely to be involved in planning and administration and less likely to be involved in the control and surveillance of labour. Organizational theorists tell us that this is the expected outcome when capitalist competition intensifies.[1] The routinization of work and centralization of control enhance profitability only in those industries at an advanced stage of the product cycle where core technologies are well understood, product markets are stable, and there is little pressure to innovate. Where capitalist competition requires flexibility or innovation either in response to changing markets or new technologies, the routinization of work and centralization of control impede profit maximization. Under conditions of uncertainty, the search for profits drives firms to decentralize, eliminate standardized routines, and increase employee control over the labour process. These same processes tend to be associated with the third major shift in the relations of ruling: the emergence of a new labour aristocracy.

3 *The New Labour Aristocracy* The rise of a new labour aristocracy of knowledge workers, direct producers of goods and services who do not participate directly in the administration of either capital or labour (except their own), is among the defining features of postindustrial labour markets. The result in the second half of the twentieth century is a bewildering array of new occupations and work sites (advertising agencies, business consultancies, software firms, health-care clinics). For class theorists, this development has been troubling. In view of their typical work conditions and life chances, incorporating the new "labour aristocracy" of school teachers, designers, and software programmers into the ranks of the working class created a conceptual problem for class theorists as well as a political problem for organized labour. Should they be counted as potential allies or as enemies in the struggles of the working class?

In classical Marxist thought, the division between skilled and unskilled labour posed a political, but not a conceptual, problem. Craftworkers tended to be more conservative than industrial workers,

bent more on protection of craft privilege than on building proletarian solidarity, hence a political problem. They were workers nonetheless, *direct producers* of commodities, carrying out the functions of labour. In the long run the political problem, it was thought, would be
resolved by the tendency of capitalism to eliminate skilled work. The
rapid destruction of the traditional craft occupations confirmed this
expectation. But postindustrialism has released the genie from the
bottle once again. The "postindustrial crafts" associated with such activities as the design and marketing of goods and the high-end human services in health, education, and welfare create both political
problems for labour and theoretical problems for class theory.

Like their industrial predecessors, the new labour aristocracy is
more conservative than other workers (chapter 5), hence its members pose a political problem for organized labour and political parties originally organized to represent an industrial, predominantly
male working class. Because their (re)appearance on the stage of
capitalist development was theoretically unexpected, they also raise
an intellectual challenge for conventional class theory. Especially
during the seventies, when many class theorists were persuaded by
Harry Braverman's claims concerning the inevitable degradation of
labour under capitalism, to admit these new knowledge workers to
the ranks of the working class would have posed a profound intellectual conundrum. The conundrum was neatly avoided by elevating
the division between the new knowledge workers and the less skilled
to a "new class" boundary. For the Ehrenreichs, these employees became part of the "professional-managerial class" and for Nicos Poulantzas, part of the "new petite bourgeoisie," manipulators of knowledge who regulate a working class whose jobs are increasingly empty
of intellectual content.[2] As we have highlighted in chapter 4, as an
empirical description of postindustrial relations of ruling, Poulantzas's conceptualization was simply wrong. Many "knowledge workers" do indeed rise to the ranks of management, where they participate in the control of capital and labour. But a significant number
(approximately a fifth of the working class) are "direct producers" of
goods and services; in short, *workers*.

4 *The Expansion of the New Middle Class*   A distinct issue has been the
emergence of a full-blown "new" class, located with the pyramid of
work between the executives and direct producers, whose job is to
direct and oversee the labour of others according to the policies set
by the executive. This intermediate class has expanded enormously
in postindustrial societies, especially in the "people-intensive" service
sectors. This class is ambiguous since it both oversees others and is

itself directed by more powerful actors, to whom it is obliged. Members of the new middle class are employees but brought into the command and planning structure of workplace bureaucracies. Their material position places them "between" employers and labourers with the potential to be pulled either way in their alliances.

Expansion of the new middle class has been the greatest in the state sector, especially in Sweden, where 57 per cent of that class is located there. In Canada the state sector and capitalist services have been equal as locations for the new middle class (39 per cent in each). The same level occurs in the United States for the capitalist service sector but somewhat less in the state sector (32 per cent). These expansions have provided the best jobs for women, who have captured half of all the new-middle-class places in North America in the capitalist services and state sectors and in the large Swedish state sector. The "coming into its own" of the new middle class with postindustrialism poses challenges to traditional class and gender dynamics.

Sweden provides an important example of stress introduced by the new organization of work and the rise of the new middle class. The new middle class has not posed a threat to the union movement in Sweden; on the contrary, it has become as unionized as the working class, even more so for women, and at world record levels (over 80-per-cent density). The threat has come to the old structures of the labour movement. Traditionally, the Swedish labour movement was dominated by the blue-collar workers' labour central (LO), which had an intimate relationship with the dominant Social Democratic Party. LO's place has become threatened by the rise of the salaried workers' union (TCO) and the union of university-educated employees (SACO), which together are now approaching LO in size.[3] Are these unions equipped to deal with the postindustrial world of work? One indicator is the flexibility embedded in employees through training, a flexibility that has become renown in Sweden through what is called the "active labour market" policy, which has traditionally paid to retrain and relocate employees from redundant jobs. We now know that blue-collar workers in Sweden are vulnerable to both new technologies and structural changes in a way other workers are not. "One out of two university graduates gets further training on the job every year, as does one out of four white-collar workers. But only one out of ten blue-collar workers gets such training and, once they have started working, a large proportion of all workers in manufacturing never see the inside of a school again."[4] There are new stresses introduced within the world's most solidaristic labour movement as it is confronted by postindustrialism's implications.

Results such as these suggest the new middle class will be better prepared to deal with the flexibility demands of postindustrial labour markets, locking the working class into dead-ends and promoting interunion rivalries even in Sweden. The new middle class remains the most volatile actor in the postindustrial world, poised to go in a multitude of political directions or enter into a variety of class alliances.

5 *The Feminization of the Class Structure*   A further point of convergence in postindustrial labour markets is at once the most striking and the least well comprehended by conventional class theory. In retrospect, it is really quite stunning that while class theorists of all stripes were debating the status of the new middle class during the 1970s and 1980s, the remarkable transformation of the working class, by then almost complete, called for little more than a footnote or occasional specialized article. While these theorists had their eyes focused on the "shop floor" on the one hand and the growing ranks of managers and knowledge workers on the other, the "new working class" of women sales clerks, office workers, and personal-service workers went largely unnoticed.

The feminization of the labour force means that in modern capitalism the "worker" has two prototypes rather than one: the male, blue-collar worker of industrial capitalism and the postindustrial, female service worker. Indeed the identity in the composition of the working class across countries is one of the most striking examples of "postindustrial convergence" (Table 10.1). In all five countries, blue-collar men constitute about a third of the working class and women in clerical sales and service jobs about the same. The inverse situation – blue-collar females and men in clerical sales and service occupations – each represent only about a tenth or less of the working class.

If it now seems strange that such a momentous change in the social composition of the labour force went largely unnoticed by class theorists, it is important in retrospect to recognize that this neglect was not entirely uninformed about the class-gender nexus. While much has been made of the absence of women in the social mobility studies of the 1960s and 1970s, the neglect was not entirely unreasonable in light of the problematic that oriented these studies. Their concern was with the transmission of power and privilege across generations. In a patriarchal society where power and privilege, like the family farm, are transmitted from male to male, women are only atypically part of the process. John Goldthorpe caused considerable stir in the 1980s when he defended the "conventional view" of excluding women from "class analysis" along similar lines.[5] His main point was that, given the nature of gender relations in contemporary capitalist

Table 10.1
Composition of the Working Class by Sex and Occupation

	United States	Canada	Norway	Sweden	Finland
CRAFTS, OPERATIVES, & LABOURERS					
Women	11	7	6	7	6
Men	30	30	30	30	33
CLERICAL, SALES, AND SERVICE					
Women	35	31	29	34	37
Men	10	12	9	8	6
PROFESSIONAL, TECHNICAL, AND "MANAGERIAL"*					
Women	7	10	14	11	7
Men	7	10	11	10	6
Total	100	100	100	100	100

* Employees classified in managerial occupations but with no managerial powers.

societies, the class experience of most women and the way women are incorporated into processes of class formation are over-determined by the class experiences of the men with whom they live. Women's relation to the "class struggle" is mediated by their subordination within patriarchal households rather than by their own class experiences. The wives of British coal-miners have played a critical and often determining role in shaping outcomes in labour disputes. But, of course, that is precisely Goldthorpe's point: when they went into the streets to take part in the struggle they went as the "wives of ..." Studies of the political attitudes of British and American women have also highlighted the fact that employed women have traditionally assumed the class attitudes of the men they are married to rather than developing views reflecting their own class position.[6] The furore raised by the Goldthorpe thesis pointed to a number of flaws in the argument, but the flaws need not blind us to its important, if now anachronistic, insight.

In *industrial* capitalism, class struggles usually (though not always) took the form of men struggling with other men, and women's involvement was usually (though not always) mediated through their relations to men. The *industrial* strike most typically involved a confrontation between male workers and their male bosses struggling over male wages and working conditions. Few women were to be found in either the union hall or the boardroom. Issues related to pay equity, child care, and paid absences to care for family members rarely if ever appeared on the bargaining table. As in the traditional patriarchal societies described by Mann, the public sphere was a male sphere: public life was conducted by male patriarchs. Except under exceptional circumstances (e.g., during wars), women remained "hidden in the household."

Postindustrialism, however, changes all this. The "postindustrial strike" (by school teachers, nurses, office clerks) brings mainly women to the picket lines, sometimes to confront women bosses. Postindustrial unions bring new issues to the bargaining table, and political parties that would represent the "working class" build new planks into their political platforms. This occurs, not despite, but because of patriarchy. The patriarchal organization of households means that most women sell their labour power under conditions very different from those of most men. The burden of the "double day" of paid labour and unpaid domestic labour circumscribes both how much labour power women can sell in the market and the timing of its availability. As a result, the focus of labour's struggles expands to include new labour-force practices and state policies – day care, flexible work schedules – intended to enhance the bargaining power of women in the market. The feminization of the labour market transforms the material interests of the working class when it confronts capital and hence the conditions under which the capital-labour wage relation is negotiated. The feminization of the labour force also feminizes the "class struggle." Both employers and labour unions, if not class theorists, have learned that they "neglect" this fact at their peril.

But women's struggles in the workplace are not reducible to struggles with employers for better pay and working conditions; they are also struggles against men. The target of affirmative-action, pay-equity, and sexual-harassment policies is not class power but male power. To pursue the analogy of previous chapters, when women move from the domestic to the public sphere, their struggle against patriarchy moves with them. The labour market and the workplace are now sites not only for "class struggle" but also for "gender struggle" or, more accurately, for a struggle *about* gender and gender relations.

Like African Americans, women have struggled to gain access to the construction site and the shop floor, as well as to the executive suite. And as with African Americans, their success until now has been limited even, as we have seen (chapter 6), when the executive suite is in a predominantly female job ghetto. The reason for this can not be chalked up entirely to domestic patriarchy, the fact that male privilege in the household imposes limits on women's participation in public life. As we were able to show in chapter 6, production rela-

tions continue to be organized not only to sustain rule by capital and
the property right but also to prevent the rule of women over men.

POSTINDUSTRIAL DIVERGENCE

The transition to postindustrialism is a product of the enormous
growth in productivity that has characterized most industrialized
capitalist economies in this century. Productivity growth brings the
opportunity either to increase the amount of goods and services
available or to produce the current amount of output with less labour. Changes in the mix of employment (the "service economy"), in
employment levels, and in patterns of paid work time are outcomes
of this process. But the precise nature and mix of these outcomes are
indeterminate: postindustrial economies come in a variety of sizes
and shapes. Revolutionizing the "forces of production" means old
ways will be left behind but does not determine what will come after.

1 *The Role of the State*   The major force shaping postindustrial differences until now has been the state. In Sweden the labour released
by rising productivity in goods production and the movement of
women from the household to the market has been channelled into
state-supported services in health, education, and welfare. In the
United States and Canada, postindustrial service growth is concentrated in business and personal services (chapter 2). High levels of
state employment also impose a hard upper limit on the extent to
which postindustrialism marks a return of the "old middle class"
(chapter 3). The two facts are connected. Big welfare states tend to
"crowd out" low-wage personal services and small employers who depend on low-wage labour. If people pay high taxes for comparatively
luxurious social services, there is less discretionary income for other
things. Consequently, through much of the postwar period, levels of
self-employment have been higher in North America than in the
Nordic countries. This pattern has been diminished only since the
mid-1980s as the restructuring of the welfare states in Sweden and
Finland have provided new space for self-employment to flourish.

2 *The Role of Unions*   The quality and types of employment in a service economy are not simply a matter of the mix of services since the
same service can be provided in radically different ways. In social services, for example, there are two alternative models available for the
day-care industry to emulate: low-wage, unskilled baby-sitting services or high-wage, skilled educational services. Day care can be provided by highly qualified teachers with advanced degrees in child

development or by minimum-wage child-minders. In North America, retail sales clerks are typically associated with the low end of the labour market, requiring minimal skills and drawing low wages. In some European countries, retail clerks serve apprenticeships and are considered skilled workers. Primary school teachers in Canada and the northern United States earn "middle class" salaries, while in the southern United States they earn "lower class" salaries.

These differences among countries and regions are largely a result of differences in the power of organized labour to impose a bottom line on the conditions under which labour is employed. In the Nordic countries, postindustrial service workers are almost completely unionized (chapter 4). In North America, the strength of organized labour is split along the public-private divide. The public sector is typically highly unionized, while organized labour is virtually absent in private services. Not surprisingly, public-sector services are seen as providing "good jobs" and private services "bad jobs." Where public-sector unions are weak or absent (as in the American South), the positive connotations associated with public-sector jobs are also weak or absent.

When labour is expensive, employers must find ways to recoup the wages paid in one of two ways: through investments in physical capital that increase the productivity of labour or through investments in human capital (job skills) that increase the productivity of labour. Relative to manufacturing, the potential for productivity gains through investments in physical capital (e.g., machines) is limited in the service sector. Hence service employers tend to pay higher wages only to their more skilled employees. As we saw in chapter 2, the anomaly of semi-skilled workers earning high wages found in manufacturing is largely absent in the service sector. As a result, where strong unions can deny employers access to a low-wage labour force, only high-end services can flourish. For all their mechanization, North American fast-food chains could not survive paying the union wages found in auto production.

3 *The Role of History: 1. Production Relations*   In all of the countries we have examined, postindustrial services tend toward more dispersed participation in decision making and greater reliance on skilled labour. But postindustrialism does not develop in an historical vacuum. National practices developed in the era of industrial capitalism to organize relations of ruling are not obliterated by postindustrialism. Thus the "American way," which combines relatively unskilled labour with high levels of managerial surveillance of workers, is evident not only in goods production, but in services as well.

Postindustrial services provide more skilled jobs than goods production, but postindustrialism's effects on the labour process are more muted in some countries than others.

Esping-Andersen's claim that such differences are a result of different "postindustrial trajectories" – a different material division of labour – captures only part of the story behind these differences. Sweden has a larger welfare state than the United States, and this is one reason why the "new labour aristocracy" is larger in the former than in the latter country. But it is also the case that the same material activities (e.g., welfare-state services) can be embedded within different relations of ruling that largely reflect past practice and historical precedent.

The Canada–U.S. contrast provides the most striking evidence for the claim that the same material division of labour can be embedded within very different relations of ruling. The mix of postindustrial services in the two North American countries is virtually identical, yet production relations in Canadian services more closely resemble Nordic than American patterns. Indeed, the Canadian case is the most dramatic instance of where postindustrialism has brought a break with the industrial past. And this too is for historical and institutional, not technical, reasons. Production relations in the Canadian goods sector emulate the American pattern as a result of Canada's history of "dependent industrialization": American owners brought American practice for organizing workplace relations to the Canadian factory. In services, where American ownership has been traditionally weak or non-existent, very different relations of ruling prevail.

4 *The Role of History: II. The Politics of Class* Our greatest scepticism about postindustrialism's homogenizing effects on class life among nations is reserved for the consequences of postindustrialism on class culture. In general, our results in chapter 5 show that nation-specific class attitudes have been either resilient in the face of, or reinforced by, postindustrialism. In North America, postindustrialism has brought a consolidation of the populist centre at the expense of both the left and the right. The new middle class, women, public-sector workers, and young people all tend toward distrust of both organized labour and big business. Similarly, our results indicated that new Nordic "social democratic hegemony" has by and large absorbed postindustrial divisions.

None of this means there is nothing new about postindustrialism. Our emphasis on continuities with the past concerns the way in which interests become represented in public life. In Sweden, issues related to gender, the environment, and even culture tend to enter public debate through class-based institutions or not at all. Women's issues become class issues. In North America, where organized labour is a weak, and sometimes hostile, vehicle for representing women or environmental interests, independent organizations emerge to represent those voices previously unrepresented in public life.

PATRIARCHY AND THE POSTINDUSTRIAL HOUSEHOLD

Women's particular workplace has changed with the postindustrial world, including adjustments to the domestic sphere. We have sought to identify some of those developments in terms of "unconventional" domestic situations, where women earn as much or more than their partners and which lead to altered attitudes about feminist issues, albeit with fewer changes in men's behaviours (chapter 7). Consequently, activist women have been forced to take matters into their own hands by seeking to socialize the costs of child care. Households have adjusted to postindustrial society, in part through greater "commodification" of domestic labour and in part by greater "socialization" of the tasks associated with child rearing. To gain greater "breadwinner" power women have pressed governments for greater pay-equity legislation. It seems that change has occurred more as a result of state policy and the creation of markets for commodified domestic labour than because men have altered their behaviour in the household.

The rise in women's labour-force participation rates across postindustrial societies means money mediates labour more than ever. The income women now bring into the household has become a source of domestic power. As a result, the household has become a contested terrain of interests. More power for women means a less privileged place for men, both inside the home and in paid work. Both public and private patriarchy are challenged as the conditions under which women supply their labour power are confronted: there are demands for day care, since fathers do not share the work of child care. There are also demands for more equal structures of pay, enforced by governments as pay-equity legislation or by unions as solidaristic wages, *and* demands for equal opportunities in promotions because the market as constructed by men disadvantages women. These constitute some of the most significant political demands of contemporary society, and they will intensify with the movement away from industrialism.

We sought in our analysis of households to understand unconventional situations likely to be more common in postindustrial societies. These include situations when women are empowered either by earned income or the ability to negotiate a more equitable sharing of domestic labour. We wanted to know whether such households make a difference? Are "modern" households likely to influence the relations of ruling? We stressed that it is in the nexus of the public and private spheres that most change is needed since that relationship privileges men and diminishes women.

Analysis of the division of domestic labour showed that women's economic power influenced the sharing of domestic work but that a fundamental division between the sexes persisted (chapter 8). Modern households, where men do a major share of the domestic work, are still rare, but there are more transitional households, where women earn half or more of the income, especially in Sweden. New-middle-class women are more likely to be modern and less traditional in their households, while working-class women are in the most traditional arrangements. Nevertheless, new-middle-class men are more traditional and more reluctant than working-class men to share domestic responsibilities. We found that women's attitudes and experiences are influenced both by their class position and by that of their spouse. Being middle class clearly matters for women's influence over how their spouses think and their own career disruptions. As women's class power increases, this leads to more progressive households. The opposite is true for men: new-middle-class men are more demanding and draining than working- class men, who tend to be more supportive of their spouses both ideologically and in action.

Men and women live in the same households but share them unequally. The postindustrial work world is one where women's labour-force participation will be as high as men's regardless of children. Households will have to adapt to this new reality and so too will the labour market. A major development, for example, has been the rise of part-time work, which now is borne nearly universally by women. Such work will have to gain entitlements equivalent to full-time work, including not only benefits but career and training opportunities. Swedish women have gained the former but not the latter; North American women have gained neither, but both will surely be on their postindustrial agenda.

We find the conditions for conflict between the sexes to be greatest in conventional households, where men earn most of the money. In these households there is the greatest gap between the views of men and women about gender issues. The greater women's share of household income, the more likely men are to have views compatible with feminism. There will also have to be a bringing into line of attitudes and behaviour. Swedish men speak progressively about what "should be" the case but are weak on sharing child care, behind even the more traditional United States. In examining household tasks we have discovered a "universal law of domestic practices" whereby women cook, clean, and launder while men help somewhat after meals and with some shopping.

Our results show Nordic families to be the least patriarchal in terms of decision making. Canadian families tend to resemble Nordic ones, while in the United States most men retain exclusive "executive powers" over major financial decisions. Everywhere the propertied classes are more patriarchal than the employed classes, especially so in North America. Men's attitudes are changed when their spouses earn as much or more than they do. This suggests that a change in women's material conditions will be followed by more progressive male attitudes. The exception is the United States, where men seem more prepared to change with respect to public patriarchy than its private counterpart.

Will the higher education levels accompanying postindustrialism lead to greater enlightenment about gender issues? The answer is mixed. More-educated men are threatened by women contending for positions of power. But generally more education equals more progressive views on gender issues, especially where they concern domestic matters.

Just as postindustrialism will likely have a complex relationship to education, so too are we likely to find a persistence of "preindustrial" social cleavages built around race, sex, and region (chapter 9). Racial and ethnic cleavages, along with national struggles, are as strong as ever. They continue to influence the way people think, including, as we have demonstrated, about gender issues.

The politics of gender have given us an analytical window on the intranational complexities of North America in terms of race/ethnicity and nation/region. Such divisions appear *not* to have been dismantled by postindustrial society. The homogeneity some expected by the reduction of ascriptive characteristics in favour of meritocracies has not been born out.

We also demonstrated racial differences in the United States whereby union involvement was positive toward feminism for women of colour but negative for men of all races. The United States has no single national pattern of gender attitudes. It is highly regionalized with, for example, progressive working-class men on both coasts but a very traditional centre running from the Midwest to the South.

How the feminist project links to class actors and unions is a contingent issue. We have shown in Canada, for instance, that the union movements in Ontario and Quebec have reacted quite *differently* to the rise of feminism. Both have been progressive for women, but for men in Ontario there has been a backlash. The feminist cause has been led, our data indicate, by new-middle-class women in Ontario and working-class women in Quebec.

We argued that North America divides into three zones for gender attitudes: a progressive Quebec, a traditional middle America, and a middle ground occupied by the rest of Canada and coastal America, all with remarkably similar profiles. In a larger context, we have shown that unions have been progressive for the feminist cause in the Nordic countries and Quebec but in the rest of Canada and the United States, they are on a collision course with a backlash by men against the claims of women.

Relations of ruling in all advanced capitalist societies are constructed around both class and gender but also include the social cleavages of ancestry and place. Each social formation is a complex construction demanding individual and comparative understanding. We have begun to advance some avenues of exploration, especially in the domains of dividing household responsibilities and their relationship to paid labour, and have made some beginnings around the culture of gender. We have only scratched the surface, but even these "scratchings" reveal the potential richness of such undertakings. Still concealed, however, are the so-called conjunctural levels of specific historical practices beyond the scope of this immediate project.

A FINAL WORD

Much remains to be done. In effect, the results we report upon here are point-in-time "snapshots" of five countries. We have come to think of them as historical residues, that is, the outcomes of processes that have been going on for some time. They are results which themselves need to be accounted for and explained in terms of processes currently underway that we have grouped under the notion of "postindustrialism." But what will this new world look like? What institutions, practices, and actors will influence the outcomes? What will be common and what distinctive in various countries? The answers to such questions require more information than is presently available. We come away with new projects and research agendas suggested by our evidence but not yet satisfied.

But then again, we should never be satisfied as observers of social life. As the last few years have so dramatically taught us, much can change and very rapidly. We will always need to investigate the processes underlying such changes and the links between structures and practices. The privilege of being able to do so in a comparative context is rewarding. Our claim is that the relations of ruling associated with class and gender must remain at the core of such accounts, even in postindustrial societies.

APPENDIX ONE

Methodological Notes

1 SAMPLES AND DATA

Data used through this analysis were gathered in conjunction with the Comparative Project on Class Structure and Class Consciousness. Questionnaire surveys containing identical "core" questions, as well as nation-specific questions, were administered across five nations in the early 1980s.[1] Information on sample sizes, survey methods, and so on for each of these nations are summarized in Figure A1.1.

2 WEIGHTS

The Canadian data are weighted to reflect sample design and post facto adjustments for age and sex composition by region and employment status, based on the 1981 census distribution of households and the March 1983 Labour Force Survey conducted by Statistics Canada.

The United States data are weighted to correct for the over-representation of respondents with high levels of education and high occupation status, and were designed in such a way as not to alter the number of employed labour-force respondents.[2] Weights were not used for the other countries.

Figure A1.1
Survey Design and Sample Characteristics for Five Nations

Sample Characteristics	United States	Canada	Norway	Sweden	Finland
Agency Conducting Survey	Survey Research Center, University of Michigan	Canadian Facts	Norges Markedsdata		
Survey Date	1980 (Summer)	1982/83 (Winter)	1982	1980 (Fall)	1981 (April-Sept.)
Sample Size	1,761	2,577	2,532	1,145	1,435
Sample Size (Currently Employed)	1,498	1,785	1,713	1,145	988
Type	2-stage systematic cluster	Multi-stage probability, stratified by region and community size	Random stratified by region and municipality	Random sample from national list of the population	2-stage cluster and random
Sample Population	Adults over age 16 working in the labour force, living in coterminus United States	Non-institutionalized, non-disabled adult population (ages 15–65) living in 10 provinces, representative with respect to sex and labour-force status	Men and women aged 16–66 representative of the entire Norwegian population	Adults aged 16–65 currently employed in the workforce	Adults aged 18–65, representative with respect to occupational structure and community size
Administration of Survey	Telephone	Personal interviews	Personal interviews	Mailed questionnaires and telephone	Personal interviews
Response rate	78%	76%	100%	76%	74%

3 LABOUR-FORCE COMPARISONS

Throughout the book, labour-force comparisons are based on the universe of the *currently employed* population. The universe for Canada is somewhat different. It consists of the currently employed population plus the subgroup of "experienced unemployed," that is, respondents currently unemployed but who had worked at a regular job in the eighteen months prior to the survey. This adjustment was made because the Canadian survey was fielded later than other surveys, during the depths of the 1982–83 recession, and reflects an uncommonly high level of unemployment. Using the experienced labour force for Canada allowed us to limit the effects of the recession on our findings and to use a larger sample population. The subgroup of experienced unemployed adds 327 unweighted cases to the 1,785 unweighted cases of currently employed.[3]

4 VARIABLE CONSTRUCTION

a *Class Location*   The theoretical underpinnings of our class typology are discussed extensively in chapter 1. From that discussion the following criteria were developed to operationalize our class categories:

Capitalist-Executive   (A) If self-employed *or* has paid employees *and* number of permanent employees is three or more;

OR (B-1) respondents make decisions about such things as the products or services delivered, the total number of people employed, budgets, and so forth;

and are personally involved in decisions to increase or decrease the total number of people employed in the place where they work;

or about policy decisions to change significantly the products, programs, or services delivered;

or the policy concerning the routine pace of work or the amount of work performed in the work place as a whole;

or about policy decisions to change significantly change the basic methods or procedures of work used in a major part of the workplace;

or deciding the overall size of the budget;

or in general policy decisions about the distribution of funds within the overall budget of the workplace;

AND (B-2) if for any of these, the respondents make the actual decisions themselves or make the decisions as voting members of a group;

AND (B-3) respondents are located within the organization as top, upper, or middle managers.

New Middle Class   (A) If, as an official part of their main jobs, the respondents supervise the work of other employees;

and decide how fast they work, how long they work, or how much work they have to get done;

or grant a pay raise or promotion to a subordinate;

or prevent a subordinate from getting a pay raise or promotion because of poor work or misbehaviour;

or fire or temporarily suspend a subordinate;

or issue a formal warning to a subordinate;

OR (B) if, as in B-1 above, and for any of B-1, the respondents make the actual decisions, as voting members of a group

or make the decisions subject to approval.

Old Middle Class   If self-employed and not more than two people are employed by the respondents on a permanent basis.

Working Class   If employed by someone else or work without pay and not included above.

Note: The logic of this operationalization requires that each set of requirements occur in succession, so if the requirements for capitalist-executive are met, the person is not eligible for the new middle class, and those meeting these conditions are not eligible for the old middle class and, finally, the working class.[4]

b *Occupational Classification*   In each country, data was gathered and coded to match Standard Occupational Classifications in that country. The participating national studies then agreed upon a two-digit occupational classification consisting of twenty-seven categories that have been collapsed further into the nine categories used in this analysis.

1 *Professionals*
physicians and dentists
accountants, auditors, actuaries
teachers: university, social scientists, librarians
mathematicians, engineers, architects, natural and physical scientists
lawyers and judges

2 *Semi-Professionals*
other medical and paramedical
teachers: elementary and secondary
technicians: draftsmen, embalmers, etc.
public advisers: clergymen, personnel relations, social workers, etc.
arts and entertainment
government protective workers

3 *Managers*
managers: public and quasi-public
managers: corporate
managers: other (e.g., funeral directors)

4 *Clerical*
secretaries
other clerical

5 *Sales*
sales

6 *Supervisors and craftworkers*
supervisors
crafts

7 *Blue-collar*
transportation workers
operatives except transportation
labourers except farm labourers

8 *Service*
white-collar services
skilled manual services (barbers, etc.)
unskilled services

9 *Farm*
farm workers (labourers, foremen)
farmers

Occupational classification of the people in the experienced labour force was done on the basis of their primary occupation within the preceding eighteen months.

c *Industry Classification* The industry classification used in this analysis is not based on that found in other studies using the comparative class structure data set.[5] Instead the detailed industrial codes for all five countries were recoded[6] to a nine-sector industrial classification scheme as follows:

1 *Agriculture*
2 *Natural Resource–Based*
forestry
fishing/trapping
metal mines
mineral fuels
non-metal mines
quarries and sand-pits
services to mining
wood industries
paper and allied
primary metals
petroleum and coal
electric power, gas, water
3 *Construction*
general contractors
special trade contractors
services to construction
4 *Distributive Services*
transportation
storage
communications
wholesale trade

5 *Consumer Services*
retail trade
amusement and recreational
services
personal services
accommodation and food
miscellaneous services
6 *Business Services*
finance industries
insurance carriers
insurance/real estate
services to business management
7 *Health, Education, and Welfare*
education and related
health and welfare
religious organizations
8 *Public Administration*
federal administration
provincial administration
local administration
other government

APPENDIX TWO

Identifying Skilled Jobs

The focus on skill as a significant dimension of production relations in recent neo-Marxist debates derives historically from Marx[1] but more immediately from Harry Braverman's analysis of the capitalist labour process.[2] For Braverman, the division of conception from execution – the former done by managers and planners, the latter by proletarianized workers – is the essence of deskilling and the "degradation of labour." Because the workers' *knowledge* is made redundant, *control* over the labour process passes from workers to their employers.

This concept of deskilling, as Ken Spenner, Craig Littler, and others have observed, has two referents.[3] The first is the notion of workers as possessing a complex body of knowledge and practices of which they are dispossessed; the second is the erosion of autonomy and self-direction in work that accompanies this development. As Spenner notes, the debate over deskilling has often conflated two distinct concepts: skill as *job complexity* – "the level, scope, and integration of mental, interpersonal, and manipulative tasks on a job" – and skill as *autonomy-control* (or self-direction), the notion that "the structure of work roles provides more or less room for the worker to initiate and conclude action, to control the content, manner and speed with which a task is done."[4] For deskilling to occur in Braverman's sense, change must occur along both dimensions.

This distinction is one on which Erik Wright's original effort to identify "knowledge workers," new and old, *apparently* floundered. For craftworkers and laboratory researchers who retain control over

how they do their work and at least some control over what they produce, Wright created the category of "semiautonomous employee"
and a set of operational procedures to identify such people.[5] Semiautonomous *employees* who could not otherwise be allocated to the
new middle class of managers and supervisors were assigned their
own contradictory class location, that of semiautonomous *workers*.
This became the most contested of his categories and was subsequently abandoned by Wright.[6] The critique had two dimensions,
one theoretical, the other empirical. The first focused on the theoretical logic underlying the constitution of *semiautonomous workers* as a
distinct "contradictory class location" in the class structure. The empirical attack was on the adequacy of the actual operational procedures used to identify *semiautonomous employees*.[7]

We have no intention of resurrecting the semiautonomous worker
to a distinct location in the class structure. We do intend, however, to
resurrect the category of semiautonomus employees as a measurement strategy to identify "skilled" jobs. As we show below, the operational procedures originally outlined by Wright provide a demanding measure of skilled labour, possibly too demanding.

To identify semiautonomous employees, respondents were asked:
"Is yours a job in which you are required to design important aspects
of your own work and to put your ideas into practice? Or is yours a
job in which you are not required to design important aspects of your
own work or to put your ideas into practice, except perhaps in minor
details?" Those who said, "Yes, required," were then asked for an example of how they design their work and put their ideas into practice. The examples were then coded to identify those who clearly
demonstrated that this self-direction involved more than routine
problem solving to ensure that the cognitive, as well as the volitional,
element of skilled work was being captured by the measure. The examples were coded as follows:

1 *High* Design/plan significant aspects of the final product or service, not just procedures used in one's own work;
   or problem solving with non-routine solutions is a central aspect of
   the work, not just an occasional event.
2 *Probably high* Same as 1, only less certain about the coding.
3 *Medium* Design/plan most of the procedures used in one's work,
   but only have influence on very limited aspects of the final product or service;
   or problem solving is a regular aspect of work, but generally of a
   routinized character or not a central activity in one's work.
4 *Probably medium* Same as 3, only less certain about the coding.

5 *Low*   Design or plan at most a limited aspect of procedures, with virtually no influence over aspects of the final product or service; *or* problem solving is at most an occasional/marginal aspect of work.

6 *None*   Very marginal involvement with designing procedures. Most work activities highly routinized with rare problem solving.

The ensuing debate over the measurement properties of this procedure focused on the cognitive ("job complexity") dimension. Both Wright (in his auto-critique) and his critics pointed out that some jobs with relatively minor cognitive requirements, such as office cleaners, may enjoy considerable discretion on the job.[8] Conversely, in some occupations (e.g., airline pilots) there are high cognitive demands but limited discretion except under unusual circumstances. The implication is that Wright's "semiautonomous employees" include a large number of false positives (such as office cleaners) and false negatives (such as airline pilots). As we show below, the first assumption is certainly incorrect. The dilemma of the semiautonomous office cleaner is a pseudo-problem that can be laid to rest.

Whether the procedure also results in too many false negatives – skilled "knowledge workers" who are not counted as semiautonomous employees – remains open to debate. Any effort to reduce errors of the first sort (false positives) increases the risk of the second type of error (false negatives) by making the measurement criteria too demanding. There is a trade-off involved. As Wright and his colleagues emphasize, they were prepared to accept this trade-off.[9] Their objective was to create a "pure semiautonomous employee" category by eliminating excessive claims to autonomy. Our results show that not only were they successful but also that their caution was warranted.

Our conclusions are based on a special supplement on job skills included in the Canadian version of the survey. Using as a model the work of Melvin Kohn, we asked respondents a battery of questions concerning the skill content of their jobs.[10] Here we report on five of these items to determine whether the respondents we coded as autonomous also consistently claimed high levels of job complexity. The questions asked of respondents were as follows:

Q68 Could you tell me how much your job requires
1 CREATIVITY, such as thinking of new or different ways to do things?
2 Understanding based on EXPERIENCE?
3 An ability to make decisions (DECISION MAKING)?
4 ABSTRACT KNOWLEDGE about the ideas behind your work, such as

the application of general principles or theories to solve a problem?

The response set for these items was a five-level Likert scale ranging from "none" to "a great deal."

Q70 *Complex Problem Solving*. Respondents were asked: We would like to know about the kinds of problems which normally arise in your job and the amount of thought and attention you need to deal with them. I am going to show you some statements and ask you to pick the one which best describes the thought and attention your job normally demands of you.

a *Little* thought and attention (My work is usually routine and problems seldom arise)
b *Some* thought and attention (Problems which arise normally require straightforward solutions)
c *Simple* problem solving (Unforeseen problems arise which require some practical experience)
d *Difficult* problem solving (Difficult problems arise which require considerable experience and careful analysis to solve)
e *Complex* problem solving (Highly complex problems arise which require a high level of abstract knowledge and theory to solve)

Based on the responses to these questions respondents were classified into three categories as follows:

False positives   are semiautonomous employees with responses in the two lowest skill levels (e.g., "little" or "some");

False negatives   are employees with responses in the two highest skill levels (e.g., "difficult" or "complex") but not classified as autonomous;

Ambiguous   are employees with a response in the middle of the skill range.

As a further check, we examined skill distributions using a skill measure based on the judgment of independent job analysts rather than respondents' self-reports. The General Educational Development scale (GED) is one of a family of measures used to evaluate the skill requirements of census occupations.[11] The GED ranks each of the 486 (four-digit) occupational census titles on a six-point scale on the basis of general reasoning and mathematical and language requirements. The associated verbal descriptions provide a hierarchy of task requirements from the very simple (level 1: apply common sense understanding to carry out simple one- or two-step instructions) to the

Table A2.1
Per Cent of Employees Incorrectly Coded as Autonomous (False Positives) and Not
Autonomous (False Negatives) on Six Measures of Job and Occupational Skill Level,
Canada

Skill Measure	False Positive (Low-Skill Coded Autonomous)	False Negative (High-Skill Not Coded Autonomous)
SELF-REPORTED		
1 Creativity	6	35
2 Experience	2	50
3 Decision making	1	41
4 Abstract knowledge	5	42
5 Complex problem solving	7	38
WORKER TRAIT		
6 General educational development (GED)	6	10

very complex (level 6: apply scientific thinking to a wide variety of
intellectual and practical problems). The descriptions for level 4 and
higher correspond to what would generally be considered as cogni-
tively complex work ("apply principles of rational systems to solve
practical problems in situations where only limited standardization
exists"). On the GED scale:

False positives   are autonomous employees with GED scores of 1 and
                  2;
False negatives   are employees with GED scores of 4 or higher who
                  are not autonomous;
Ambiguous   are employees with a GED score of 3.

The false positives and false negatives from the five self-reported
skill measures and the GED are reported in Table A2.1.

It is evident that the problem of "false positives" – autonomous
employees in unskilled jobs – is minimal. Over the five self-report
measures, the average share of autonomous employees who claim
low levels of job complexity is about 4 per cent. On the GED scale, 6
per cent are false positives. In contrast, the percentage of false negatives on the self-report items – those who claim high levels of job
complexity but were not coded as autonomous – ranges between 35
and 50 per cent.

In the construction of the autonomy variable, the presumption
was that employees are more likely to inflate the skill requirements of
their work than to understate them; thus caution is needed in accepting claims to high skill levels. Results for the GED scale suggests that

this caution was justified. When skill content is based on independent occupational evaluations, the percentage of false negatives is quite small (10 per cent).

Notes

PREFACE

1 Erik Olin Wright, "Rethinking, Once Again, the Concept of Class Structure," in *The Debate on Classes*, ed. E.O. Wright (London: Verso, 1989), 269.
2 G.A. Cohen, *Karl Marx's Theory of History: A Defence* (Princeton, N.J.: Princeton University Press, 1978), 79.
3 Ibid, 63. As Cohen points out, it is convenient to represent production relations in this sense as relations of ownership since to own an object is to enjoy a range of rights with respect to the use and situation of that object. But "ownership" cannot be reduced to legal ownership since the presence or absence of legal ownership is not always associated with the presence or absence of real powers over that which is owned.
4 Raymond Williams, *Politics and Letters* (London: New Left Books, 1979), 170.

CHAPTER ONE

1 G.A. Cohen, *Karl Marx's Theory of History: A Defence* (Princeton, N.J.: Princeton University Press, 1978), 63.
2 See John Kenneth Galbraith, *The New Industrial State* (Boston: Houghton Mifflin, 1967).
3 For an overview, see Martin Carnoy, *The State and Political Theory* (Princeton: Princeton University Press, 1984).

4 Among the more well known mainstream political theorists who develop this point is Charles Lindblom in his *Politics and Markets* (New York.: Basic Books, 1977).

5 See Michael Mann, "A Crisis in Stratification Theory? Persons, Households/Families/Lineages, Genders, Classes and Nations," in *Gender and Stratification* ed. Rosemary Crompton and Michael Mann (Cambridge: Polity Press, 1986), 40–56.

6 See, for example, Heidi Hartmann, "Capitalism, Patriarchy and Job Segregation by Sex," *Signs* 3 (1976): 137–68; Natalie Sokoloff, *Between Money and Love* (New York: Praeger Publishers, 1980); Natalie Sokoloff, "Contributions of Marxism and Feminism to the Sociology of Women and Work," in *Women Working*, ed. Ann H. Stromberg and Shirley Harkess, 2d ed. (Mountain View, Calif.: Mayfield Publishing Company, 1988), 116–31.

7 For an excellent overview of these various positions, see Nicholas Abercrombie and John Urry, *Capital, Labour and the Middle Classes* (London, George Allen and Unwin, 1983).

8 On this, see Erik Olin Wright, ed., *The Debate on Classes* (London: Verso, 1989), 318; Gordon Marshall, Howard Newby, David Rose, and Carolyn Vogler, *Classes in Modern Britain* (London: Hutchinson, 1988); Michael Emmison, "Wright and Goldthorpe: Constructing the Agenda of Class Analysis," in *Class Analysis in Contemporary Australia* ed. Janeen Baxter, Michael Emmison, and John Western (South Melbourne: MacMillan, 1991), 33–65.

9 See Wright, *Debate on Classes*, 348.

10 See Ira Katznelson, *City Trenches: Urban Politics and the Patterning of Class in the United States* (Chicago: University of Chicago Press, 1981).

11 E.P. Thompson, *The Making of the English Working Class* (Harmondsworth: Pelican, 1968), 9–10.

12 John Goldthorpe, with C. Llewellyn and C. Payne, *Social Mobility and Class Structure in Modern Britain*, 2d ed. (Oxford: Clarendon Press, 1987).

13 See Paul Boreham, Wallace Clement, and Geoff Dow, *Understanding Political Economies: Contemporary Transformations of Capital, Labour and the State* (London: Routledge Chapman and Hall Limited, Academic Publishing Division, forthcoming 1994).

14 Nicos Poulantzas, *Classes in Contemporary Capitalism* (London: New Left Books, 1975), 33.

15 See Mark Western, "Class Structure and Demographic Class Formation in Australia" (Ph.D. diss., Department of Anthropology and Sociology, University of Queensland, 1991).

16 The traditional male, blue-collar workers who occupy the pages of much Marxist historiography got their jobs as young men and spent

all, or a good part of, their lives in the same job or circulating between a limited set of similar jobs within the same community. Since they spent most, or a significant part, of their lives in this "class," they had an interest in its fate, they developed social bonds with other blue-collar workers, and they formed unions and parties to pursue their collective interests. The transitional character of many new, unskilled service jobs in the fast-food and other personal-service industries makes it unlikely that a similar process of demographic class formation will occur among this new, "postindustrial" proletariat. The subject of demographic class formation among unskilled service workers is the subject of a soon-to-be-published comparative study co-ordinated by Gösta Esping-Andersen, European University Institute, Florence, Italy. The results indicate that, with the exception of Germany, the expanding low-wage service jobs provide relatively temporary "stop-gap" employment and entry-level jobs for young workers.

17 See Erik Olin Wright, *Classes* (London: Verso, 1985), chap. 2 and 3.

18 Some Marxists, including Wright, are made uncomfortable by the fact that domination-based class categories sound remarkably like the neo-Weberian emphasis on authority relations. As Adnan Turegun has argued, this analyticial discomfort is misplaced. The work of domination done by *capitalists* (and employees who participate in this work) follows directly from the core problem for *capital*, that of transforming labour power into surplus labour and profit. See Adnan Turegun, "Exploitation and Domination in Wright's Class Theory: A Critical Evaluation" (photocopy; Ottawa: Carleton University, 1989).

19 See Erik Olin Wright, *Class, Crisis and the State* (London: New Left Books, 1978), 64–74.

20 For a fuller discussion, see Wallace Clement, "Class and Property Relations: An Exploration of the Rights of Property and the Obligations of Labour," in *Class, Power and Property: Essays on Canadian Society* (Toronto: Methuen, 1983).

21 See Harry Braverman, *Labor and Monopoly Capital: The Degradation of Work in the Twentieth Century* (New York: Monthly Review Press, 1974).

22 See ibid., 217–9.

23 Alfred D. Chandler Jr, *Strategy and Structure: Chapters in the History of the American Industrial Enterprise* (Cambridge, Mass.: The MIT Press, 1962), 8.

24 Ibid., 11.

25 Guglielmo Carchedi, *On the Economic Identification of Social Classes* (London: Routledge & Kegan Paul, 1977), 3.

26 Ibid., 5.

27 Ibid., 69.

28 Ibid., 70.

29 Stewart Clegg, Paul Boreham, and Geoff Dow, *Class, Politics and the Economy* (London: Routledge & Kegan Paul, 1986), 146.

30 Nicos Poulantzas, "The New Petty Bourgeoisie," in *Class and Class Structure*, ed. A. Hunt (London: Lawrence and Wishart, 1977), 118.

31 Ibid., 123.

32 Poulantzas, *Classes in Contemporary Capitalism*, 18–19.

33 Wright, *Class, Crisis and the State*, 68.

34 Ibid., 70.

35 See Wallace Clement, *The Struggle to Organize: Resistance in Canada's Fishery* (Toronto: McClelland and Stewart, 1986), esp. chap. 5; and Wallace Clement, "Property and Proletarianization: Transformation of Simple Commodity Producers in Canadian Farming and Fishing," in *Class, Power and Property*.

36 For a direct comparison between the class scheme developed here and Wright's, see Wallace Clement, "Comparative Class Analysis: Locating Canada in a North American and Nordic Context," *Canadian Review of Sociology and Anthropology* 27, (1990): 469–71.

37 See Clement, *Struggle to Organize*, 92.

38 While recognizing that unpaid spouses and children (e.g., on farms or in shops) may occupy a similar "class situation" to that of the owner of the enterprise and be important for questions of "class formation," such "situations" are mediated by patriarchal social relations, so that such persons do not typically have the same "effective powers" over the forces of production as the owner of the enterprise. In short, they do not occupy the same position in the relations of production as the owner. The number of such persons, moreover, is in large measure an artifact of the tax regime, which may or may not allow owners to count family members as paid employees (i.e., workers) for tax purposes.

39 Guglielmo Carchedi, *Class, Analysis and Social Research* (Oxford: Basil Blackwell, 1987), 113.

40 Ibid., 114.

41 See Michael Piore and Charles Sabel, *The Second Industrial Divide* (New York: Basic Books, 1984).

42 For an account of Canada's relationship to the United States and the relations of both to Britain, see Wallace Clement, *Continental Corporate Power: Economic Elite Linkages between Canada and the United States* (Toronto: McClelland and Stewart, 1977).

43 See Göran Ahrne and Håkon Leiulfsrud, "The Development of Social Stratification and Class Structure in Norway, Sweden and Finland from 1920," in *Class and Social Organization in Finland, Sweden and Norway*, ed. Göran Ahrne, et al. (Uppsala: Almquist and Wiksell International, 1988), 16–23.

44 Göran Ahrne, Raimo Blom, Harri Melin, and Jouko Nikula, "The Change of Class Structure and Social Hegemony: Conclusions," in *Class and Social Organization*, 129.

CHAPTER TWO

1 G.A. Cohen, *Karl Marx's Theory of History: A Defence* (Princeton, N.J.: Princeton University Press, 1978), 79.
2 Ibid, 63.
3 See John Myles, Garnett Picot, and Ted Wannell, *Wages and Jobs in the Eighties: Changing Youth Wages and the Declining Middle*, Research Paper no. 17, Analytical Studies Branch, Statistics Canada (Ottawa, 1988), 52.
4 See Joachim Singelmann, "The Sectoral Transformation of the Labor Force in Seven Industrialized Countries, 1920–1970," *American Journal of Sociology* 83, 5 (1978): 1224–34.
5 Ibid., 1233.
6 Anthony Giddens, "Classical Social Theory and the Origins of Modern Social Theory," *American Journal of Sociology* 81 (1976): 703–29.
7 The best-known examples are Clark Kerr, J.T. Dunlop, F. Harbison, and C. Myers, *Industrialism and Industrial Man* (New York: Oxford University Press, 1964); and Daniel Bell, *The Coming of Post-Industrial Society* (New York: Basic Books, 1973).
8 See Fred Block, *Revising State Theory: Essays in Politics and Postindustrialism* (Philadelphia: Temple University Press, 1987), 27.
9 Ibid., 107.
10 See Jane Jenson, " 'Different' but not 'Exceptional': Canada's Permeable Fordism," *Canadian Review of Sociology and Anthropology* 26 (1989): 69–94.
11 See Rianne Mahon, "From Fordism to ? New Technology, Labour Markets and Unions," *Economic and Industrial Democracy* 8 (1987): 5–60.
12 See Stephen Cohen and John Zysman, *Manufacturing Matters: The Myth of the Post-Industrial Economy* (New York: Basic Books, 1987).
13 For a review of this literature, see Nicholas Abercrombie and John Urry, *Capital, Labour and the Middle Classes* (London: George Allen and Unwin, 1983).
14 See Cohen, *Marx's Theory*.
15 "Sensitive dependence on initial conditions" – the notion that small differences in initial conditions can be magnified into dramatically different outcomes – is one of the key concepts to emerge from the new science of "chaos theory." For a popular account, see James Gleick, *Chaos: Making a New Science* (New York: Penguin, 1987).
16 Gösta Esping-Andersen, *The Three Worlds of Welfare Capitalism* (Cambridge: Polity Press, 1990).

272 Notes to pages 28–34

17 See ibid.
18 Our industry classifications are reconstructed from the detailed industry codes for the five countries and cannot be reconstituted from the
collapsed industry categories made available with five-nation data set.
The classification scheme is based on Myles, Picot, and Wannell, *Wages
and Jobs*, and is designed to capture key industry divisions with respect
to wages and job skills (see Chart 2.2).
19 See Tom Elfring, *Service Sector Employment in Advanced Economies* (Alder-
shot: Avebury Press, 1988); Esping-Andersen, *Three Worlds*.
20 See Esping-Andersen, *Three Worlds*, part 2.
21 On the distribution of earnings and wages, see John Myles, Garnett
Picot, and Ted Wannell, "The Changing Wage Distribution of Jobs,
1981–86," *Canadian Economic Observer* 1 (Nov. 1988): 4.1–4.33. On the
skill distribution of jobs, see John Myles and Gail Eno, *Job Skills and the
Service Economy* (Ottawa: Economic Council of Canada, 1990); and
John Myles, "The Expanding Middle: Some Canadian Evidence on the
Deskilling Debate," *Canadian Review of Sociology and Anthropology* 25, 3
(1988): 335–64.
22 Skill levels are measured with the General Educational Development
(GED) scale, one of a family of measures widely used in Canada and the
United States to indicate skill requirements of detailed (four-digit) occupational categories. "Low skill" refers to occupations with a GED
score of 1 or 2 on a 6-point scale. The data source is the 1986 census
of Canada. While differing in detail, very similar inter-industry patterns are found using a wide variety of "objective" and "subjective"
measures of occupational and job skill requirements; see Myles, "The
Expanding Middle"; John Myles and Gail Fawcett, *Job Skills and the Service Economy*, Working Paper no. 4 (Ottawa: Economic Council of Canada, 1990). Wage results are from Statistics Canada's 1986 Labour
Market Activity Survey. "Low wage" jobs include all those with an
hourly pay rate of $6.76 and hour or less in 1986 and roughly corre-
sponds to the bottom quintile of the wage distribution. For full details
see Myles, Picot, and Wannell, *Wages and Jobs*.
23 Harry Braverman, *Labor and Monopoly Capital: The Degradation of Work
in the Twentieth Century* (New York: Monthly Review Press, 1974), 408.
24 But this also means that there is no single typology that can provide an
all-purpose tool for class analysis.
25 Cohen, *Marx's Theory*, 70.
26 See Charles Sabel and Jonathan Zeitlin, "Historical Alternatives to
Mass Production: Politics, Markets and Technology in Nineteenth Century Industrialization," *Past and Present* 108 (Aug. 1985): 133–76.
27 For detailed analysis of the Canadian case see Monica Boyd, Mary Ann

Mulvihill, and John Myles, "Gender, Power and Postindustrialism," *Canadian Review of Sociology and Anthropology* 28, 4 (1991): 407–36.

28 See Joan Acker, "Gender, Class and the Relations of Distribution," *Signs* 13:3 (1988): 473–97.

29 See Heidi Hartmann, "Capitalism, Patriarchy and Job Segregation by Sex," *Signs* 3 (1976): 137–68.

30 See Acker, "Gender, Class," 482.

31 See Robert Erikson and Rune Åberg, *Welfare in Transition: A Survey of Living Conditions in Sweden, 1968–81* (Oxford: Clarendon Press, 1987); Rachel Rosenfeld and Arne Kalleberg, "The Gender Gap in Earnings: A Cross-National Comparison" (Photocopy; Department of Sociology, University of North Carolina, 1989).

32 See C. Jonung, *Patterns of Occupational Segregation by Sex in the Labour Market* (Meddelande: Department of Economics, University of Lund, 1983), 89.

33 See Rosenfeld and Kalleberg, "The Gender Gap in Earnings."

CHAPTER THREE

1 C. Wright Mills, *White Collar* (New York: Oxford University Press, 1951), 5.

2 Karl Marx and Friedrich Engels, *Collected Works*, vol. 6, 1845–48 (New York: International Publishers, 1976), 491–2.

3 In this chapter our unit of analysis is both the old middle class, as defined in chapter 1, as well as "petty capitalists." By petty capitalists we are referring to individuals who own and operate their own firms and who control the labour power of a small number of workers.

4 See Val Burris, "Class Formation and Transformation in Advanced Capitalist Societies: A Comparative Analysis," *Social Praxis* 7, 3/4 (1980): 147–79.

5 Mills, *White Collar*, 54. See also Seymour Martin Lipset, *Political Man: The Social Bases of Politics* (New York: Doubleday & Company Inc., 1960), esp. chap. 5; Nicos Poulantzas, *Fascism and Dictatorship* (London: Verso Books, 1979), part 5; and J.F. Conway, "Agrarian Petit-Bourgeois Responses to Capitalist Industrialisation: The Case of Canada," in *The Petite Bourgeoisie: Comparative Studies of the Uneasy Stratum*, ed. F. Bechhofer and Brian Elliott (London: MacMillan Press Ltd., 1981).

6 Organization for Economic Cooperation and Development (OECD), *Labour Force Statistics, 1970–1990* (Paris: OECD, 1992).

7 See OECD, "Employment in Small and Large Firms: Where Have the Jobs Come From?" *Employment Outlook*, September 1985, 64–82; for Canada see Ted Wannell, "Trends in the Distribution of Employment

by Employer Size," Research Paper no. 39, Analytical Studies Branch, Statistics Canada (Ottawa, 1991); for the United States and Sweden see Mark Granovetter, "Small is Bountiful: Labor Markets and Establishment Size," *American Sociological Review* 49 (1984): 323–34.

8 Once again, however, there are cross-national differences and some disagreement about cases. The OECD does not show increasing small-firm employment in the United States but Granovetter does, a conclusion confirmed in more recent studies by Davis and Haltiwanger and by Brynjolfsson and his colleagues, among others.

9 See also OECD, *Labour Force Statistics*; Granovetter, "Small is Bountiful"; S.J. Davis and J. Haltwinger, "The Distribution of Employees by Establishment Size: Patterns of Change and Movement in the United States" (photocopy, Nov. 1989); E. Brynjolfsson, T. Malone, V. Gurbaxani, and A. Kambil, "Does Information Technology Lead to Smaller Firms" (photocopy, Center for Coordination Science, MIT, Nov. 1989).

10 An establishment is a single location, such as a factory, office, or mine, where economic activity takes place. A company is legal entity; it may be comprised of a single establishment or many establishments, such as a head office in one location and a factory in another. Company employment includes the number of workersin all establishments owned by the company.

11 OECD, "Self-employment in OECD Countries," *Employment Outlook*, Sept. 1986, 53.

12 Gary L. Cohen, *Enterprising Canadians: The Self-Employed in Canada*, Statistics Canada, Labour and Household Surveys Analysis Division, Cat. #71–536 (Ottawa: Supply and Services Canada, October 1988); calculated from Tables 1A and 1D, pp. 90–1, 96–7.

13 See Oliver Hagan, Carol Rivchun, and Donald Sexton, *Women-Owned Businesses* (New York: Praeger, 1989); Richard Cuba, David Decenzo, and Andrea Anish, "Management Practices of Successful Female Business Owners," *American Journal of Small Business Management* 8, 2 (1983) 40–46; Eleanor Bradley Schwartz, "Entrepreneurship: A New Female Frontier," *Journal of Contemporary Business* 5, 1 (1976): 47–76; Carole Scott, "Why More Women are Becoming Entrepreneurs," *Journal of Small Business Management* 24, 4 (1986): 37–44; Stanley Cromie and John Hayes, "Towards a Typology of Female Entrepreneurs," *Sociological Review* 36, 1 (1988): 87–113; R. Goffee and R. Scase, *Women in Charge* (London: Andre Deutsch, 1985); R. Goffee and R. Scase, "Business Ownership and Women's Subordination: A Preliminary Study of Female Proprietors," *Sociological Review* 31 (1983): 625–47.

14 See John Goldthorpe, "The Current Inflation: Towards a Sociological Account," in *The Political Economy of Inflation*, ed. Fred Hirsch and John Goldthorpe (Cambridge: Harvard University Press, 1978), 186–214.

15 See George Steinmetz and Erik Olin Wright, "The Fall and Rise of the Petty Bourgeoisie: Changing Patterns of Self-Employment in the Post War United States," *American Journal of Sociology* 94, no. 5 (March 1989): 973–1018.

16 See Wannell, "Trends in the Distribution of Employment."

17 See ibid.

18 See Steinmetz and Wright, "Petty Bourgeoisie," 1007.

19 See Brynjolfsson et al., "Does Information Technology Lead to Smaller Firms."

20 See OECD, "Self-Employment in OECD countries," 43–63.

21 See for example, Canadian Labour Force Survey results that correct for this underestimation show that actual levels of self-employment in Canada were 13.4 per cent in 1983, almost identical to the 13.7 per cent (rounded to 14 per cent in Table 3.1) found in the Canadian survey. See Ian Macredie, "Self-Employment in Canada: An Overview," *The Labour Force*, Statistics Canada, 71–001 (Ottawa, Feb. 1985), 89.

22 To estimate the number of working owners in the economy, we have not followed the practice of counting unpaid family workers among the self-employed. Instead, we include only employers and own-account workers. Unpaid family workers are counted later in our analysis when we consider the familial relationship to capital ownership. Whether family members employed in a family-owned enterprise are classified as unpaid family workers or as employees has more to do with differences in national taxation practices than with actual production relations.

23 State employment is higher in most sectors of the Nordic economies and especially in Sweden. In distributive services (transportation, etc.), for example, 47 per cent of Swedish employees, compared to 18 per cent of American employees, are in the state sector according to our sample estimates. In health, education, and social services the figure is 97 per cent in Sweden and 78 per cent in the United States. In all five countries, however, the proportion of state employees is low in the goods sector (ranging from 3 per cent in the U.S. to 18 per cent in Norway), business services (ranging between 4 per cent in Canada and 10 per cent in Sweden and Norway), and personal and retail services (ranging from 6 per cent in the United States andCanada to 23 per cent in Sweden).

24 These and subsequent "what if" experiments make use of standardization techniques, a familiar demographic method used to "control" the effect of one variable on another. First, we adjust the industry-specific levels of state employment of the other four countries to those of Sweden and recalculate self-employment levels in each country. This is equivalent to asking, What would the overall level of self-employment

be if each country had the Swedish level of state employment within sectors but retained their own sectoral mix of services? Similarly, we recalculate self-employment levels after standardizing the other four countries to the Swedish distribution of employment among sectors of the service economy. This is equivalent to asking, What would happen if each country retained its own industry-specific levels of state employment but developed a sectoral mix identical to that of Sweden? Finally, we estimated the cumulative effect of the two variables by standardizing on both distributions simultaneously (i.e., on their joint distribution). These standardizations were estimated using James Davis's CHIP program; see James Davis, *Social Differences in Contemporary America* (New York: Harcourt Brace Jovanovich Inc., 1987). For conceptual reasons, however, we have made use of "indirect," rather than "direct," standardization for this exercise, that is, we adjust the distributions to that of one of the five countries rather than to the "total" distribution, which in comparative research of this sort is a hypothetical distribution that does not, and is unlikely to, exist.

25 The joint effect of differences in industry mix and level of state employment within industries is calculated by standardizing to the joint distribution of the two variables.

26 See International Labour Office, *The Promotion of Self-Employment* (Geneva: International Labour Conference, 77th Session, 1990), 14.

27 Göran Ahrne and Wallace Clement, "A New Regime? Class Representation within the Swedish State," *Economic and Industrial Democracy* 13 (1992): 455–79.

28 Bengt Johanisson, "Entrepreneurship in a Corporatist State: The Case of Sweden," in *Entrepreneurship in Europe*, ed. R. Goffee and R. Scase (London: Croon Helm, 1987), 131–43.

29 OECD, *Employment Outlook* (Paris: OECD, July 1992) 188, Table 4.A.4.

30 Ibid.

31 Ibid.

32 See Marc Linder and John Houghton, "Self-Employment and the Petty Bourgeoisie: Comment on Steinmetz and Wright," *American Journal of Sociology* 96, 1 (1990): 727–35. See also Angela Dale, "Social Class and the Self-Employed," *Sociology* 20, 3 (1986): 430–4.

33 See Economic Council of Canada, *Employment in the Service Economy* (Ottawa: Economic Council of Canada, 1991), 79–81.

34 See Wallace Clement, *Class, Power and Property* (Toronto: Methuen, 1983); Wallace Clement, *The Struggle to Organize: Resistance in Canada's Fishery*, (Toronto: McClelland and Stewart Ltd, 1986): Al Rainnie, "Small Firms, Big Problems: The Political Economy of Small Businesses," *Capital and Class* 25 (1985): 140–68.

35 See George Steinmetz and Erik Wright, "Reply to Linder and Houghton," *American Journal of Sociology* 96, 3 (1990): 737–8.

36 See Gary L. Cohen, *Enterprising Canadians*, 90–1, 96–7, Tables 1A and 1D.

37 See Wannell, "Trends in the Distribution of Employment," 7.

38 See Steve Johnson, "The Small Firm and the UK Labour Market in the 1980s," in *Farewell to Flexibility*, ed. Anna Pollert (Oxford: Basil Blackwell Ltd, 1991), 239–55.

39 See R.F. Imrie, "Work Decentralisation from Large to Small Firms: A Preliminary Analysis of Subcontracting," *Environment and Planning A* 18, 7 (1986): 949–65; John Holmes, "The Organization and Locational Structure of Production Subcontracting," in *Production, Work, Territory: The Geographical Anatomy of Industrial Capitalism*, ed. A. Scott and M. Storper (Boston: Allen & Unwin, 1986).

40 See René Morissette, "Canadian Jobs and Firm Size: Do Small Firms Pay Less?" Research Paper no. 35 Analytical Studies Branch, Statistics Canada, (Ottawa, 1991), 29, Table 6.

41 See Wesley Mellow, "Employer Size and Wages," *Review of Economics and Statistics* 54, 3 (Aug. 1982): 497; Walter Oi, "Heterogeneous Firms and the Organization of Production," *Economic Inquiry* 21 (April 1983): 151.

42 See Mellow, "Employer Size and Wages"; Morissette, "Canadian Jobs and Firm Size."

43 G. Picot and J. Baldwin, "Patterns of Quits and Layoffs in the Canadian Economy – Part II," *Canadian Economic Observer* 3 (Dec. 1990): 5.1–5.21.

44 The classic statement of this position can be found in Michael Piore and Charles Sabel, *The Second Industrial Divide* (New York: Basic Books, 1984).

45 The North American literature on this topic is now immense. For the seminal American study of this question, see Bennett Harrison and Barry Bluestone, *The Great U-Turn: Corporate Restructuring and the Polarizing of America* (New York: Basic Books, 1988). For Canada, see John Myles, Garnett Picot, and Ted Wannell, *Wages and Jobs in the Eighties: Changing Youth Wages and the Declining Middle*, Research Paper no. 17, Analytical Studies Branch, Statistics Canada (Ottawa, 1988).

46 See Myles, Picot, and Wannell, *Wages and Jobs.*

47 See Wannell, "Trends in the Distribution of Employment," 24.

48 Piore and Sabel, *Second Industrial Divide*, 279.

CHAPTER FOUR

1 Harry Braverman, *Labor and Monopoly Capital: The Degradation of Work in the Twentieth Century* (New York: Monthly Review Press, 1974).

2 Daniel Bell, *The Coming of Post-Industrial Society* (New York: Basic Books, 1973).

3 The historical question of postindustrialism's effects on the "proletari-

anization" of labour in the Canadian context has been addressed by John Myles and colleagues at Statistics Canada in a separate series of studies. For a synthesis of these studies, see John Myles, Garnett Picot, and Ted Wannell, "Does Postindustrialism Matter: Evidence from the Canadian Experience," in *Changing Classes*, ed. Gösta-Esping Andersen (London: Sage, 1993), forthcoming.

4 Gösta Esping-Andersen, *The Three Worlds of Welfare Capitalism* (Princeton: Princeton University Press, 1990), 202–8.

5 See, for example, Val Burris, "Class Formation and Transformation in Advanced Capitalist Societies: A Comparative Analysis," *Social Praxis* 7, 3–4 (1980): 147–79; Carlo Carboni, "Observaciones comparativas sobre la estrutura de clase de los paises capitalistas avanzados," *Revista Espanola de Investigaciones Sociologicas* 26, (Abril–Junio 1984): 129–49; Esping-Andersen, *Three Worlds*, 202–8.

6 Ken LeClair, "Report on the Industrial and Occupational Distributions of the Project Countries' Labour Forces: 1951–1981" (photocopy; Ottawa: CarletonUniversity, 1983).

7 Samuel Bowles, David Gordon, and Thomas Weisskopf, *Beyond the Wasteland: A Democratic Alternative to Economic Decline* (Garden City, N.Y.: Doubleday, 1983).

8 Stephen Hymer, "The Multinational Corporation and the Law of Uneven Development," in *Economics and the World Order from the 1970s to the 1990s*, ed. J. Bhagwati (London: Collier-MacMillan, 1972), 113–40; Burris, "Class Formation and Transformation in Advanced Capitalist Societies."

9 For Canada, see Monica Boyd, "Sex Differences in Occupational Skill: Canada, 1961–86," *Canadian Review of Sociology and Anthropology* 27, 3: (1990): 285–315; and John Myles, "The Expanding Middle: Some Canadian Evidence on the Deskilling Debate," *Canadian Review of Sociology and Anthropology* 25, 3 (1988): 335–64. For the United States see D.R. Howell and E.N. Wolff, "Skill Changes in the U.S. Labor Force, 1960–85," *Industrial and Labor Relations Review*, forthcoming. For a fine discussion of this entire issue, see Lawrence Mishel and Ruy Teixeira, *The Myth of the Coming Labor Shortage* (Washington, D.C.: Economic Policy Institute, 1990).

10 Burris, "Class Formation"; David Livingstone, *Class Ideologies and Educational Futures* (Sussex: Falmer, 1983); Bowles, Gordon, and Weisskopf, *Beyond the Wasteland*; Carboni, "Observaciones comparativas."

11 Hymer, "The Multinational Corporation"; Burris, "Class Formation."

12 Livingstone, *Class Ideologies*, 62.

13 Bowles, Gordon, and Weisskopf, *Beyond the Wasteland*.

14 Michael Piore and Charles Sabel, *The Second Industrial Divide* (New York: Basic Books, 1984).

15 Bowles, Gordon, and Weisskopf, *Beyond the Wasteland*.

16 Esping-Andersen, *Three Worlds*, 202–8.

17 Braverman, *Labor and Monopoly Capital*, 67.

18 Our aim in constructing the executive category was to identify those real powers of economic ownership. Decision-makers who were not part of the management hierarchy and those whose decisions were subject to approval or made only as a voting member of a larger group were excluded.

19 Policy decisions to change products, programs, or services and decisions to increase or decrease the number of persons employed.

20 Both the size of the budget and its distribution within the enterprise.

21 Significant policy decisions on the methods and procedures of work and the amount or pace of work for the organization as a whole or some major part of it.

22 Assigning tasks, deciding on work procedures and the pace of work; excludes those who supervise only one clerical employee.

23 Influence pay raises and promotions, suspensions, and firings or issue formal warnings to subordinates.

24 Wallace Clement, *Continental Corporate Power: Economic Linkages Between Canada and the United States* (Toronto: McClelland and Stewart, 1977).

25 John Crispo, *The Canadian Industrial Relations System* (Toronto: McGraw-Hill Ryerson, 1978).

26 See Don Black and John Myles, "Dependent Industrialization and the Canadian Class Structure: A Comparative Analysis of Canada, the United States and Sweden," *Canadian Review of Sociology and Anthropology* 23, 2 (1986): 157–81.

27 Braverman, *Labor and Monopoly Capital*; Piore and Sabel, *Second Industrial Divide*.

28 Piore and Sabel, *Second Industrial Divide*, 114.

29 Michael Burawoy, *Manufacturing Consent: Changes in the Labor Process under Monopoly Capitalism* (Chicago: University of Chicago Press, 1979), chap. 7.

30 Piore and Sabel, *Second Industrial Divide*, chap. 6.

31 For Canada, see Boyd, "Sex Differences," 285–315; and Myles, "The Expanding Middle," 335–64. For the United States, see Howell and Wolff, "Skill Changes in the U.S. Labor Force, 1960–85." For a fine discussion of this entire issue, see Mishel and Teixeira, *The Myth of the Coming Labor Shortage*.

32 See the essays by Jerry Jacobs (for the United States) and by John Myles, Garnett Picot, and Ted Wannell (for Canada) in *Changing Classes*, ed. Esping-Andersen.

33 See Stephen Cohen and John Zysman, *Manufacturing Matters: The Myth of the Post-Industrial Economy* (New York: Basic Books, 1987); Piore and Sabel, *Second Industrial Divide*.

34 Braverman, *Labor and Monopoly Capital*, 425, emphasis added.

35 Ibid., 45–51.

36 Kenneth Spenner, "Deciphering Prometheus: Temporal Change in the Skill Level of Work," *American Sociological Review* 48 (1983): 829; see also Craig Littler, *The Development of the Labour Process in Capitalist Societies* (London: Heinemann, 1982), 8.

37 See Melvin and Carmi Schooler, *Work and Personality: An Inquiry into the Impact of social Stratification* (Norwood, N.J.: Ablex, 1983).

38 See Erik Olin Wright, *Class, Crisis and the State* (London: New Left Books, 1978), 79–83; and Erik Olin Wright, Cynthia Costello, David Hachen, and Joey Sprague, "The American Class Structure," *American Sociology Review* 47 (1982): 709–26.

39 See Erik Olin Wright, *Classes* (London: Verso, 1985), 55; and Gordon Marshall, David Rose, Howard Newby, and Carolyn Vogler, *Social Class in Modern Britain* (London: Unwin Hyman, 1989), 40.

40 As Reinhard Bendix pointed out, Taylorism was a method designed to routinize and "deskill" the labour process of managers and supervisors as well as that of workers, a fact that led to managerial, as well as worker, resistance to his methods. See Reinhard Bendix, *Work and Authority in Industry* (New York: Wiley, 1956).

41 Robert Kuttner, "The Declining Middle," *Atlantic Monthly*, July 1983, 60–72. For the more scholary version of this perspective, see Barry Bluestone and Bennett Harrison, *The Deindustrialization of America* (New York: Basic Books, 1982).

42 For the Canadian experience, see John Myles, Garnett Picot, and Ted Wannell, *Wages and Jobs in the Eighties: Changing Youth Wages and the Declining Middle*, Research Paper no. 17, Analytical Studies Branch, Statistics Canada, (Ottawa, 1988). A review of American evidence can be found in Gary Loveman and Chris Tilly, "Good Jobs or Bad Jobs: What Does the Evidence Say?" *New England Economic Review* Jan./Feb. 1988, 46–65. A variety of national experiences are presented in *Changing Classes*, ed. Esping-Andersen.

43 The share of postindustrial service employment acounted for by health, education, and social services is 61 per cent in Sweden, 49 and 46 per cent in Finland and Norway respectively, and 34 per cent in both Canada and the United States.

44 The presence of an interaction term is indicative of a correlation between the underlying "effects," and the estimates of effect parameters can be highly misleading. It is even possible that reversing the order of decomposition (Sweden–U.S. instead of U.S.–Sweden) could reverse the order of magnitude of the effects and lead to opposite conclusions. In this instance, the magnitude of the effects are lower in the Sweden–U.S. decomposition, but their relative size is not changed. The results

for the Sweden–U.S. decomposition are as follows: (total difference) 9.5 = 3.9 (sector) + 3.2 (labour process) + 2.4 (interaction).

45 The classification of managerial and supervisory occupations is based on Peter Pineo, John Porter, and Hugh A. McRoberts, "The 1971 Census and the Socioeconomic Classification of Occupations," *Canadian Review of Sociology and Anthropology* 14, 1 (1977): 71–9.

46 This conclusion is based on a shift-share analysis (not shown) identical to the one presented for the working class in Table 4.9.

47 Gösta Esping-Andersen, *Politics against Markets: The Social Democratic Road to Power* (Princeton, N.J.: Princeton University Press, 1985).

48 All figures on union density are from Pradeep Kumar, *Industrial Relations in Canada and the United States: From Uniformity to Divergence*, Working Papers Series, School of Industrial Relations, Queen's University (Kingston, 1991).

49 Ibid, 23.

50 Esping-Andersen, *Three Worlds*, 227.

51 Michael Burawoy, *The Politics of Production* (London: Verso, 1985).

52 Ibid., 147.

53 Ibid., 133.

54 Albert O. Hirschmann, *Exit, Voice and Loyalty: Responses to Declines in Firms, Organizations and States* (Cambridge, Mass.: Harvard University Press, 1970).

55 See especially John Goldthorpe, *Social Mobility and Class Structure in Modern Britain* (Oxford: Clarendon Press, 1980).

56 Ibid.

57 Hirshmann, *Exit, Voice and Loyalty*, 106.

58 Louis Hartz, *The Liberal Tradition in America* (New York: Harcourt, Brace and World, 1955), pp. 64–5.

CHAPTER FIVE

1 Seymour Martin Lipset, "Whatever Happened to the Proletariat? An Historic Mission Unfulfilled," *Encounter* 56 (1981): 18–34.

2 John Zipp and Joel Smith, "A Structural Analysis of Class Voting," *Social Forces* 60 (1982): 738–59; Robert Brym, Michael Gillespie, and Rhonda Lenton, "Class Power, Class Mobilization, and Class Voting: The Canadian Case," *Canadian Journal of Sociology* 14 (1989): 25–44.

3 Harold Chorney and Phillip Hansen, "The Falling Rate of Legitimation," *Studies in Political Economy* 4 (1980): 85–6.

4 Ira Katznelson, *City Trenches* (Chicago: University of Chicago Press, 1981), 9.

5 See especially Gad Horowitz, *Canadian Labour in Politics* (Toronto: Uni-

versity of Toronto Press, 1968); and Seymour Martin Lipset, *Continental Divide: The Values and Institutions of the United States and Canada* (New York: Routledge, 1990). For a review of this literature, see Robert Brym with Bonnie Fox, *From Culture to Power: The Sociology of English Canada* (Toronto: Oxford University Press, 1989).

6 See *Unions in Transition: Entering the Second Century*, ed. Seymour Martin Lipset (San Francisco: ICS Press, 1986).

7 Brym with Fox, *From Culture to Power*, 59.

8 John Myles and Dennis Forcese, "Voting and Class Politics in Canada and the United States," *Comparative Social Research* 4 (1981): 3–31.

9 Keith Banting, "The Welfare State and Inequality in the 1980s," *Canadian Review of Sociology and Anthropology* 24, 3 (1985): 311–38; David Cameron, "The Growth of Government Spending: The Canadian Experience in Comparative Perspective," in *State and Society: Canada in Comparative Perspective*, ed. Keith Banting (Toronto: University of Toronto Press, 1986), 21–52; Julia O'Connor, "Welfare Expenditure and Policy Orientation in Canada in Comparative Perspective," *Canadian Review of Sociology and Anthropology* 26, 1 (1989): 127–50.

10 Jane Jenson, "Representations in Crisis: The Roots of Canada's Permeable Fordism," *Canadian Journal of Political Science* 23, 4 (1990): 653–83.

11 Adam Przeworski, *Capitalism and Social Democracy* (Cambridge: Cambridge University Press, 1985), 69.

12 Ibid., 71; emphasis added.

13 Katznelson, *City Trenches*, esp. chap. 3.

14 In the Swedish survey, the word "physically" was omitted from the first question because forming picket lines and physically preventing scab labour from entering a work site is largely absent from current labour practice. The result is likely to inflate the Swedish tendency to take a pro-labour position on this item. Since, however, the Norwegian and North American versions were identical, the Norwegian response set to these items will provide us with a good indicator of the extent of bias introduced by this difference in wording.

15 For a fine study of public attitudes toward unions corporations and the state, see Gary Bowden, "Labour Unions in the Public Mind: The Canadian Case," *Canadian Review of Sociology and Anthropology* 26, 5 (1989): 723–42.

16 See John Conway, "Populism in the United States, Russia and Canada: Explaining the Roots of Canada's Third Parties," *Canadian Journal of Political Science* 11 (1978): 99–124.

17 Sam Bowles and Herb Gintis, *Democracy and Capitalism* (New York: Basic Books, 1986), 8.

18 Gareth Stedman Jones, *Language of Class: Studies in English Working Class History* (Cambridge: Cambridge University Press, 1983), 106.

19 Quoted in Conway, "Populism," 78.
20 Gösta Esping-Andersen, *Politics against Markets: The Social Democratic Road to Power* (Princeton, N.J.: Princeton University Press, 1985).
21 Conway, "Populism," 121. See also Peter Sinclair, "The Saskatchewan CCF: Ascent to Power and the Decline of Socialism," *Canadian Historical Review* 54 (1973): 419–33.
22 Seymour Martin Lipset, "Radicalism in North America: A Comparative View of the Party Systems in Canada and the United States," *Transactions of the Royal Society of Canada*, ser. 4, 16 (1976): 40.
23 Ibid., 42.
24 Janine Brodie and Jane Jenson, *Crisis, Challenge and Change: Party and Class in Canada* (Toronto: Methuen, 1980), 228–43 and 278–90.
25 On the relation between the Democrats and organized labour, see Thomas Edsall, *The New Politics of Inequality* (New York: W.W. Norton, 1984), chap. 4.
26 Bowden, "Labour Unions."
27 Paul Stevenson and Michael Ornstein, "On the Psychology of Political Change and Crisis: A Critique of New Themes in Bourgeois Political Sociology," (Toronto: Institute for Behavioural Research, York University, 1982), 24.
28 Tom Langford, "Workers' Subordinate Values: A Canadian Case Study," *Canadian Journal of Sociology* 11, no. 3 (1986): 269–91
29 Göran Ahrne and Wallace Clement, "A New Regime? Class Representation within the Swedish State," *Economic and Industrial Democracy* 13 (1992): 455–79.
30 First, an anti-corporate index was constructed by summing respondent scores on their response to two questions: "Corporations have too much power" and "Corporations benefit owners at the expense of consumers and workers." The anti-corporate category was assigned to all those who scored higher than the mid-point on the scale. The pro-corporate category was assigned to all those scoring less than or equal to the mid-point. The pro-labour index was similarly constructed from the two questions: "During a strike, management should be prohibited by law from hiring workers to take the place of strikers" and "Striking workers are generally justified in physically preventing strikebreakers from entering the place of work."
31 John Logue, "Social Welfare, Equality, and the Labor Movement in Denmark and Sweden," *Comparative Social Research* 6 (1983): 248.
32 Robert Alford, *Party and Society* (Chicago: Rand McNally, 1963). Alford calculated an index of class voting by taking the difference between the percentage of blue-collar and white-collar workers voting for left parties. Later studies followed in this tradition by examining a multitude of attitudes and behaviours to determine whether "class matters,"

more recently by estimating "class effects" in multivariate regression models.

33 The index of dissimilarity shows the extent two distributions are different; the higher the index, the greater the difference. It is calculated by taking the sum of the absolute differences in the distribution divided by two. In this instance, the indices tell us the degree of difference in the class orientation of the reference class (workers) and each other class. They can be interpreted as indicating the percentage of capitalists (or of the old middle class) who would have to shift their orientation in order to have a distribution identical to that of workers.

34 This is the measure employed by Alford in his voting analysis. Conceptually and methodologically, it is equivalent to the unstandardized regression coefficient showing the "effect" of class location on class attitudes.

35 See Jill Quadagno, *Creating the Great Society: Inequality and Social Policy in the Turbulent Sixties* (New York: Oxford University Press, 1994); and Margaret Weir, *Politics and Jobs: The Boundaries of Employment Policy in the United States* (Princeton, N.J.: Princeton University Press, 1992), chap. 3.

36 Brym with Fox, *From Culture to Power*, 59.

37 For reviews of this literature see Brym with Fox, *From Culture to Power*; and David Bell and Lorne Tepperman, *The Roots of Disunity: A Look at Canadian Political Culture* (Toronto: McClelland and Stewart, 1979).

38 Seymour Martin Lipset, "North American Labor Movements: A Comparative Perspective," in *Unions in Transition*, 421–52.

39 Bowden, "Labour Unions," 724–5. Since 1986, however, Canadian unionization levels have also begin to drift downward.

40 For a critical review of the Lipset thesis and alternative accounts of Canada–U.S. divergence, see *Unions in Transition*. For an alternative explanation of the decline of organized labour in the United States, see Michael Goldfield, *The Decline of Organized Labour in the United States* (Chicago: University of Chicago Press, 1987).

41 Bowden, "Labour Unions."

42 Ibid., 734.

43 The shifting strategies and role of labour during this period are exhaustively analyzed in Miriam Smith, "Labour without Allies: The Canadian Labour Congress in Politics" (Ph.D. diss., Yale University, 1990). See also Rianne Mahon, "Canadian Labour in the Battle of the Eighties," *Studies in Political Economy*, Summer 1983, 149–75.

44 Mike Davis, "The Political Economy of Late-Imperial America," *New Left Review* 143 (Jan.-Feb. 1984): 6–38.

45 See Brym with Fox, *From Culture to Power*; and Zipp and Smith, "A Structural Analysis of Class Voting."

46 See Zipp and Smith, "A Structural Analysis of Class Voting"; Robert

Brym, "Incorporation versus Power Models of Working Class Radicalism: with Special Reference to North America," *Canadian Journal of Sociology* 11 (1986): 227–51; and Brym, Gillespie, and Lenton, "Class Power, Class Mobilization, and Class Voting."

47 See for example B. Bruce-Briggs, *The New Class?* (New Brunswick, N.J.: Transaction Books, 1979); and Barbara Ehrenreich and John Ehrenreich, "The Professional-Managerial Class, in *Between Labour and Capital*, ed. Pat Walker (New York: Monthly Review, 1979), 5–45.

48 Ironically, Lipset himself has made one of the strongest cases for this similarity between Canada and the United States. See Lipset, "Radicalism in North America," 19–55.

49 For the United States see Thomas Edsall, *The New Politics of Inequality* (New York: W.W. Norton, 1984); for Canada see David Langille, "The Business Council on National Issues and the Canadian State," *Studies in Political Economy* 24 (1987): 41–85.

50 Bowden, "Labour Unions," 730.

51 See Trond Petersen, "A Comment on Presenting Results from Logit and Probit Models," *American Sociological Review* 50, 1 (1985): 130–1.

CHAPTER SIX

1 For example, Gösta Esping-Andersen, *Politics against Markets* (Princeton, N.J.: Princeton University Press, 1985).

2 See Ann Orloff, "Gender and the Social Rights of Citizenship: State Policies and Gender Relations in Comparative Perspective" (paper presented at the meetings of the Research Committee on Poverty, Social Welfare and Social Policy (RC 19) of the International Sociological Association, University of Bremen, Sept. 1992).

3 Michael Mann, "A Crisis in Stratification Theory?" in *Gender and Stratification*, ed. Rosemary Crompton and Michael Mann (Cambridge: Polity Press, 1986), 41.

4 Ibid., 55

5 Ibid., 44–5.

6 Whether or not the growing prevalence of single-parent households headed by females should be counted as an erosion of the traditional patriarchal form is a matter of some importance, but one which we shall not take up. It is important to point out, however, that for most women, single-parenthood is eventually followed by marriage or remarriage and, in many countries, the interval of single-parenthood is characterized by low income and poverty. The key question to be answered is the extent to which single-parenthood becomes a viable alternative, socially and financially, to entering a domestic relationship with a male partner.

7 Joan Acker, "From Sex Roles to Gendered Institutions," *Contemporary Sociology*, Sept. 1992, 567.

8 Wally Seccombe, "Reflections on the Domestic Labour Debate and Prospects for Marxist-Feminist Synthesis," in *The Politics of Diversity: Feminism, Marxism and Nationalism* ed. Roberta Hamilton and Michele Barrett (Montreal: Book Centre, 1986), 204–5.

9 See John Myles and Gail Fawcett, *Job Skills and the Service Economy*, Working Paper no. 4 (Ottawa: Economic Council of Canada, 1990).

10 Seccombe, "Reflections on the Domestic Labour Debate," 205–6.

11 Cynthia Cockburn, *In the Way of Women: Men's Resistance to Sex Equality in Organizations* (Ithaca: ILR Press, 1991).

12 At the outset, gender issues were considered important in two ways. First, a major portion of the study was devoted to collecting information on "relations of ruling" in the household. But the "world of work" was largely considered a "class world," with different outcomes for men and women but driven by a class logic. Second, we were greatly concerned with gathering information on the link between the domestic and public spheres. These concerns led to the the analyses presented in chapters 7 through 9. We were, of course, concerned with sex differences in class outcomes but only in a limited way with the gendered structure of relations of ruling in the workplace. We asked some fairly rudimentary questions on the gender of superiors and subordinates, reported later in this chapter. That we did so was entirely a result of the fact that Erik Wright had realized the problem we faced after conducting the American survey and suggested that this could be an important addition to the analysis.

13 The strategy of wage compression is not directed at women *per se*. Rather, gender equality in earnings is a by-product of a more general labour strategy to reduce differentials in earnings and wages across the whole of the labour market. See Mary Ruggie, "Gender, Work and Social Progress: Some Consequences of Interest Aggregation in Sweden," in *Feminization of the Labour Force: Paradoxes and Promises*, ed. Jane Jenson, Elizabeth Hagen, and Ceallaigh Reddy (Cambridge: Polity Press, 1988), 173–88.

14 Ylva Ericsson, "Sweden," in *Women Workers in Fifteen Countries* (Ithaca, N.Y.; ILR Press, Cornell University, 1985), 139.

15 See OECD, *Employment Outlook* (Paris, Sept. 1988), 21–2.

16 Ibid., 13.

17 The definition of part-time employment tends to be country-specific, making cross-national comparisons from official sources difficult. The OECD's *Employment Outlook* (Paris, Sept. 1988) reports 1987 part-time employment in Canada and Norway as 30 hours or less and in Sweden and the United States as 35 hours or less. In view of these definitional

differences, as well as the time difference for the estimates, the official estimates are remarkably close to our sample estimates. Part-time employment accounted for 25 per cent of female employment in Canada in 1987, 26 per cent in the United States, 43 per cent in Norway, and 45 per cent in Sweden. Finland is the exception among Nordic countries in this regard. In 1981 only 16 per cent of women were employed less than 35 hours per week.

18 Our Finnish sample has very few cases of part-time workers, reflecting low levels of part-time employment in that country (see note 17). Consequently, "removing" part-time workers in this analysis produces virtually no change in levels of representation.

19 Neil Smelser, *Social Change in the Industrial Revolution* (London: Routledge and Paul, 1959).

20 See for example, John Porter, *The Vertical Mosaic: An Analysis of Social Class and Power in Canada* (Toronto: University of Toronto Press, 1965); and Wallace Clement, *The Canadian Corporate Elite* (Toronto: Mclelland and Stewart, 1975).

21 See William Bielby and James Baron, "Men and Women at Work: Sex Segregation and Statistical Discrimination," *American Journal of Sociology* 91, 4 (1986): 759–99.

22 Ibid., 790.

23 It should be emphasized that these results refer only to the respondent's *immediate* superior. Many respondents will be at the end of longer chain of command with a different sex composition than that indicated here.

24 See Monica Boyd, Mary Ann Mulvihill, and John Myles, "Gender, Power and Postindustrialism," *Canadian Review of Sociology and Anthropology* 28, 4 (1991): 407–36.

25 To demonstrate that the claim is warranted as a causal statement – that the process generating this result is endogenous to the work site – requires firm level data. For an example, see Cockburn, *In the Way of Women*; and Bielby and Baron, "Men and Women at Work."

26 See Rosabeth M. Kanter, *Men and Women of the Corporation* (New York: Basic Books, 1977), 206.

27 Stinchcombe, A.L., "Social Structure and Organizations," in *Handbook of Organizations*, ed. J.G. March (Chicago: McNally, 1965).

28 James Baron and Andrew Newman, "For What It's Worth: Organizations, Occupations and the Value of Work Done by Women and Non-whites," *American Sociological Review* 55 (1990): 155–75.

29 See Monica Boyd and Elizabeth Humphreys, *Labour Markets and Sex Differences in Canadian Incomes*, Discussion Paper no. 143 (Ottawa: Economic Council of Canada, 1979). Margaret Denton and Alfred A. Hunter, *Equality in the Workplace Economic Sectors and Gender Discrimina-*

tion in Canada, Discussion Paper, Ser. A, no. 6 (Ottawa: Labour Canada, Women's Bureau, 1982).

30 See Myles and Fawcett, *Job Skills and the Service Economy.*

31 In technical terms, tests for interactions across industrial sectors are not statistically significant.

32 Boyd, Mulvihill, and Myles, "Gender, Power and Postindustrialism."

33 Acker, "Gendered Institutions," 565.

34 As in Cockburn, *In the Way of Women.*

35 See Paula England, "Women and Occupational Prestige: A Case of Vacuous Sex Equality," *Signs* 5, 2 (1979): 252–65.

CHAPTER SEVEN

1 Dorothy E. Smith, "Feminist Reflections on Political Economy," *Studies in Political Economy* 30 (Autumn, 1989): 53.

2 Joan Acker, "The Problem with Patriarchy," *Sociology* 23, 2 (May 1989): 235–6.

3 Heidi Hartmann, "The Family as the Locus of Gender, Class, and Political Struggle: The Example of Housework," *Signs* 6, 3 (1981): 368–9.

4 Ibid., 372.

5 Wally Seccombe, "Reflections on the Domestic Labour Debate and Prospects for Marxist-Feminist Synthesis," in *The Politics of Diversity: Feminism, Marxism and Nationalism*, ed. Roberta Hamilton and Michele Barrett (Montreal: Book Centre, 1986), 205–6.

6 See Christina Jonung, "Patterns of Occupational Segregation by Sex in the Labour Market," in *Sex Discrimination and Equal Opportunity: The Labour Market and Employment Policy*, ed. Gunther Schmid and Renate Weitzel (Berlin: wzb Publications, 1984).

7 See Michèle Barrett, *Women's Oppression Today: Problems in Marxist Feminist Analysis* (London: Verso, 1980), 180, 192, 206, 225; and Johanna Brenner and Maria Ramas, "Rethinking Women's Oppression," *New Left Review* 144 (Mar./Apr. 1984): 38, 48, 62.

8 Sylvia Walby, "Theorising Patriarchy," *Sociology* 23, 2 (May 1989): 221.

9 Dorothy Smith, "Women, Class and Family," in *Women, Class, Family and the State*, ed. Roxanna Ng (Toronto: Garamond, 1985), 6.

10 Ibid., 37–8.

11 Meg Luxton, "Two Hands for the Clock: Changing Patterns in the Gendered Division of Labour in the Home," *Studies in Political Economy* 12 (Fall 1983): 35.

12 Ibid.

13 Bonnie Fox, "Conceptualizing 'patriarchy,'" *Canadian Review of Sociology and Anthropology* 25, 2 (May 1988): 176.

14 Meredith Edwards, *Financial Arrangements within Families: A Research Re-*

port for the National Advisory Council (Canberra, Australia, February 1981), 4.

15 Ibid., 128.

16 A further aspect of household decision making involves family "allocative systems" of money management between members. Several patterns have been identified, including "one purse," "independent," and "alliance" systems. These help reveal particular household power relations, but unfortunately our data do not allow such an analysis. See Susan McRae, "The Allocation of Money in Cross-Class Families," *Sociological Review* 4 (1987): 97–122. David Rose and Heather Laurie of the University of Essex are currently conducting a household panel study in Britain, "The Relevance of Household Allocative Systems for Class Analysis" (Paper presented at the Social Stratification Research Committee 28, XII World Congress of Sociology, Madrid, 9–13 July 1990).

17 OECD, *Economic Outlook* (Paris, September 1988), 21, 40.

18 See Jo-Anne B. Parliament, "Women Employed Outside the Home," *Canadian Social Trends* 13 (Summer 1989): 3.

19 See Maureen Moore, "Dual-Earner Families: The New Norm," *Canadian Social Trends* 12 (Spring 1989): 25–6; also see Raj K. Chawla, "The Changing Profile of Dual-Earner Families," *Perspectives on Labour and Income* (Ottawa: Statistics Canada, Summer 1992), 22–9.

20 Maureen Moore, "Wives as Primary Breadwinners," *Perspectives on Labour and Income*, Spring 1990, 65.

21 Annemette Sorenson and Sara McLanahan, "Married Women's Economic Dependency, 1940–1980," *American Journal of Sociology* 93, 3 (Nov. 1987): 683.

22 Ibid., 685.

23 Barbara Hobson, "No Exit, No Voice: Women's Economic Dependency and the Welfare State," *Acta Sociologica* 33, 3 (1990): 235.

24 Ibid., 236–7.

25 Ibid., 243–4.

26 See Harriet Rosenberg, "Motherwork, Stress and Depression: The Cost of Privatized Social Reproduction," in *Feminism and Political Economy: Women's Work, Women's Struggles*, ed. H.J. Maroney and M. Luxton (Toronto: Methuen, 1987).

27 Ann Duffy, Nancy Mandell, and Norene Pupo, *Few Choices: Women, Work and Family* (Toronto: Garamond Press, 1989), 36.

28 Heidi Hartmann, "The Family as the Locus of Gender, Class, and Political Struggle: The Example of Housework," *Signs* 6, 3 (Spring 1981): 377.

29 We thank an anonymous reader for bringing this insight to our attention and crediting Meg Luxton with it.

30 "Part-time" is defined here as under 35 hours of paid employment per week.

31 Phyllis Moen, *Working Parents: Transformations in Gender Roles and Public Policies in Sweden* (Madison: University of Wisconsin Press, 1989), 20. Also see L. Haas, "Domestic Role Sharing in Sweden," *Journal of Marriage and the Family* 43 (Nov. 1981): 957–69; L. Haas, "Determinants of Role-Sharing Behavior," *Sex Roles* 7 (1984): 747–60; K. Sandqvist, "Swedish Family Policy and Attempts to Change Parental Roles," in *Reassessing Fatherhood*, ed. C. Lewis and M. O'Brian (London: Sage Publications, 1987), 144–60; J. Holland, *Women's Occupational Choice: The Impact of Sexual Divisions in Society* (Stockholm Institute of Education, 1980).

32 Paula England and Barbara Stanek Kilbourne, "Markets, Marriages, and Other Mates: The Problem of Power," in *Beyond the Marketplace: Rethinking Economy and Society*, ed. Roger Friedland and A.F. Robertson (New York: Aldinede Gruyter, 1990), 163.

33 Ibid., 169.

CHAPTER EIGHT

1 Martin Meissner et al., "No Exit for Wives: Sexual Division of Labour and the Cumulation of Household Demands," *Canadian Review of Sociology and Anthropology* 12, 4, part 1 (1975): 425, For a general overview of the literature on household labour, see Susan Clark and Marylee Stephenson, "Housework as Real Work," in *Work in the Canadian Context*, 2d ed., ed. K.L.P. Lundy and Barbara Warme (Toronto: Butterworths, 1986).

2 Pat and Hugh Armstrong, *Theorizing Women's Work* (Toronto: Garamond Press, 1990), 87.

3 Ann Duffy, Nancy Mandell, and Norene Pupo, *Few Choices: Women, Work and Family* (Toronto: Garamond Press, 1989), 105–6.

4 The only possible exception is a few men (13 cases) who are part-time (under 20 hours), a third of whom have had some career disruption.

5 Pat and Hugh Armstrong, *The Double Ghetto: Canadian Women and Their Segregated Work* (Toronto: McClelland and Stewart, 1978), 141.

6 Ibid., 143.

7 Wally Seccombe, "Reflections on the Domestic Labour Debate and Prospects for Marxist-Feminist Synthesis," in *The Politics of Diversity: Feminism, Marxism and Nationalism*, ed. Roberta Hamilton and Michele Barrett (Montreal: Book Centre, 1989), 197–8.

8 Duffy, Mandell, and Pupo, *Few Choices*, 10.

9 See OECD, *Employment Outlook* (Paris, September 1988), 40, Table 1.15.

10 The class profile for the "short-term" part-timers tends to be more er-

291 Notes to pages 184–92

ratic. In the United States 38 per cent (of 47 cases) belong to the property class, indicating a very high proportion of self-employed, possibly running their own businesses selling cosmetics or household goods. In Canada this practice does not appear. Instead, the working class rises to 77 per cent (+ 11 percentage points more than full-time). There is little change in the Nordic countries.

11 Elisabet Nasman, *Work and Family – A Combination Made Possible by Part-Time Work and Parental Leaves?* Arbetslivscentrum F24 (Stockholm, April 1986), 8.

12 Marianne Sundström, *A Study in the Growth of Part-Time Work in Sweden* (Stockholm: Arbetslivscentrum, 1987), 26.

13 See ibid., 15–16.

14 Gisela Pettersson, "Working Hours in Sweden: Trends and Background to the Current Discussion," *Working Life in Sweden* 37 (Sept. 1989): 3.

15 We thank an anonymous review for this point.

16 Inga Persson, "The Third Dimension – Equal Status between Swedish Women and Men," in *Generating Equality in the Welfare State: The Swedish Experience*, ed. Inga Persson (Oslo: Norwegian University Press, 1990), 230.

17 Sundström, *Part-Time Work*, 170–1.

18 Ibid., 234. Non-market work in the time-budget study includes household tasks, repairs, and maintenance as well as active child care.

19 Ibid., 235.

20 See Duffy, Mandell, and Pupo, *Few Choices*, 73.

21 See, for example, Jean Gardiner, "Women's Domestic Labour," *New Left Review* 89 (Jan./Feb. 1975): 47–58.

22 Pat Connelly, *Last Hired, First Fired: Women and the Canadian Work Force* (Toronto: The Women's Press, 1978), 63.

23 Ibid., 66.

24 Pat and Hugh Armstrong, "Beyond Sexless Class and Classless Sex: Toward Feminist Marxism," *Studies in Political Economy* 10 (Winter 1983): 25–6.

25 See Eric Plutzer, "Work Life, Family Life, and Women's Support of Feminism," *American Sociological Review* 58 (August 1988): 644, 647.

26 See Ethel Klein, *Gender Politics* (Cambridge: Harvard University Press, 1984), 36, 69, 92.

27 Gordon Marshall, David Rose, Howard Newby, and Carolyn Vogler, *Social Class in Modern Britain* (London: Unwin Hyman, 1989), 64.

28 Ibid., 85.

29 See J.H. Goldthorpe, "Women and Class Analysis in Defence of the Conventional View," *Sociology* 17 (1985): 465–88; Håkon Leiulfsrud and Alison Woodward, "Women at Class Crossroads: Repudiating Conventional Theories of Family Class," *Sociology* 21 (1987): 393–412;

Håkon Leiulfsrud, *Det familjara klass-samhallet* (The familial class society) (Lund: Arkiv Avhandlingsserie, 1991).

30 Janeen Baxter, in "Gender and Class Analysis: The Position of Women in the Class Structure," *Australia and New Zealand Journal of Sociology* 24, 1 (March 1988): 106–23, attempts to examine "cross-class" families using preliminary data from the Australian class-structure project by distinguishing homogeneous from heterogeneous class composition in families. As she notes, this is not very satisfactory methodologically since it fails to include the class positions of housewives and submerges class-based gender differences within the family.

31 See Erik Olin Wright, "Women in the Class Structure," *Politics and Society* 17, 1 (1989): 36–66.

32 Meg Luxton, "Taking on the Double Day: Housewives as a Reserve Army of Labour," *Atlantis* 7, 1 (Fall 1981): 18.

33 Ibid., 19.

34 Household classes with a working-class man and new-middle-class women have only 14 cases in Sweden but 72 in Canada, 44 in Norway, and 49 in the United States.

35 Kathleen Gerson, "Emerging Social Divisions among Women: Implications for Welfare State Politics," *Politics and Society* 15, 2 (1986–87): 218–9.

36 Nancy J. Davis and Robert V. Robinson, "Men's and Women's Consciousness of Gender Inequality: Austria, West Germany, Great Britain, and the United States," *American Sociological Review* 56 (Feb. 1991): 72–84.

37 In Canada the difference between pre-secondary and secondary schooling is especially strong in the working class, raising the gender index for both men (+.29) and women (+.31).

CHAPTER NINE

1 Patricia Armstrong and Patricia Connelly, "Feminism and Political Economy: An Introduction," *Studies in Political Economy* 30 (Autumn 1989): 5.

2 The question within the gender-attitude scale that most strongly divides the populations by age concerns traditional families. In Canada, which is indicative of the other nations, only 16 per cent of the eldest group of men are progressive, followed by 36 per cent for the middle group and 54 per cent for the youngest; for women, the proportions run from 21 to 46 to 57 per cent. None of the other questions are nearly as divisive by age, although the tendency toward more progressive attitudes for youth remains on all questions.

3 Armstrong and Connelly, "Feminism and Political Economy," 6.

4 Danielle Juteau-Lee and Barbara Roberts, "Ethnicity and Femininity," *Canadian Ethnic Studies* 13, 1 (1981): 7.

5 Floya Anthias and Nira Yuval-Davis, "Contextualizing Feminism – Gender, Ethnic and Class Divisions," *Feminist Review* 15 (Nov. 1983): 67.

6 See John Porter, *The Vertical Mosaic: An Analysis of Social Class and Power in Canada* (Toronto: University of Toronto Press, 1965). Also, see his *The Measure of Canadian Society: Education, Equality and Opportunity* (Ottawa: Carleton University Press, 1987; original ed., 1979).

7 One paper that does relate women to ethnicity is Frances Abele and Daiva Stasiulis, "Canada as a 'White Settler Colony': What about Natives and Immigrants," in *The New Canadian Political Economy*, ed. W. Clement and G. Williams (Montreal: McGill-Queen's University Press, 1989), 240–77.

8 In a review of Canadian census data between 1931 and 1971, E. Hugh Lautard and Donald S. Loree conclude that "measurement of the relative occupational status of ethnic groups confirms that the ethnic mosaic remains a vertical one." Moreover, they find "that patterns differ for males and females, and that separate analyses by gender are called for." See "Ethnic Stratification in Canada," *Canadian Journal of Sociology* 9, 3 (1984): 333, 342.

9 See Hubert Guindon, *Quebec Society: Tradition, Modernity, and Nationhood* (Toronto: University of Toronto Press, 1988).

10 Peter Li, *Ethnic Inequality in a Class Society* (Toronto: Wall and Thompson, 1988), 140–1.

11 Anthias and Yuval-Davis, "Contextualizing Feminism," 69.

12 Grace Hartman, "Women and the Unions," in *Women in the Canadian Mosaic*, ed. Gwen Matheson (Toronto: Peter Martin Associates, 1976), 248.

13 See Heather Jon Maroney and Meg Luxton, "From Feminism and Political Economy to Feminist Political Economy," in *Feminism and Political Economy: Women's Work, Women's Struggles*, ed. H.J. Maroney and M. Luxton (Toronto: Methuen, 1987), 7; and Isabella Bakker, "The Political Economy of Gender," in *The New Canadian Political Economy*, 102–4.

14 See Linda Briskin, "Women and Unions in Canada: A Statistical Overview," in *Union Sisters: Women in the Labour Movement*, ed. Linda Briskin and Lynda Yanz (Toronto: The Women's Press, 1983), 30, 36.

15 See Hélène David, "Action Positive in the Quebec Trade Union Movement," in *Union Sisters*, 91.

16 See Françoise David, "Women's Committees: The Quebec Experience," in *Union Sisters*, 285–92.

17 Heather Jon Maroney, "Feminism at Work," in *Feminism and Political Economy*, 89.

18 William D. Coleman, "The Political Economy of Quebec," in *The New Canadian Political Economy*, 171.

19 "Interview with Madeleine Parent," *Studies in Political Economy* 30 (Autumn 1990): 27, 28, 31.

20 While we do not have sufficient cases to reliably report the situation for unionization and the middle-class Québécois, in the rest of Canada the results reinforce our findings for the working class. Middle-class women with union experience (1.02) are more progressive (+.16) than those without union experience (.86). New-middle-class men outside the union movement (.75) are more progressive (.−11) than those with union experience (.64), giving even greater confidence to the earlier findings that illustrate the contradictory influence the union movement has had for men's and women's gender attitudes in the rest of Canada.

21 See Michèle Barrett and Roberta Hamilton, "Introduction," in *The Politics of Diversity: Feminism, Marxism and Nationalism* (Montreal: Book Centre, 1986), 23–27.

22 Bakker, "The Political Economy of Gender," 103.

23 Winnie Ng, "Immigrant Women: The Silent Partners of the Women's Movement," *Canadian Women's Studies* 4, 2 (Winter 1982): 87.

24 Alejandra Cumsille, Carolyn Egan, Gladys Klestorny, and Maria Terese Larrain, "Triple Oppression: Immigrant Women in the Labour Force," in *Union Sisters*, 212–21.

25 Abele and Stasiulis, "Canada as a 'White Settler Colony,'" 267.

26 Monica Boyd et al., *Ascription and Achievement: Studies in Mobility and Status Attainment in Canada* (Ottawa: Carleton University Press, 1985), 441.

27 Results (not shown here) on the foreign-born versus native-born pattern of difference are robust for both sexes, irrespective of education, age, and country of origin. Foreign-born women in our sample tend to be slightly less educated and somewhat older than the native-born yet still more progressive in each age category and among the best educated.

28 Regionalism has been examined within the Comparative Class Structure Project in Finland by Raimo Blom, by dividing that country by provinces into three areas – south, central, and north – then within each into rural and urban areas. He finds considerable differences in class structure, with more self-employed further north because of more farms, fewer managerial-supervisory positions, and a smaller working class. See Raimo Blom, "Class Theories and the Class Structure of Finnish Society," Working Paper no. 11, Comparative Project on Class Structure and Class Consciousness, Sociology, University of Wisconsin (Madison, 1982), 30–35.

29 Barrett and Hamilton; *The Politics of Diversity*, 6.

295 Notes to pages 226–32

30 See Guindon, "Social Unrest, Social Class and Quebec's Bureaucratic Revolution," in *Quebec Society*.

31 Rosemary Warskett, "Defining Who We Are: Solidarity through Diversity in the Ontario Labour Movement," in *Culture and Social Change*, ed. Colin Leys and Marguerite Mendell (Montreal: Black Rose Books, 1992), 116–17.

32 Ibid, 117.

33 See, for example, T.B. Edsall and M.D. Edsall, *Chain Reaction: The Impact of Race, Rights, and Taxes on American Politics* (New York: W.W. Norton & Co., 1992).

34 bell hooks, *Ain't I a Woman?* (Boston, Mass.: South End Press, 1981), 140.

35 See Leslie Cagan, "Something New Emerges: The Growth of a Socialist Feminist," in *They Should Have Served that Cup of Coffee*, ed. D Cluster (Boston: South End Press, 1979).

36 Bonnie Thorton Dill, "Race, Class, and Gender: Prospects for an All-Inclusive Sisterhood," *Feminist Studies* 9, 1 (Sept. 1983): 136.

37 See Catherine E. Ross, "The Division of Labor at Home," *Social Forces* 65 (1987): 828–9.

38 Josefina Figueira-McDonough has derived a series of propositions about sex, race, and class for feminism in the United States. Our data supports some of her basic propositions, such as that "women will rank higher than men in feminist orientation (Proposition 1)" and that "black women to rank higher than white women on feminist orientation (Proposition 2)," but not that "greater convergence in feminist orientations among blacks than whites (Proposition 3)," or that "black males will rank lower in feminist orientation than white males ... (Proposition 4)." None of her propositions suggesting that "lower-classes" are more feminist than "higher-classes" are supported, but her argument that "higher- and middle-class white women will have a higher feminist orientation than their lower-class counterparts (Proposition 8)" is supported. See "Gender, Race and Class: Differences in Levels of Feminist Orientation," *Journal of Applied Behavioral Science* 21, 2 (1985): 123–6.

39 Sheva Medjuck, "Ethnicity and Feminism: Two Solitudes?" *Atlantis* 15, 2 (Spring 1990): 3.

40 The claim that the United States has greater regional effects on gender attitudes than does Canada is based upon an analysis of difference using four political regions in each country by sex and class. It is reinforced by findings (not reproduced here) for class orientations (see chapter 5), where there were twice as many differences of at least 10 percentage points between the two main classes, sex, and four regions in the United States as in Canada.

41 Since our analysis focuses upon the gender attitudes associated with variously specified areas, in the following we have chosen to identify respondents with the area where they lived at 16 years of age to better reveal formative regional influences on orientations.

CHAPTER TEN

1 For an example see P.R. Lawrence and J.W. Lorsch, *Organization and Environment: Managing Differentiation and Integration* (Boston: Harvard University Press, 1967). For theoretical discussion of these matters see James Thompson, *Organizations in Action* (New York: McGraw-Hill, 1967).
2 Barbara Ehrenreich and John Ehrenreich, "The Professional-Managerial Class," in *Between Labor and Capital*, ed. Pat Walker (New York: Monthly Review, 1979), 5–45; Nicos Poulantzas, *Classes in Contemporary Capitalism* (London: New Left Books, 1975).
3 See Göran Ahrne and Wallace Clement, "A New Regime? Class Representation within the Swedish State," *Economic and Industrial Democracy* 13 (1992): 460–1.
4 Göran Brulin and Anders Victorin, "Improving the Quality of Working Life: The Swedish Model," in *New Directions in Work Organisation: The Industrial Relations Response* (Paris: OECD, 1992), 164.
5 John Goldthorpe, "Women and Class Analysis: In Defense of the Conventional View," *Sociology* 18 (1984): 465–88.
6 See Rianne Mahon, "From Fordism to ? New Technology, Labour Markets and Unions," *Economic and Industrial Democracy* 8 (1987): 5–60.

APPENDIX ONE

1 For a brief overview of the intellectional history of the project, see Erik Olin Wright, *Classes* (London: Verso, 1985), 25–6.
2 Ibid., 159–61.
3 For further details on data collection, sample design, etc., and weighted procedures, see Comparative Project on Class Structure and Class Consciousness, User's Guide for Machine-Readable Data File, *Five Nation Tape Code Book, vol. 1.1, Table of Contents and Core Variables* (Madison, Wis.: Institute for Research on Poverty, 1986).
4 For a comparison and discussion of the relationship between our scheme and Wright's, see Wallace Clement, "Comparative Class Analysis: Locating Canada in a North American and Nordic Context," *Canadian Review of Sociology and Anthropology* 27, 4 (1990):462–86. Included there is a table comparing the two schemes for five nations (Table III) and a detailed appendix on variable construction for class (pp. 485–6).

5 Comparative Project on Class Structure and Class Consciousness, *Five Nation Tape Code Book*, vol. 1.1, variable #536, reference 536.

6 Ibid., variable #13, reference #13, was used in this recoding.

APPENDIX TWO

1 Marx demarcated phases of capitalist development in terms of the transition from the "formal" to the "real" subordination of labour. The former refers to a strictly legal relationship in which direct producers are separated from ownership of their means of production. The direct producers are brought into the factory, but there they reproduce their traditional patterns of work organization, retaining control of their own labour process. The real subordination of labour begins when employers begin to take control of and reorganize the way work is done.

2 Harry Braverman, *Labor and Monopoly Capitalism* (New York: Monthly Review Press, 1974).

3 Kenneth Spenner, "Deciphering Prometheus: Temporal Change in the Skill Level of Work," *American Sociological Review* 48 (1983): 829; Craig Littler, *The Development of the Labour Process in Capitalist Societies* (London: Heinemann, 1982), 8.

4 Spenner, "Deciphering Prometheus," 829.

5 See Erik Olin Wright, *Class, Crisis, and the State* (London: New Left Books, 1978), 79–83; and Erik Olin Wright, Cynthia Costello, David Hachen, and Joey Sprague, "The American Class Structure," *American Sociology Review* 47 (1982): 709–26.

6 See the collection of papers in *The Debate on Classes*, ed. Erik Olin Wright (New York: Verso, 1989).

7 See especially Wright, Costello, Hachen, and Sprague, "American Class Structure," 715–6.

8 See Erik Olin Wright, *Classes* (London: Verso, 1985), 55; and Gordon Marshall, David Rose, Howard Newby, and Carolyn Vogler, *Social Class in Modern Britain* (London: Unwin Hyman, 1989), 40.

9 Wright, Costello, Hachen, and Sprague, "American Class Structure," 716, esp. note 9.

10 See Melvin Kohn and Carmi Schooler, *Work and Personality: An Inquiry into the Impact of Social Stratification* (Norwood, N.J.: Ablex, 1983).

11 For a discussion of these measures, see Spenner, "Deciphering Prometheus," and John Myles, "The Expanding Middle: Some Canadian Evidence on the Deskilling Debate," *Canadian Review of Sociology and Anthropology* 25, 3 (1988): 335–64.

Index

Abele, Francis, 224
Acker, Joan, 38, 127, 140, 142
African Americans, 22, 245
age cohorts, 109, 176, 212
agrarian society, 132
Ahrne, Göran, 51
Alford, Robert, 102
American Civil War, 228, 232
"American exceptionalism," 91–2, 107, 113
Anthias, Floya, 216, 217
anti-matriarchy, 134, 137
Armstrong, Hugh, 161, 175, 178, 179, 189
Armstrong, Pat, 161, 175, 178, 179, 189, 211, 212
Asplund, Gisele, 131
attitudes: towards business, 95, 97; towards gender. *See* gender attitudes; towards labour, 94–6, 97, 108
autonomy. *See*

occupational skill: components of

Bakker, Isabella, 223
Baldwin, John, 58
Baron, James, 133, 136
Barrett, Michèle, 226
Bell, Daniel, 26, 27, 31, 63, 71
Bielby, Bill, 133
Block, Fred, 25
Bowden, Gary, 108, 114
Bowles, Sam, 64, 65, 98
Boyd, Monica, 134, 139, 224
branch plants, 20, 69. *See also* Canada: dependent industrialization in
Braverman, Harry, 26, 31, 63, 66, 73–7 passim, 82, 241, 261
Brym, Robert, 109
Brynjolfsson, E., 62
Burawoy, Michael, 71, 87
Burris, Val, 65, 66

Cagan, Leslie, 229
Canada: dependent industrialization in, 20,

69, 108, 248; ethnicity and immigration, 215–19, 224; labour movement, 84–5, 106–8, 219–20, 252; politics in, 91–3, 98–100, 106–9, 113–15; regionalism, 93, 211, 226–8. *See also* Ontario; Quebec
Canadian Union of Public Employees, 219
capitalism: as mode of production, 7, 9–10. *See also* industrial capitalism; postindustrialism
capitalist-executive class, 10, 239; compared to Wright, 18; decision making, 11, 67–8; definition of, 15–19; formal and real economic ownership of, 10–11, 83
Carboni, Carlo, 65
Carchedi, Mino, 6, 11–13, 18
Catholic Confederation of Labour, 220

Seccombe, Wally, 127, 144, 179
self-employment: aspirations to, 44–5; national variations in, 45–6, 48–9; and populism, 112; postindustrial variants and, 44; rise of, 41–2, 45–7
semi-autonomous employees. *See* occupational skill: components of
service economy: rise of, 23–6, 46, 64–5, 75
Singelmann, Joachim, 24
skill. *See* occupational skill
Sloan, Alfred, 10
Sloanism, 10, 72
small firms, 239; employment in, 42, 44, 57–9; wages and earnings, 58, 60, 240
Smelser, Neil, 132
Smith, Adam, 24
Smith, Dorothy, 142, 145
Social Credit Party, 106
Social Democratic Party, 21, 51, 92, 99, 242
social mobility, 8
Sombart, Werner, 88, 91
Spenner, Ken, 74, 261
Stasiulis, Daiva, 224
state: employment in, 78–9, 83, 136, 242; growth of, 114–15; limits on employment structures, 48–50, 246; and property, 4–5; theories of, 5; women and, 124
Steinmetz, George, 47, 54
Stevenson, Paul, 100
Stinchcombe, Arthur L., 136
strikes, 70, 86, 94–6, 244. *See also* attitudes: towards labour
subcontracting, 47, 53

Sundström, Marianne, 185, 186
surplus value/labour, 12
Sweden: economic development in, 20–1; erosion of corporatism in, 51; female labour force, 130; labour movement, 29–30, 84, 92, 99, 105, 110; occupational structure, 63–4; part-time employment, 186–7
Swedish Confederation of Professional Associations (SACO), 86, 110, 242
Swedish Employers' Confederation (SAF), 51
Swedish Trade Union Confederation (LO), 86, 242

Taylor, Frederick, 10, 70
Taylorism, 10, 70, 72
technology, 47, 62, 239
Thompson, E.P., 7
Toryism, 107

unemployment, 46
unions, 33, 37, 57, 71, 84–5, 92, 106–8, 111, 114–15, 186, 242, 246; and gender attitudes, 213–15, 218, 221, 225, 227, 230, 235–6, 251. *See also* labour movement
United Fishermen and Allied Workers' Union, 18
United States: female labour force, 130; individualism, 89; labour movement, 84–5, 106–8, 231; politics in, 91–2, 98–100, 106–9, 113–15; race, 215, 228–31, 251; region, 232–4;

surveillance of labour, 60–70, 87
unpaid family workers, 18, 270 n38

Waffle group, 114
wage polarization, 75
wage solidarity, 86, 186, 249
Walby, Sylvia, 145, 146
Wannell, Ted, 47, 54, 60
Warskett, Rosemary, 227
Weber, Max, 6, 124
Weisskopf, Tom, 64
welfare state. *See* state
Western, Mark, 8
women, 83: distributions in classes, 128–9, 137–8; employment status, 181–7; immigrant women, 224–6; income relative to men, 39, 136, 153–5; labour-force participation, 23, 34, 86, 123, 145, 152, 181, 243–5, 249; and populism, 110–11; in self-employment, 42–3, 48; subordination in labour market, 127–8; women of colour, 229–31. *See also* occupations: sex segregation
working class: definition of, 15–19; feminization of, 86, 244; fractions within, 109; in industrial capitalism, 22–3; "maturity" of, 45–6; politics of, 91–3; in postindustrialism, 34–5, 83; women in, 35
Wright, Erik Olin, 6, 7, 9, 14, 18, 31, 47, 54, 75, 261–3

Yuval-Davis, Nira, 216, 217